100
Literacy Hours

YEAR 1

Published by Scholastic Ltd,
Villiers House,
Clarendon Avenue,
Leamington Spa,
Warwickshire CV32 5PR

SERIES CONCEPT
Chris Webster

AUTHORS
Kathleen Taylor
David Waugh
Wendy Jolliffe

EDITOR
Lorna Gilbert

ASSISTANT EDITOR
Irene Goodacre

SERIES DESIGNER
Joy White

DESIGNER
Sarah Rock

COVER ARTWORK
Val Biro

ILLUSTRATIONS
Denise Elliott

Text © 1999 Kathleen Taylor, David Waugh and
Wendy Jolliffe
2 3 4 5 6 7 8 9 9 0 1 2 3 4 5 6 7

British Library Cataloguing-in-Publication Data
A catalogue record for this book is available from the British Library.

ISBN 0-590-53977-9

ACKNOWLEDGEMENTS

The publishers gratefully acknowledge permission to reproduce the following copyright material:
Colin and Jacqui Hawkins for the use of illustrations and text from *Zug The Bug* and illustrations from *Tog The
Dog* and *Zen The Hen* in the boxed set called *Pat The Cat and Friends* (ISBN: 0-7513-5356-6) © 1988, Colin and
Jacqui Hawkins (1995, Dorling Kindersley).
David Higham Associates for the use of 'Another Day' by John Cunliffe from *A Very First Poetry Book*
compiled by John Foster © 1984, John Cunliffe (1984, OUP) and 'Cats' by Eleanor Farjeon from *The
Children's Bells* by Eleanor Farjeon © 1957, Eleanor Farjeon (1957, OUP) original copyright 1938,
renewed by Eleanor Farjeon in 1966.
Vernon Scannell for the use of 'Cat' from *The Apple-Raid and Other Poems* by Vernon Scannell ©
1974, Vernon Scannell (1974, Chatto & Windus).
Macmillan Children's Books for the use of text and illustrations from *Peace At Last* by Jill Murphy
© 1982, Jill Murphy (1982, Macmillan).
Mallinson Rendel Publisher, New Zealand for the use of illustrations and text from *Hairy
Maclary from Donaldson's Dairy* by Lynley Dodd © 1983, Lynley Dodd (1983, Spindlewood)
Peters Fraser and Dunlop Group on behalf of Michael Rosen 'A busy day' by Michael Rosen
from *A Very First Poetry Book* compiled by John Foster © 1984, Michael Rosen (1984, OUP).
Walker Books Ltd for the use of extracts from *Can't You Sleep Little Bear?* by Martin Waddell
and © 1988 Illustrations, Barbara Firth © 1988, Martin Waddell and © 1988 Illustrations,
Barbara Firth (1988, Walker Books Ltd) and *Let's Go Home, Little Bear* by Martin Waddell and
Barbara Firth © 1991, Martin Waddell and © 1991, Illustrations, Barbara Firth (1991,
Walker Books Ltd); for the use of text from *We're Going on a Bear Hunt* by Michael Rosen
and Helen Oxenbury © 1989, Michael Rosen and © 1989, Illustrations, Helen Oxenbury
(1989, Walker Books Ltd); for the use of the poem 'The Grass House' from *Out and About*
by Shirley Hughes © 1988, Shirley Hughes (1988, Walker Books Ltd) and text from
Handa's Surprise by Eileen Browne © 1994, Eileen Browne (1994, Walker Books Ltd).

Contents

INTRODUCTION

ABOUT THE SERIES

100 Literacy Hours is a series of year-specific teachers' resource books that provides a core of material for the teaching of the English curriculum within the context of the *National Literacy Strategy Framework for Teaching* and within the structure of the Literacy Hour. Each book offers term-by-term lesson plans, complete with objectives and organization grids and accompanied, where relevant, by photocopiable texts and activity sheets. The materials are ready-to-use, and their adaptable format enables them to be used as flexibly as possible. The 100 hours provided offer a balance of both reading and writing, and of range: fiction and poetry and non-fiction. However, it is expected that you will wish to personalize the material – altering the order, interleaving lesson plans with complementary materials from your school's existing schemes, consolidating work by using the structure of a lesson plan as a model for a lesson with different content, and so on. The loose-leaf format of each book, with hole-punched, perforated, tear-out pages, makes the integration of other tried-and-tested and favourite material into the core very easy.

USING THIS BOOK

The materials

This book provides 100 literacy hours for Year 1, presented as 'units' of between 1 and 5 hours. There is a balance of reading and writing units, most of which are linked in order to demonstrate and reinforce the close relationship. The units are fully supported with detailed lesson plans and integrated photocopiable resources. Together, these materials should be regarded as a core, and a starting point for developing your own personalized folder for the year.

Adapting and personalizing the materials

During the trialling of these resources, wide differences in ability were found in classes of the same year group in different schools. This means that the precise content of the plans and resources will almost certainly need modification to suit the children in a particular school. One way to do this is as follows:
■ Separate the pages of the book and place them in an A4 ringbinder.
■ Adjust the level of the photocopiable resource sheets to match the needs of the pupils in your year group.
■ 'Trade' materials with higher or lower year groups so that the average level matches that of the target year group.
■ Add your own favourite teaching materials in the appropriate places.
■ Substitute materials for others if necessary (for example, if you have a set of books which you wish to use instead of one of the ones recommended).
You will then have created a tailor-made folder of plans and resources for your year group.

Preparing a scheme of work

All schools are required to write detailed schemes of work, and these materials have been designed to facilitate this process. The termly Overview Grids on pages 14–19 have been compiled by extracting the 'Objectives' grids from each teaching unit to provide you with what are, essentially, medium-term plans. These grids are photocopiable so, should you wish to alter the order of units and/or add your own, they can be copied, cut and pasted to make your own plans.

ORGANIZATION OF TEACHING UNITS

Each term is divided into teaching units comprising between 1–5 hours. Each of the main units has either a reading or a writing focus (although there is, of course, overlap) and a fiction, poetry or non-fiction content. The units are organized as follows:

OBJECTIVES GRID

Outlines the word-, sentence- and text-level objectives of the unit.

UNIT	SPELLING/ VOCABULARY	GRAMMAR/ PUNCTUATION	COMPREHENSION/ COMPOSITION
READING FICTION 'The Little Box' by Kathleen Taylor.	Investigate, read and spell words by onset and rime, drawing on knowledge about initial consonant letter blends and word endings.	Reinforce knowledge through reading of the term 'sentence'.	Re-tell stories to give the main points in sequence and to pick out significant incidents.

ORGANIZATION GRID

Outlines the key activities for each part of each hour.

INTRODUCTION	WHOLE-CLASS SKILLS WORK	DIFFERENTIATED GROUP ACTIVITIES	CONCLUSION
HOUR 1 Shared reading of 'The Little Box' story on photocopiable page 189.	Identify story structure and main events.	1: Sequence events in the story to a story pattern. 2: Put sections of story text in correct order. 3*: Track story text to find sentences.	Selected pupils re-tell the story.
HOUR 2 Tell the story of 'The Little Box' from memory with some deliberate mistakes to test pupils' memory skills.	Spell words using onsets and rimes.	1*: Re-tell the story using prompt cards. 2*: Sort out true statements from false. Re-write false statements to make them true. 3: Make and spell words using onsets and rimes.	Selected pupils from Group 2 explain their work and reinforce how to structure sentences.

UNIT LESSON PLANS

Each unit of lesson plans is written to the following headings:

Resources
Provides a list of what you need for teaching the whole unit. Where appropriate, in the longer units, these have been grouped into paragraphs for ease of reference, for example: common classroom resources, photocopiable pages, other items.

Preparation
Outlines any advance preparation needed before the hour(s) begins. Where appropriate, in longer units, these have been grouped by hour.

Each hour is then set out as follows:

Introduction
Describes the activities for the whole-class shared reading/writing session.

Whole-class skills work
Describes the activities for the whole-class word- and sentence-level skills session. (See page 8 for further information about whole-class skills work.)
[NB: Sometimes Introduction and Whole-class skills work have been combined under one heading.]

Differentiated group work
Describes the group activities for the guided or shared group and independent work session. (See page 9 for further information about differentiated group work.)

Conclusion
Sets out what to do in the whole-class plenary session.

Photocopiables
Photocopiable texts and activity sheets are provided to support each unit. These can be found at the end of each relevant unit and are marked with the photocopiable symbol. Many of the sheets have more than one application and are therefore referred to in several units.

READING UNITS

These teaching units have three aims:

- ■ to develop basic reading skills across a wide range of texts – fiction, poetry and non-fiction
- ■ to develop skills of comprehension at a literal and inferential level
- ■ to encourage enjoyment of reading.

Using the texts
Some texts are provided on photocopiable resource sheets. In addition, the following popular texts will also be needed:

- *Hairy Maclary* by Lynley Dodd
- *Zug the Bug, Jen the Hen, Tog the Dog* by Colin Hawkins and Jacqui Hawkins
- *Where's Spot? and Spot Bakes a Cake* by Eric Hill
- *Have You Seen the Crocodile?* by Colin West
- *Handa's Surprise* by Eileen Browne
- *Farmer Duck* by Martin Waddell and Helen Oxenbury
- *Peace at Last* by Jill Murphy
- *School* by Carol Watson
- *We're Going on a Bear Hunt* by Michael Rosen and Helen Oxenbury
- *Can't You Sleep, Little Bear?* and *Let's Go Home, Little Bear* by Martin Waddell and Barbara Firth
- *How Cows Make Milk* from Magic Bean series (See also NLFS list of non-fiction)
- *Polar Bear, Polar Bear, What Do You Hear?* (Big Book and small versions) and *Brown Bear, Brown Bear, What Do You See?* by Bill Martin and Eric Carle
- *Mr Magnolia* by Quentin Blake
- *Mr McGee Goes to Sea* by Pamela Allan
- *Funnybones, The Black Cat, Dinosaur Dreams, Mystery Tour, The Pet Shop* by Janet and Allan Ahlberg
- *Alex and Roy* by Mary Dickinson
- Versions of *The Three Little Pigs* and *The Three Billy Goats Gruff*
- Modern stories with thematic links to *The Three Little Pigs,* such as *Alfie Gives a Hand* and *Moving Mollie* by Shirley Hughes
- Fairy stories with repeated phrases: *Goldilocks, Little Red Riding Hood, The Little Red Hen, Chicken Licken, The Gingerbread Man, The Runaway Pancake*
- Multiple copies of simple dictionaries
- Early fiction and non-fiction readers with contents pages and indexes.

Full details of these texts appear in the resources section of each unit. All the texts are intended for use as shared texts; that is to say, texts for whole-class and/or guided reading. Use of appropriate teaching methods enables children to read and understand texts beyond their independent reading level. The methods suggested in these materials include:

- ■ preparation: for example, giving the background to a story, prior study of difficult words
- ■ shared reading to the whole class with children following the text
- ■ differentiated follow-up activities which allow the most able children to respond independently to the text while further support is given to weaker readers
- ■ guided reading, in which the teacher takes groups of children through the text helping them with phonic or contextual clues (less able readers), or higher-level reading skills (more able readers).

Additional suggestions are given, where relevant, in the detailed lesson plans – for example, use of different versions of the same story. It is assumed that children will be following a programme of guided reading alongside their reading of these shared texts.

Written comprehension

Most written tasks included in these materials encourage a creative response to reading. These often reveal children's comprehension of the text as clearly as any formal comprehension, and, like the oral and dramatic activities, they are just as effective in developing comprehension skills. Activities included in the units will support the development of these skills.

WRITING UNITS

The writing units provide a series of structured writing experiences throughout the year. Some writing will be done with the teacher or another adult, and some will be done with the teacher modelling writing, but using the children's suggestions. These shared writing sessions should enable the teacher to use the vocabulary of writing and to discuss approaches to presentation. The teacher should also be able to demonstrate that writing can be revised and redrafted to make it more accessible to an audience.

There are also many opportunities for children to write independently, but at Key Stage 1 it is particularly important to provide props such as word banks (see Additional Resources, page 10) and frameworks which children can draw upon. These props should enable the children to become more independent to allow the teacher more time to work with children during differentiated group sessions.

Cross-curricular writing

Many opportunities for non-narrative writing occur in other curriculum areas. Therefore, when the necessary skills have been introduced through one of the non-fiction units, they should be applied to another curriculum area soon afterwards.

SPEAKING AND LISTENING

Speaking and Listening is also an essential part of literacy, and development of skills in this important area has been integrated into the units for both reading and writing. Speaking and listening is the most important way of developing reading skills. Children need to explore texts through discussion, role play and other forms of oral 'comprehension' before they can write with greater understanding. Brainstorming, sharing ideas, helping each other to check work and so on, will all help children to write more effectively.

TIMING OF THE LITERACY HOUR

A brisk pace is an important feature of an effective literacy hour. The following suggestions will help to keep things moving:

■ Train children to work independently. Stress that you cannot help them while you are working with a group – their turn will come. In the meantime, they must find out for themselves, or ask a friend or a classroom assistant.
■ Keep explanations brief. Get children on task as soon as possible, and give further clarification and help in the context of the activity. The use of a Task Management Board may help by acting as a visual reminder of group tasks. This uses symbols to denote activities (which can be created by the class) and 'T' to denote when working with the teacher. Groups are listed or named down the left-hand side of the board and the symbols put along side each group. If the symbols are laminated and backed with Velcro or Blu-Tack, they can be easily moved around and re-used.
■ Don't let skills sessions over-run, unless there is a good reason which has been planned for previously. Skills will be revised and practised several times throughout the year within the context of other slots in the Literacy Hour and in other lessons in English and other curricular areas.
■ When starting group activities sessions, give a clear message about what you want children to have achieved in the time allocated, and encourage them to work efficiently – ask them to concentrate on written tasks and complete illustrations later.

■ When working with a group, sit in a position so that the rest of the class can be seen.
■ Break off group work immediately to deal with any disruption. Ensure that children are aware that they are being supervised even when you are working with a group.

Introductory session: Shared reading

The following procedure is recommended:

■ Select a specific focus in advance (for example, rhyming words).
■ Begin by predicting the contents of the text from the cover and title (and blurb if appropriate).
■ Discuss words in the title, look at the title page and other illustrations. (This is an important step in activating children's prior knowledge, which is vital in a meaningful learning context.)
■ Read the text at a brisk expressive pace with the children joining in, and use a pointer to point to the words as you read. This will help to emphasize the one-to-one correspondence of one spoken word to one written word, and focus the children to the text. Ensure that you use a pointer, as fingers will mask the text.
■ During reading, stop occasionally (but not so frequently that the meaning is lost) to ask questions or predict what will happen next.
■ Demonstrate using different cues, for example, picture cues or graphophonic cues, ie 'How can we work out this tricky word?' You can also demonstrate reading on and leaving a word out, but guessing it later, or reading back to find out a difficult word, depending on the position of the word in the sentence.
■ After reading, respond to the text by asking questions to ensure understanding of the content. Extend by asking questions which require an inferential understanding.
■ Focus on specific sentence or word-level aspects after ensuring an understanding of the whole text.
■ Use a variety of guided and independent tasks to deepen understanding, and to explore word- and sentence-level aspects. The units contain a large number of tasks of this nature.

Whole-class skills work

It is during these sessions that grammar, punctuation, spelling, vocabulary and phonic skills are taught, with an emphasis on word-level work at Key Stage One. The main principle is that the skills arise from the shared text and will also be used in the related writing unit. Over the year, key skills should be revisited many times so that the children's mastery of them grows incrementally.

Although the materials in this book include spelling activities based on spelling rules and patterns arising from the texts, they cannot take the place of a programme of individualized spelling for children. The children could collect, in a spelling book, a list of words they need to learn. This could be supplemented at least once a week with words from a standard list to make a list of, say, ten (or more for more able/older children). Children then learn their lists using the 'Look, say, cover, write, check' strategy. Pairs of children can test each other on their own lists. Any words not learned can be carried over into the next list.

At Key Stage One there should be considerable emphasis on the following:

■ listening to the sounds within words and identifying phonemes
■ identifying initial sounds
■ simple mnemonics to help children to remember spellings
■ spelling patterns
■ segmenting words into onset and rime and into graphemes which represent phonemes.

A NOTE ON TEACHING PHONICS
There are three main strands in the teaching of phonics:

Phonological awareness
Children must be able to hear and discriminate sounds in words accurately. It is important to assess children's ability to do this and provide plenty of opportunities to

develop the use of rhythm, rhyme and alliteration for those who have not yet developed good phonological awareness.

Sound/symbol (Phoneme/grapheme) correspondence
One teaching programme which helps develop this correspondence is THRASS. This stands for Teaching Handwriting Reading and Spelling Skills. Central to THRASS is the chart which shows how all 44 sounds (phonemes) of spoken English are represented by letters (graphemes). THRASS focuses on knowledge of the alphabet and the naming of the lower-case letters and their capitals, using the correct terms from the beginning (eg phoneme and grapheme). THRASS also teaches that it is not always one letter which makes one sound (a graph); it may be two letters (a digraph) or three letters (a trigraph).

Mnemonics: Many phonic schemes (for example, *Letterland*, or *The Phonic Handbook*: *Jolly Phonics*) utilize mnemonics to help children to remember the sound/symbol relationship. These are useful as an interim measure in helping children to recall the letter and the sound(s) it makes.

Blending/segmenting sounds
Children need to be taught to blend individual phonemes into words when reading and to segment words into sounds for spelling in order to use phonics successfully.

Differentiated group activities

For most group activities, three levels of differentiation are suggested:

Group 1:   above average pupils
Group 2:   average pupils
Group 3:   below average pupils.

The ability groups may be further subdivided according to size of class and ability of the children. Groups do not have to be of equal size and there may be some flexibility of groupings.

In the average Key Stage One class, group sizes would be between 8–10 (with some trade-off between groups according to the spread of ability in the class). This is fine for organizational purposes and working with the teacher, but too large for most collaborative activities. These groups will therefore need to be subdivided into smaller groups of fours or pairs for some activities.

Try to divide your teaching time equally between all groups over the course of the week – the most able need help just as much as the least able if they are given suitably demanding tasks.

[NB: An asterisk (*) after the group number is used on the grids and in the lesson plans to show which groups the teacher should be working with during the group activities session.]

Finally, it is important to stress that even when you are working intensively with one group, the first priority is always the overall work rate of the whole class. See 'Timing of the Literacy Hour' (page 7) for suggestions on how to keep the session moving at a brisk pace.

Finishing off

At the end of the group activities, it may be that some children have not completed their work. If this is the case, children could complete short tasks as homework. Some tasks may be completed over several sessions, for example if they are making their own books. However, it is important to stress to children what they are expected to finish within the time and thereby ensure the pace of work.

Conclusion

The key objective in most of these sessions is to review the teaching points of the lesson and ensure that the work of selected children, pairs or groups is shared with the class for discussion and evaluation. Enough should be heard to exemplify the variety of work produced, but not so much that it becomes boring, or takes too much time. Keep a record of who has presented what to ensure that all children have the opportunity to present their work in due course.

ASSESSMENT

Regular and on-going assessment of pupils' achievements and progress is, of course, essential. These materials assume that you and your school have satisfactory methods and systems of assessing and recording already in place and therefore don't attempt to suggest an alternative. However, what these materials also assume is that your current procedures are based on clearly stated teaching objectives. Therefore the objectives grids at the beginning of each unit should be invaluable in providing you with a framework for on-going assessment.

In addition, to facilitate individual pupil conferencing at the end of each half-term, a photocopiable record sheet has been provided on page 20. Specific targets for reading and writing can be set for each pupil at the end of the previous half-term and recorded on the sheet in the left-hand column. Interim progress towards these targets can be assessed when appropriate and noted in the middle column. Then, at the end of each half-term, during the conference, pupil and teacher together can record achievement and agree further targets for the next half-term.

ADDITIONAL RESOURCES

The following additional equipment and resources are invaluable in delivering the Literacy Hour, and are referred to in a number of units:
- Big Book stand
- Whiteboard/magnetic board and letters
- Pointer (a home-made one will do!)
- OHP and acetate sheets
- 'Post-it' notes
- Masking cards – which slide to reveal particular words (see below for details)
- Selection of ready-made blank cards for writing key vocabulary
- Listening centre and headphones
- Blank Big Books
- Bank of frequently used resources for independent group work, such as word wheels, word dice, rhyming pictures, letter dice, words squares, sight word recognition games, for example lotto and pairs. A range of these resources is provided in these materials for specific activities
- Resource box for each table, containing, for example, spelling resources (spelling cards, dictionaries, personal dictionaries, 'have a go' books), pencils, crayons, sharpeners, rubbers, scissors, glue, highlighters.

Big Books
Big Books are an essential resource for many of the literacy hour lessons. When purchasing commercially-made versions (some are specifically recommended in the units), ensure that the print is large enough to be seen by the whole class and look for examples which will provide a rich resource for different activities.

Making Big Books from published books
It is possible to make your own Big Books using published picture books. You will need to cut the book up into pages (if the book has pictures on both sides of the pages, you will need two copies). Then retype the text using 48-point font size and double spacing in between the words. Stick the pictures onto A3 size card or stiff paper and stick the appropriate enlarged words underneath. Laminate the pages and include the cover, title page and so on, so the whole book is reproduced. Now bind the book, using either a spiral binder, or several binding rings. Note that only one Big Book (not multiple copies) may be made for any one published picture book.

Making a blank Big Book
You will need sheets of standard-sized large card (64cm by 45cm), sheets of buff sugar paper cut to fit the card so that a 3cm margin remains all the way round, and some sticky-backed plastic cut into strips measuring 8cm wide and slightly longer than the length of the pages.
   Use one side only of the buff sugar paper pages when scribing the story for the children (write in large print), and decide together on the amount of illustration space.

Once the illustrations have been completed, mount each sugar paper page onto a sheet of card in the correct order, using both sides of the card, to make the pages of the book. Take a strip of sticky-backed plastic and carefully lay the edge of the cover page about 3cm into the strip leaving a little at the top and bottom (Figure 1a). Place the edge of the second page alongside the edge of the first page and make a seam with a second length of sticky-backed plastic (Figure 1b). Do this until all the pages are linked together with the sticky-backed plastic seams. Finish by sticking the remaining width of sticky-backed plastic to the back cover.

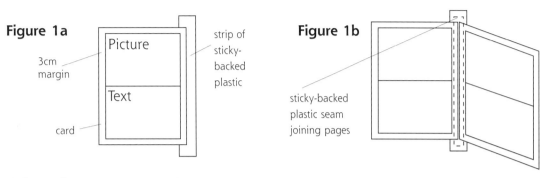

Figure 1a

3cm margin

Picture

Text

card

strip of sticky-backed plastic

Figure 1b

sticky-backed plastic seam joining pages

Enlarged texts
A large variety of enlarged texts can be used for shared reading. For example, commercially produced posters, nursery rhyme cards and poems are available from publishers. Home-made posters and shaped poem cards can also be made by typing the text (again in 48-point font size) and adding illustrations from photocopiable sheets or children's own illustrations. Shaped poem cards are made by using an enlarged shape, for example of a pig, and then fixing on a suitable poem or rhyme. Laminate or cover in sticky-backed plastic for extended use. With the text extracts provided in this book you can make enlarged A3 versions using the photocopier.

Storyboards
An enlarged storyboard on which you can fix characters and objects from a story is useful to focus young children on the story and help fix the details in their minds. To make one, use a large sheet of chipboard or hardboard measuring about 75cm high by 90cm wide and cover in felt. Now cut appropriate characters to fit the story out of different coloured felt, or use cardboard and attach a patch of Velcro to the back (you can build up a selection of characters for traditional tales). The characters will stick to the felt board. Alternatively, if you have a magnetic board, cut the characters or objects out of stiff cardboard and colour or paint them, then fix magnetic tape to the back of them.

Word banks
Word banks can take many forms. You can provide lists of words which children will need for general use (for example, the high frequency lists in the *National Literacy Strategy Framework for Teaching)* and/or lists of words for specific activities or topics.

The words may be provided on sheets of paper or they may be displayed so that children can refer to them constantly and use them as part of their 'Look, say, cover, write, check' strategy.

You could make a pocket wall display. This will consist of a large piece of cloth (such as very strong cotton) approximately 1.5m wide and 1m long, onto which are stitched pockets large enough to house high frequency words printed onto card. The letters of the alphabet in lower and upper case will need to be displayed on the outside of the pockets. (You could combine x y z on one pocket.) Alternatively this could be made from strong card with cardboard pockets. (See Figure 2.)

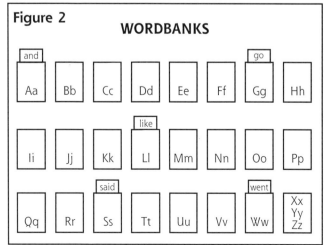

Figure 2

WORDBANKS

and						go	
Aa	Bb	Cc	Dd	Ee	Ff	Gg	Hh

			like				
Ii	Jj	Kk	Ll	Mm	Nn	Oo	Pp

		said				went	
Qq	Rr	Ss	Tt	Uu	Vv	Ww	Xx Yy Zz

When new words are added, use the opportunity to discuss spelling and alphabetical order and ask the children to help you place the new words in the correct positions. Encourage the children to go to the word bank to see if spellings they need are displayed rather than asking for your help. Discuss the words regularly and make sure that children become increasingly familiar with them.

Masking cards

The use of masking cards is a device that helps to focus children's attention on specific words or phrases and helps teaching 'that crucial eye-voice-ear link which makes print intelligible in the earliest stages of reading' (Don Holdaway, *The Foundations of Literacy*, 1979). Don Holdaway's work has become an established rationale for using Big Books which is at the very heart of teaching within the literacy hour.

The sliding mask allows the teacher to gradually reveal words or phrases that are to be focused on. These can be made in two ways, either as a sliding mask (which will require a sliding strip to be cut and a card loop fixed to the back to pull it through – see Figure 3a), or as a cut-out or 'fixed' mask which can be used to emphasize repeated phrases or refrains in a story (Figure 3b). Put Blu-tack on the back in order to fix the card to the page of text.

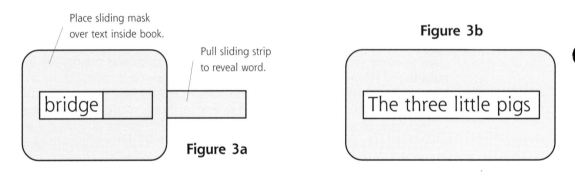

Figure 3b

Place sliding mask over text inside book.

Pull sliding strip to reveal word.

bridge

The three little pigs

Figure 3a

GENERAL BOOK MAKING

A range of book-making activities is used in the units. Instructions for these are follows:

Zigzag book

Cut a strip of thick paper or thin card. This can be half a sheet of A3 cut lengthwise or bigger or smaller as required. Make even folds in the paper to create a concertina effect (Figure 4). Extra zigzag strips can be joined on with adhesive tape if more pages are required.

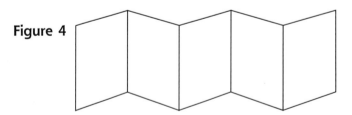

Figure 4

Stapled book

Also known as 'little books', these are invaluable for story sequencing or story writing activities and can be made in different sizes and shapes. Start by working out how many pages are needed – remember that one folded sheet of paper will provide four pages. Take the appropriate number of sheets and fold each one exactly in half. Staple along the centre fold (Figure 5). To make a firmer cover, replace the outside sheet of paper with a piece of card. A laminated cover will help the book to last longer.

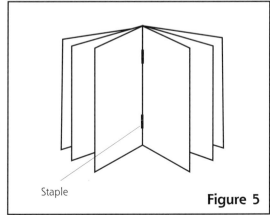

Staple

Figure 5

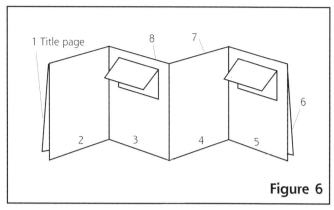

Lift-the-flap book

Fold a sheet of A3 paper in half lengthways. Fold this in half again widthways and in half again (Figure 6). Cut flaps carefully with a craft knife or sharp scissors on alternate pages, making a total of three flaps.

Figure 6

Shape book

Make a card template of the shape you wish to use (keep the shape as simple as possible). Fold a sheet of card for the cover and enough cartridge paper to make the inside pages for one book, then use the template as an outline to cut through the whole book in one go (Figure 7a) and staple together.

Alternatively, you can make books with shaped covers only. To do this, trace round the template and cut several covers at once from card. Staple or sew each cover over the inside pages (Figure 7b).

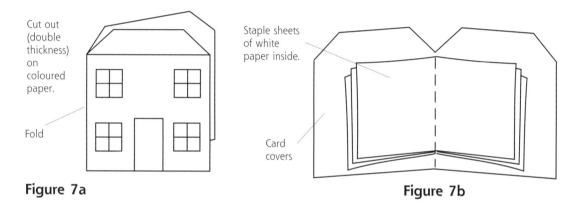

Figure 7a

Figure 7b

USE OF AN OVERHEAD PROJECTOR

Having the use of an overhead projector (OHP) is ideal for whole-class work. Photocopiable texts and skills activities can then be copied onto acetate sheets to make overhead transparencies (OHTs) which can be projected onto a screen or a bare, white or light-coloured wall, or a whiteboard which can then be written on. Where an OHP is not available, photocopiable sheets should be enlarged to at least A3 size with 48 point text.

INFORMATION AND COMPUTER TECHNOLOGY

■ For skills practice, using programs such as *Animated Alphabet*
■ For word processing, either by the teacher during shared or guided writing sessions, or by children using simpler word processing programmes, such as *Clicker Plus* (Crick Software) which enables the creation of grids similar to an overlay keyboard, but on screen.
■ For creating own books and developing story writing using programs such as *StoryBook Weaver* (Iona Software).
■ For developing reading skills using interactive stories on CD ROM.

A NOTE ON PHOTOCOPYING

Please note that where there is instruction to copy material from copyright texts, you need to ensure that this is done within the limits of the copying licence your school has. If children are using their own exercise books or paper for answers, then all photocopiable resources are re-usable.

OVERVIEW: YEAR 1
TERM 1

UNIT	SPELLING/ VOCABULARY	GRAMMAR/ PUNCTUATION	COMPREHENSION/ COMPOSITION
HOUR 3 READING FICTION AND POETRY *Hairy Maclary from Donaldson's Dairy* by Lynley Dodd.	Explore words with analogous sound patterns and letter patterns.	Draw on and use grammatical awareness to read with appropriate expression and intonation. Use the term 'capital letter' and recognize their use in names.	Read independently, tracking the text in the right order, page by page. Make correspondence between words said and read. Elaborate on an incident in the story.
HOUR 3 READING FICTION AND POETRY *Zug the Bug* by Colin and Jacqui Hawkins.	Discriminate and segment all three phonemes in CVC words. Blend phonemes to read CVC words in rhyming sets.	Draw on and use grammatical awareness to read with appropriate expression and intonation using puppets.	Notice difference between spoken and written forms through re-telling and re-enacting stories. Read simple stories independently.
HOUR 1 READING AND WRITING FICTION *Where's Spot?* by Eric Hill.	Blend phonemes to read CVC words.	Write simple sentences and re-read, recognizing whether or not they make sense.	Use a patterned story as a model for their own writing. Make simple 'lift-the-flap' books.
HOUR 2 READING AND WRITING FICTION *Have You Seen the Crocodile?* by Colin West.	Discover new words from shared reading and investigate their phonemic structure. Word recognition of high frequency words from list 1.	Use awareness of the grammar of a sentence in order to predict text.	Use a patterned story as a model for their own writing. Make simple 'lift-the-flap' picture books with sentences, modelling them on basic text conventions.
HOUR 5 READING AND WRITING FICTION *Handa's Surprise* by Eileen Browne.	Recognize new words from reading. Recognize critical features of words in order to predict the whole word.	Recognize full stops and capital letters when reading and name them correctly. Begin to use the term 'sentence' and identify sentences in text. Begin to use capital letters and full stops in writing.	Use phonological, contextual, grammatical and graphic knowledge to work out, predict and check meanings of unfamiliar words. Describe a story setting. Make simple books with sentences, modelled on basic text conventions.
HOUR 5 READING FICTION *The Little Red Hen* (Traditional), and *Farmer Duck* by Martin Waddell and Helen Oxenbury.	Read on sight high frequency words including: said, the, who, will, help, this. Spell these words correctly.	Use a capital letter for the personal pronoun 'I'. Write captions and simple sentences, and re-read for sense. Predict text from grammar. Predict story from cover. Compare with other stories.	Identify main features in stories. Re-enact stories in a variety of ways. Raise an awareness of the difference between spoken and written forms through retelling known stories – compare oral version with written text.
HOUR 3 READING AND WRITING FICTION *Peace at Last* by Jill Murphy.	Reinforce key words for sight vocabulary by putting words into sentences to fit into the story. Begin to locate middle sounds in words.	Be able to join in and predict words from overall sense. Write simple sentences. Use capital letters for names, for the start of a sentence and for the personal pronoun 'I'.	Predict story pattern. Recognize features, eg use of capital letters, for expression.

OVERVIEW: YEAR 1
TERM 1 (CONTINUED)

UNIT	SPELLING/ VOCABULARY	GRAMMAR/ PUNCTUATION	COMPREHENSION/ COMPOSITION
READING POETRY 'Another Day' by John Cunliffe.	Identify rhyming words, and rhyming phonemic elements. Generate new words from reading and discussion.	Use awareness of grammar to decipher new or unfamiliar words.	Read independently and point to written word, making correspondence between this and spoken version. Recite small sections of the poem.
READING AND WRITING FICTION AND NON-FICTION What's Cooking? (Recipe)	Explore new words from reading and shared experiences. Distinguish between 'onsets' and 'rimes' and invent new words using the rime -ake.	Write one-word instructions and simple sentences. Re-read for sense or to make improvements. Reinforce using capital letters at the start of names.	Read and use captions/labels. Write captions/one word instructions. Write and draw simple instructions.
READING AND WRITING NON-FICTION Our School Day.	Use 'look, say, cover, write, check' routine for learning spellings and putting words into personal word books.	Read captions and simple sentences. Check meaning by using grammatical awareness. Use lines to indicate relationship between word and items.	Use a selection of non-fiction books to read captions and pictures. Read and write captions. Read, follow and devise simple instructions.

OVERVIEW: YEAR 1
TERM 2

UNIT	SPELLING/ VOCABULARY	GRAMMAR/ PUNCTUATION	COMPREHENSION/ COMPOSITION
HOUR 5 READING FICTION *The Three Little Pigs* (Traditional story).	Use onset, rime and analogy to read unknown words. Extend initial consonant clusters.	Identify sentences and order/re-order them. Introduce speech bubbles.	Listen to and re-tell a traditional story. Identify and discuss characters and speculate about their behaviour. Compare *The Three Little Pigs* with other stories.
HOUR 5 WRITING FICTION *The Three Little Pigs* (Traditional story).	Practise and reinforce discrimination, spelling and reading of beginning, middle and final letter sounds in simple words.	Identify and compare basic story elements using appropriate story language. Recognize appropriate punctuation.	Shared writing of class story. Identify key features in plots, especially beginnings and endings. Extend rhyming and alliterative patterns.
HOUR 1 READING AND WRITING POETRY 'The Grass House' by Shirley Hughes.	Identify 's' sounds in text.	Recognize features in text that assist reading with expression.	Become aware of meanings contained in phrases of a poem. Use poem as a model for creating own poems.
HOUR 3 READING AND WRITING POETRY 'A Busy Day' by Michael Rosen.	Recognize by sight and spell some high frequency words. Spell using onset and rime.	Recognize how punctuation affects the way a poem is read, especially question marks. Predict text from grammar (prepositions).	Learn and recite a poem. Extend language patterns in the poem.
HOUR 5 READING AND WRITING FICTION *We're Going on a Bear Hunt* by Michael Rosen and Helen Oxenbury.	Investigate spelling, recognizing critical features of some words and sounding out.	Predict words from preceding sentences. Recognize the effects of different types of print.	Read, making links between texts and illustrations. Through shared and guided writing, apply phonological and graphic knowledge and sight vocabulary to spell words. Use grammatical structures as models for writing.
HOUR 5 READING AND WRITING FICTION *Can't You Sleep, Little Bear?* and *Let's Go Home, Little Bear* by Martin Waddell and Barbara Firth.	Discriminate, read and spell words with initial consonant clusters. Build words with different consonant clusters.	Use capital letters for proper nouns, and at the beginning of sentences.	Identify and discuss characters and speculate on behaviour in using text and illustrations.
HOUR 3 READING AND WRITING NON-FICTION Say Cheese! (Lists and recipes.)	Explore and generate words with initial consonant cluster *ch* and identify it in words. Develop understanding of phonemic structures and critical features of words for spelling.	Use awareness of grammatical sense to decipher new or unfamiliar words.	Develop awareness of the different layout of non-fiction text as in lists and recipes.

OVERVIEW: YEAR 1
TERM 2 (CONTINUED)

UNIT	SPELLING/ VOCABULARY	GRAMMAR/ PUNCTUATION	COMPREHENSION/ COMPOSITION
READING NON-FICTION Information books.	Blend phonemes in words with clusters. Extend vocabulary through reading. Collect words of interest, including those from topic work. Use initial letters for alphabetic organization.	Identify sentences in texts, ie those demarcated by capital letters and full stops.	Use terms 'fiction' and 'non-fiction', noting different features. Read non-fiction books and understand that reading can be selective according to readers' needs. Predict a book's contents from covers. Understand purpose of contents/indexes.
READING AND WRITING NON-FICTION Ordered texts: simple dictionaries.	Secure identification, spelling and reading of simple cvc words. Secure alphabetical order.	Expect reading to make sense when accessing information in dictionaries.	Use simple dictionaries and understand their alphabetical arrangement

OVERVIEW: YEAR 1
TERM 3

UNIT	SPELLING/ VOCABULARY	GRAMMAR/ PUNCTUATION	COMPREHENSION/ COMPOSITION
READING FICTION AND POETRY *Polar Bear, Polar Bear, What Do You Hear?* and *Brown Bear, Brown Bear, What Do You See?* both by Bill Martin and Eric Carle.	Investigate verbs with *-ed* (past tense) and *-ing* (present tense) endings. Encounter new words from reading. Spell new and familiar words using graphic and phonic knowledge.	Use awareness of grammar to decipher new and high frequency words. Identify questions and use question mark appropriately. Read with pace and expression appropriate to grammar and punctuation.	Use titles, covers and 'blurb' to predict story content. Read poetry aloud. Compose poetic sentences using imagination. Enact and tell imagined stories, with expression.
READING AND WRITING NON-FICTION Polar Bears.	Recognize words by common spelling patterns. Read and spell new words from reading. Identify special or significant words linked to the topic.	Identify questions. Read familiar texts aloud with pace and expression appropriate to the grammar. Add question marks to questions. Reinforce knowledge of the term 'sentence'.	Recognize non-fiction books. Read and write recounts and begin to recognize ordered sequence of events/words. Identify questions and use texts to find answers. Make group/class non-fiction books.
READING AND WRITING FICTION AND POETRY *Mister Magnolia* by Quentin Blake.	Explore words with different spellings of the same phoneme.	Choose and collect significant/ favourite sentences. Discuss, re-read and use to adapt and extend.	Use the context of reading and grammatical and phonemic cues to predict texts. Use a poem/ story as a model for writing by adapting the text.
READING AND WRITING FICTION AND POETRY *Mr. McGee Goes to Sea* by Pamela Allen.	Explore words with different spellings of the long vowel phonemes *ee* and *ie*.	Extend rhyming sentences. Construct sentences for given words.	Use the context of reading as a cue in conjunction with grammatical and phonemic cues to predict texts. Explore element of fantasy in story.
READING AND WRITING POETRY 'Cats' by Eleanor Farjeon and 'Cat' by Vernon Scannell.	Identify rhyming words including those which have same sounds but different spellings. Understand the terms 'vowel' and 'consonant'. Learn some of the common spellings for the long vowel phoneme *ai*.	Use awareness of grammar to decipher new or unfamiliar words.	Read a variety of poems on similar themes.
READING AND WRITING POETRY 'I Wonder' by Kathleen Taylor.	Build individual collections of words for alliterative value from given double consonant blends. Build collections of words that rhyme. Investigate spellings of vowel phonemes *ai*, *ow* and *i_e*.	Read aloud with pace and expression appropriate to grammar.	Use poem as a model for composing own poetry.
READING FICTION 'The Little Box' by Kathleen Taylor.	Investigate, read and spell words by onset and rime, drawing on knowledge about initial consonant letter blends and word endings.	Reinforce knowledge through reading of the term 'sentence'.	Re-tell stories to give the main points in sequence and to pick out significant incidents.

OVERVIEW: YEAR 1
TERM 3 (CONTINUED)

UNIT	SPELLING/ VOCABULARY	GRAMMAR/ PUNCTUATION	COMPREHENSION/ COMPOSITION
READING FICTION *Funnybones* by Janet and Allan Ahlberg.	Use the term 'phoneme' and identify phonemes in speech and words.	Reinforce knowledge of a sentence by re-writing upper case letters in lower case, placing capital letters correctly. Read familiar parts of text with expression.	Use covers to compare similarities and differences within the *Funnybones* series. Identify preferences in the different stories of *Funnybones*.
READING AND WRITING FICTION *Alex and Roy* by Mary Dickinson.	Be able to read on sight words from List 1. Investigate compound words. Investigate spellings of verbs with *-ed* and *-ing* endings.	Read familiar texts aloud with pace and expression appropriate to the grammar. Understand common uses of capitalization.	Write about significant incidents from known stories.
READING AND WRITING NON-FICTION Charts.	Learn new words linked to a topic. Use simple dictionaries to check spelling.	Add question marks to questions.	Locate information using a chart. Use the language and features of non-fiction texts. Write questions related to a chart.

PUPIL RECORD SHEET

Pupil's name:

		Class	Year group
Term	1	2	3	1st half	2nd half

TARGET(S)	INTERIM PROGRESS (inc. dates)	ACHIEVEMENT AT END OF HALF TERM
Reading		
Writing		

Term 1

HAIRY MACLARY

OBJECTIVES

UNIT	SPELLING/ VOCABULARY	GRAMMAR/ PUNCTUATION	COMPREHENSION/ COMPOSITION
READING FICTION AND POETRY *Hairy Maclary from Donaldson's Dairy* by Lynley Dodd.	Explore words with analogous sound patterns and letter patterns.	Draw on and use grammatical awareness to read with appropriate expression and intonation. Use the term 'capital letter' and recognize their use in names.	Read independently, tracking the text in the right order, page by page. Make correspondence between words said and read. Elaborate on an incident in the story.

ORGANIZATION (3 HOURS)

	INTRODUCTION	WHOLE-CLASS SKILLS WORK	DIFFERENTIATED GROUP ACTIVITIES	CONCLUSION
HOUR 1	Shared reading of *Hairy Maclary* Big Book. Pupils predict masked rhyming words.	Explore rhyming letter patterns in words.	1*: Read in pairs the whole text, making decisions regarding how to share reading aloud in order to enhance the reading of the story. 2: Match names of dogs to associated rhyming phrase in order to place in sequence in a little book. 3: Match names to dogs and do cloze exercise.	Selected pair of Group 1 pupils read story to the class.
HOUR 2	Oral session providing extended rhymes to those in story.	Identify phonemes in CVC (Consonant-Vowel-Consonant) words using medial vowel sounds *o* and *u*.	1: Extend rhyming pattern. 2*: Complete rhyming phrases by choosing appropriate rhyming word. Make lists of rhyming words. 3: Play 'Snap' game, identifying -ot and -um words.	Selected pupils from Group 3 show others how to play game. Display pupil's work from Group 1.
HOUR 3	Gather suggestions on a flip chart for a new ending to the story, so pupils can read back suggestions they have made.	Develop awareness of the uses of capital letters.	1: Invent and name nasty creatures. 2: Practise writing own and school's name using capital letters appropriately. 3*: In pairs, practise reading book aloud with expression and intonation.	Pupils from Group 2 show and read their own name and name of school. Pair from Group 3 read aloud. Display pupil's work from Group 1.

RESOURCES

Hairy Maclary from Donaldson's Dairy by Lynley Dodd (Big Book – Era Publications, Australia, ISBN 0-14-050531-8. Also, see main Introduction, page 10 for general guidance on making your own Big Books), enough small copies of *Hairy Maclary* (Puffin, ISBN 0-14-050531-8) for group work and guided reading, Blu-Tack, card, materials for making small books (see main Introduction, page 12 for guidance), a copy of the school's letterhead (optional), a board or flip-chart, writing and drawing materials.

Photocopiable pages 26 (Match it Up!), 27 (Names and Pictures), 28 (Rhyming Words) and 29 (Choose the Rhyme).

PREPARATION

Hour 1

Before the shared reading of the *Hairy Maclary* Big Book in Hour 1, mask the rhyming words *dairy*, *horse*, *spots*, *hay*, *bony* and *turn* (see main Introduction, page 12) so that the children can predict the rhymes as they follow the text. Make enough small blank six-page books for each child in Group 2 (see main Introduction, page 12, for guidance). Prepare one copy of photocopiable page 26 (Match it Up!) for each child in Group 2, and one copy of photocopiable pages 27 (Names and Pictures) and 28 (Rhyming Words) for each child in Group 3.

Hour 2
Prepare cards with additional rhymes written on as listed in the Introduction on page 24. Write a selection of *ot* and *um* words on separate cards (choose from the list below) and place in a cloth bag. Make one copy of photocopiable page 29 (Choose the Rhyme) for each child in Group 2. Devise a 'Snap' game by writing two sets of each word below on separate cards. You will need a complete set of cards for each group of three or four children in Group 3.

**got, hot, cot, rot, tot, jot, dot, lot, not, pot
gum, tum, rum, sum, bum, hum, mum**

Introduction
Display the *Hairy Maclary* Big Book and engage the children in reading the title and the name of the author. Turn the front cover over and read the inside front cover. Ask the children what they think the nasty surprise might be. Read and name the title page and then begin reading the story, selecting children to predict the covered rhyming words. Draw the children into the story by referring to what is happening in the pictures. At the end of the story, remember to ask the children if their predictions for the rhyming words were correct.

Whole-class skills work
Turn to the beginning of the book and draw the children's attention to the look of the words '*Hairy Maclary*'. Ask them to predict again the rest of the rhyme ('*from Donaldson's Dairy*'). Draw their attention to the descending *y* shape at the end of the rhyming words, for example *-ry, -airy*.
   Ask the children: Who followed Hairy Maclary? Again, draw their attention to analogous patterns, for example *-ot,* as in *B*o*ttomley, P*o*tts, *sp*ots*.
   Repeat this exercise for the other dogs mentioned, so that the children remember the sequence that occurred in the story and see the need to look for patterns of rhyming sounds.

Differentiated group activities
Children in Group 2 will each need a copy of photocopiable page 26 (Match it Up!). Each child in Group 3 will need a copy of photocopiable pages 27 (Names and Pictures) and 28 (Rhyming Words).
1*: Pairs of children should share a copy of the text and read the story to each other with expression (just as you did during the shared reading).They then have to work out how to share the task of reading the story aloud so that they can take turns as they read through the book. Ask them how they might do this so that the story sounds even better. Remind them to look at the pictures of the characters in order to 'adopt a voice' as you did earlier, for example: a light, bouncy voice for Bottomley Potts, a deep strong voice for Hercules Morse and a low voice for Schnitzel von Krumm. Explain that at the end of the lesson, you will be asking one of the pairs to present their reading to the class.
2: Children work independently to complete photocopiable page 26. They then stick the names and phrases in sequence into a six-page little book for future reading. Cover pages and illustrations can be added later if desired.
3: Children work independently to complete photocopiable page 27. They then move on to complete photocopiable page 28, in which they are asked to provide the correct rhyming words to accompany phrases taken from the story.

Conclusion
Select a pair of children from Group 1 to read the story to the class. Encourage and praise the children at points where greater expression is needed. At the end of the reading, reinforce the teaching points by referring to places in the text that give the reader clues to appropriate expression, for example:

they

saw

SCARFACE CLAW

"EEEEEOWWWFFTZ!"

Introduction

Tell the children you have added an extra little rhyme onto the rhymes in the story and that you want them to guess the new rhyming words. Read aloud each rhyme written on separate cards as follows, selecting children to guess the rhyme:

Hairy Maclary from Donaldson's Dairy
Came down the street dressed like a <u>fairy</u>.

Hercules Morse as big as a horse
Always ate dinner covered in <u>sauce</u>.

Bottomley Potts covered in spots
Came down the street with his tail tied in <u>knots</u>.

Muffin McLay like a bundle of hay
Had a ball in his mouth and wanted to <u>play</u>.

Bitzer Maloney all skinny and bony
Came down the street riding a <u>pony</u>.

Schnitzel von Krumm with a very low tum
Came down the street chewing on <u>gum</u>.

Then engage the children in thinking of ways to extend the rhymes even further. For example, for the rhyme *Hairy Maclary from Donaldson's Dairy/ Came down the street dressed like a fairy*, ask what else rhymes with *'fairy'* ('scary', 'wary'). Then experiment with inventing rhyming words, such as 'shary', 'bary', 'glary' and so on.

Whole-class skills work

Now focus on the less complex rhyming words in the text, for example *'spot'* and *'tum'*. Write *'spot'* on one side of the board and *'tum'* on the other. Select children to choose the words from the cloth bag (see Preparation) and to place them underneath the appropriate rhyming word using a little Blu-Tack. Encourage the children to listen to the sound of each word and then say the letter sounds aloud, especially the medial *o* and *u*.

Differentiated group activities

Give each child in Group 2 a copy of photocopiable page 29 (Choose the Rhyme).
1: Children work in pairs to choose from the extended rhymes on the cards and work on extending them further. Explain that a good way to start is to list as many other rhyming words as possible and then choose from these to add a further part to the rhyme.
2*: Each child reads and completes a copy of photocopiable page 29, finishing by choosing one of the rhyming words and making a list of other words, real or invented, with the same rhyme.
3: Children in threes or fours play the 'Snap' game, starting by dealing all the cards equally. The first player places a card on the table and says the word aloud, for example 'hot'. Then the next player places a card on top. If this word does not rhyme with 'hot', no-one calls out and they continue playing. When a rhyming word does occur, the first one to call out that word wins the cards.

Conclusion

Select some children from Group 3 to show the rest of the class how to play the Snap game, then place the game on a table for others to play over the week. Tell the children that the work from Group 1 will be displayed on a board so that everyone can read the rhymes this group have created.

Introduction

Display the *Hairy Maclary* Big Book and remind the children of what it says on the inside cover, as in the introduction for Hour 1. Explain that while you read the story, you want everyone to be thinking of an alternative 'nasty surprise' instead of Scarface Claw. When you reach the point in the story where it says: *out of the shadows/ they/ saw...*, ask the children to suggest their ideas on possible 'nasty' creatures. They might suggest spiders, snakes, aliens, monsters, ghosts, etc. Encourage them to think of names for their nasty creatures, similar to 'Scarface Claw'. Be prepared to support them at this point by providing a few suggestions, such as: Snapper Chops Croc, Big Bite Spider, Fork Fang Snake, Growl Face Tiger. Write these on the board or flip chart.

Whole-class skills work

Focus on specific phonemes and shapes of letters as you write the children's suggestions on the board. Then ask the children if they have noticed a difference between the letters at the beginning of the name and the other letters. Do they know what the large letters are called? Where else have they seen them used? Link the capital letters at the beginning of the names of the dogs and invented creatures in the story to the children's own names.

Differentiated group activities

1: Children work in pairs to invent nasty creatures for the story, together with appropriate names. Each pair then collaborates to choose two creatures which they draw and name.

2: Children work independently, following the example of *Hairy Maclary from Donaldson's Dairy* as a model for writing their name and the name of the school using capital letters appropriately, for example:

Louise Smith
from Oakhurst School.

If supervision is available, the children could go outside to look at the name of the school on the signboard. Alternatively, you could provide them with a copy of the school's letterhead. They should then write their home address using the same model.

3*: Children work in pairs, sharing a copy of the *Hairy Maclary* book. They read the story together and provide an alternative nasty creature which they substitute for 'Scarface Claw'. They should be encouraged to use their imagination and expressive skills when reading aloud in order to convey the full nastiness of the creature. (This could be a guided reading session.)

Conclusion

Select children from Group 2 to show and read their own names and the name of the school, and ask them to talk about where they have used capital letters. Incorporate some of their work in a display that reinforces knowledge about using capital letters. Ask a pair of children from Group 3 to read the story aloud, and encourage and praise them for the expression they use.

Display the work done by Group 1 on a board for everyone to read.

MATCH IT UP!

■ Which rhyme goes with which name? Draw a line to link each name and rhyme. The first one has been done for you.

Muffin McLay

Bottomley Potts

Hairy Maclary

Bitzer Maloney

Schnitzel von Krumm

Hercules Morse

as big as a horse

from Donaldson's Dairy

all skinny and bony

covered in spots

like a bundle of hay

with a very low tum

NAMES AND PICTURES

■ Match the names below with the pictures.

Hairy Maclary   **Bottomley Potts**   **Bitzer Maloney**

Hercules Morse   **Schnitzel von Krumm**   **Muffin McLay**

RHYMING WORDS

■ Choose the correct rhyming word from the box below.

Hairy Maclary

from Donaldson's _____

Hercules Morse

as big as a _____

Bottomley Potts

covered in _____

Muffin McLay

like a bundle of _____

Bitzer Maloney

all skinny and _____

Schnitzel von Krumm

with a very low _____

tum	hay	Dairy	spots	bony	horse

CHOOSE THE RHYME

■ Choose the correct rhyming word from the box below. Write it in the space provided.

Hairy Maclary from Donaldson's Dairy

Came down the street dressed like a _____ .

Hercules Morse as big as a horse

Always ate dinner covered in _____ .

Bottomley Potts covered in spots

Came down the street with his tail tied in _____ .

Muffin McLay like a bundle of hay

Had a ball in his mouth and wanted to _____ .

Bitzer Maloney all skinny and bony

Came down the street riding a _____ .

Schnitzel von Krumm with a very low tum

Came down the street chewing on _____ .

play	gum	Dairy	bony
knots	horse	tum	pony
hay	fairy	sauce	spots

■ Now choose one of the rhyming words above and write down some other words that rhyme with it.

_____

ZUG THE BUG

OBJECTIVES

UNIT	SPELLING/ VOCABULARY	GRAMMAR/ PUNCTUATION	COMPREHENSION/ COMPOSITION
READING FICTION AND POETRY *Zug the Bug* by Colin and Jacqui Hawkins.	Discriminate and segment all three phonemes in CVC words. Blend phonemes to read CVC words in rhyming sets.	Draw on and use grammatical awareness to read with appropriate expression and intonation using puppets.	Notice difference between spoken and written forms through re-telling and re-enacting stories. Read simple stories independently.

ORGANIZATION (3 HOURS)

	INTRODUCTION	WHOLE-CLASS SKILLS WORK	DIFFERENTIATED GROUP ACTIVITIES	CONCLUSION
HOUR 1	Make predictions about *Zug the Bug* from the cover. Shared reading of *Zug the Bug*.	Read rhyming words by onset and rime. Identify phonemes.	1*: Use *Zug the Bug* as a model for a 'flip-the-page' book; focus on using rime -*ug*. 2: Match onsets to rimes -*ug* and -*ag* to make new words. 3: Use pictures to make a word bank of rhyming words.	Select a child from Group 1 to read their own *Zug the Bug* book. Place these books in reading corner. Reinforce onset/rime work and display work from Group 3.
HOUR 2	Re-enact the story of *Zug the Bug* using puppets.	Introduce the term 'vowel' and continue onset/rime work focusing on medial vowel sound *i*.	1: Re-enact story using simple puppets. 2*: Sequence speech bubbles to make books. 3: Create words using onset and rime by playing cube game. Draw pictures of Zig and Zag.	Selected children from Group 1 re-enact story to rest of class. Display pictures of Zig and Zag.
HOUR 3	Make predictions about other stories by the same authors by looking at book covers. Shared reading of *Jen the Hen*.	Read rhyming words by onset and rime and identify phonemes.	1: In pairs, read a selection of books from the series and make comparisons. 2: Use pictures to make a word bank of rhyming words. 3*: Make simple picture and word 'flip-the-page' books.	Selected pupils from Group 1 discuss the books they have read. Display Group 2's work alongside pictures from previous sessions. Place Group 3's books in reading corner.

RESOURCES

Copies of *Zug the Bug*, *Jen the Hen* and *Tog the Dog* by Colin and Jacqui Hawkins (Dorling Kindersley, ISBN 0-7513-5356-6 – *Pat the Cat and Friends*), card, materials for making small books, board or flip chart, writing and drawing materials, photocopiable pages 34 (Word Banks) and 35 (Speech Bubbles), materials for making simple sock puppets and a collection of simple props (see Preparation).

NB: Big Book versions of these Colin and Jacqui Hawkins books are also available from Dorling Kindersley (*Zug the Bug*, ISBN 0-7513-6201-8; *Jen the Hen*, ISBN 0-7513-6198-4; *Tog the Dog*, ISBN 0-7513-6200-X; *Pat the Cat*, ISBN 0-7513-6197-6; *Mig the Pig*, ISBN 0-7513-6199-2).

PREPARATION

Hour 1

Prepare a set of cards containing the following onsets: z, sl, b, t, r, p, gl, l, j, m, sn, h.

Make a small book (four pages plus cover) for each child in Group 1 in the same format as the *Zug the Bug* book, for example with narrower pages than the covers and *ug* written on the outside margin of the back cover.

For each pair of children in Group 2, prepare two cards with the rimes *-ag* and *-ug* written on. For the same group, make one set of cards between four containing single letter onsets: b, c, d, f, g, h, j, k, l, m, n, p, r, s, t, v, w, z. You may also wish to provide a set of cards containing double consonant onsets as an extension activity:

bl, br, ch, cl, cr, dr, fl, fr
gl, gr, pl, pr, sc, sh, sl
sm, sn, sp, st, th, tr.

You will also need to make sets of blank cards for the children in Group 2 to write their own onsets. For Group 3, enlarge enough pictures of the bag and Zug from photocopiable page 34 (Word Banks) for one set per pair of children.

Hour 2
Make two sets of simple sock and finger puppets to represent the characters in the story. For Zug, use a yellow sock and attach eyes, a red felt smiley mouth and a hat with antennae. For Pug, use a blue sock, and attach dark blue floppy ears, eyes and a big red tongue. You will also need two simple pink finger puppets for slug and two green finger puppets in total for the caterpillars (this will provide a total of eight puppets for use with Group 1 in the group activities). Gather together some simple props such as a rod and line (as in the book) made from dowelling and string, a jug, a mug, and a rug. For each child in Group 2, make a little book in the same format as the *Zug the Bug* book (see above), and make one copy of photocopiable page 35 (Speech Bubbles) for each child. Each pair of children in Group 3 will need two blank cubes made from card on which to write rimes and onsets.

Hour 3
Copy enough pictures of Jen and Tog from photocopiable page 34 (Word Banks) to allow one picture of either character per pair in Group 2. Make enough four-page small books in the same format as the *Jen the Hen* and *Zug the Bug* book for each child in Group 3, writing the rime *-en* on the outside margin of the back cover, plus a set of cards denoting the onsets used in the book.

Introduction
Show the children the cover of *Zug the Bug*, point to the speech bubble that says *'I'm Zug, give me a hug!'* and ask them if they would like to give Zug a hug. Tell them who the authors of the book are and explain that it is a 'flip-the-page' rhyming book; ask the children what they think this means. What sort of a book do they think it is going to be? Gather their opinions and predictions, then proceed with reading the whole story.

Whole-class skills work
Encourage the children to sound out the rhymes, through onset and rime, as they occur in the book. Explain how the pages work in order to assist spelling, for example: *'b/ug'*, *'P/ug'*, *'t/ug'*, *'sl/ug'*. Explain any words that the children are unsure of, such as *'lug'*, then sound out each phoneme in the word *'Zug'* (*Z/u/g*). Concentrate on the medial vowel sound and use the term 'vowel' in relation to *u*. Ask the children what would happen if we were to change the *u* sound in *'Zug'* to an *a* sound (*Zag*). Can the children think of other words that rhyme with *'Zag'*? (For example: bag, hag, lag, nag, rag, sag, tag, flag, crag, snag, brag and so on.)

Differentiated group activities
1*: Give each child a little book in the same format as the *Zug the Bug* book, and allow the whole group access to the set of cards denoting the onsets from the book (see Preparation). The children each choose a card and write the appropriate onset in their book which they then use to make a whole word by adding the rime *-ug*. They follow this by drawing an appropriate picture and writing a phrase or short sentence below, for example, *'Hello, I'm Zug/Slug/Pug'* and so on. Some children may wish to make their book into a story similar to *Zug the Bug*.
2: Give each pair of children two cards with the rimes *-ag* and *-ug*, together with a set of cards containing single letter onsets (see Preparation). They should use the cards to make new words, reading them aloud and compiling a list. Also, give them a supply of blank cards and ask them to think of some onsets they could use to make their 'own' words.

3: Give the enlarged pictures of the bag and Zug from photocopiable page 34 (Word Banks) to each pair of children. Ask them to make a bank of words that rhyme with each picture, writing the words inside the picture outlines.

Conclusion

Select a child from Group 1 to read his/her *Zug the Bug* book and ask him/her to spell out loud some of the *-ug* words used. Place the books in the book corner for the other children to read. Ask children from Group 2 to share some of the words they have made from the onsets and rimes given, and other words they have made by using different onsets. Display the pictures/word banks from Group 3 so that other children can add rhyming words and build on the collection.

Introduction

Show the children the *Zug the Bug* book again, drawing their attention to the different types of text on the page, that is: 1) the story line, leading to 2) large-print rhyming words and 3) the dialogue in the speech bubbles. Explain that you are going to tell the story by reading aloud what the characters say to each other in the speech bubbles. First of all, use the book to explore the characters of Zug, Pug, Slug and the two caterpillars by looking at what they say (they provide an amusing questioning commentary). Then place the Zug and Pug puppets on your hands and show them to the class. Choose some children to wear the slug and caterpillar puppets. Go through the story using the puppets to say aloud the speech bubbles. Enjoy it!

Whole-class skills work

Remind the children of the *-ug* and *-ag* rimes from the previous session, referring to the word bank and pictures on display. Say that you are going to look at another vowel today which will change 'Zug' and 'Zag' to 'Zig'. Ask the children if they can hear the sound of the *i* in '*-ig*' - do they know what the letter for this sound looks like? Take the opportunity to write 'Zig' on the board and sound out each phoneme. Can the children think of other words that rhyme with 'Zig'?

Differentiated group activities

1: Provide sufficient puppets and props for two groups of four children to re-enact the story of *Zug the Bug*. They should practise reading what is said in the speech bubbles in the book to prepare for presenting their 'play' at the end of the session.
2*: Give each child in this group a little book made in the same way as the *Zug the Bug* book. They should then cut out the speech bubbles on photocopiable page 35 and stick them in their own books in the same sequence as they occur in *Zug the Bug*.
3: Give each pair of children two card cubes. Ask them to stick the three rimes *-ug*, *-ag*, *-ig* (two of each rime) on one cube, and six onsets on the other cube, including *z*. Then demonstrate how to make words by throwing the cubes before letting the children have a go. Some words will make sense and others will not, for example: pug, pig, pag. The children could sort them into those words that make sense and those that do not. They could finish by inventing and drawing characters for Zig and Zag.

Conclusion

One of the groups from Group 1 should re-enact the story for other children in the class. Display the pictures of Zig and Zag drawn by Group 3.

Introduction

Show the children two other books written by Colin and Jacqui Hawkins: *Jen the Hen* and *Tog the Dog*. Ask them to look closely at the pictures on the covers. What do they think the new stories will be about? Do they think they are going to like Jen the Hen and Tog the Dog as much as Zug the Bug?

Next, read *Jen the Hen* to the children, encouraging them to sound out the rhymes through onset and rime as set out in the book.

Whole-class skills work

Remind the children of the rimes they have explored in previous sessions: *-ug*, *-ag*, *-ig*. Look at the *-og* rime in *Tog the Dog* and sound it out phonemically: *o/g*. Talk about the *g* sound at the end of each of the rimes. Then provide children with the opportunity to suggest rhyming words and sound out by phonemes, for example: *l/o/g*, *f/r/o/g*. Explain that the rime in *Jen the Hen* is quite different - begin by identifying the final *n* sound and then the medial e sound. Again, ask the children to provide rhyming words to segment into phonemes.

Differentiated group activities

1: Children work in pairs to read the three books *Zug the Bug*, *Jen the Hen* and *Tog the Dog*. They should be encouraged to make comparisons and determine reasons for any preferences.

2: Give each pair of children a picture of either Tog or Jen from photocopiable page 34 (Word Banks) to create a bank of rhyming words.

3*: Give each child a four-page little book in the same format as the *Jen the Hen* book, and provide the group with the cards denoting onsets from the book. The children should use these cards to help them make a word by writing the onset on the appropriate part of the page to match the rime on the back page. They can then draw an appropriate picture for each word.

Conclusion

Ask children from Group 1 to talk about the stories they have read and their reasons for any particular preferences. Display the pictures/word banks from Group 2's activity alongside other pictures from previous sessions. Place the books made by Group 3 in the book corner for other children to read.

WORD BANKS

bag

Zug

Jen

Tog

SPEECH BUBBLES

I'm Zug
the bug.

Glug, glug.

Hi, Zug.

Hi, Pug.

It's a slug!

Help me, Zug!

Clever Pug,
give me a hug.

They're
as snug...

Will you
always lug me?

Into the jug,
slippery Slug.

...as a bug
in a rug.

WHERE'S SPOT?

OBJECTIVES

UNIT	SPELLING/ VOCABULARY	GRAMMAR/ PUNCTUATION	COMPREHENSION/ COMPOSITION
READING AND WRITING FICTION *Where's Spot?* by Eric Hill.	Blend phonemes to read CVC words.	Write simple sentences and re-read, recognizing whether or not they make sense.	Use a patterned story as a model for their own writing. Make simple 'lift-the-flap' books.

ORGANIZATION (1 HOUR)

	INTRODUCTION	WHOLE-CLASS SKILLS WORK	DIFFERENTIATED GROUP ACTIVITIES	CONCLUSION
HOUR 1	Shared reading of *Where's Spot?*, with pupils predicting what happens next in the story.	Read and segment simple CVC words.	1*: Model a story using frames from a selection of books. 2*: Model a story from a given syntactic frame. 3: Make CVC words in order to read and say aloud.	A pupil from each of Groups 1 and 2 reads their stories. Reinforce skill of blending phonemes.

RESOURCES

Where's Spot? by Eric Hill (Puffin, ISBN 0-14-050420-6), stories with a similar question and answer format such as *Baby Goz* by Steve Weatherill (Frances Lincoln, ISBN 0-7112-0651-1), *Home* (Book 4, Level 1) (Ginn 360, 0-602-25736-0) and *Where's Julius?* by John Burningham (Red Fox, ISBN 0-09920071-6); other stories such as *All Together Now* by Nick Butterworth (Collins, ISBN 0-00-664626-3), *Here* (Book 2, Level 1) and (Ginn 360, ISBN 0-602-25734-4), board or flip chart, writing and drawing materials, materials for making small books (see main Introduction, page 12 for guidance), photocopiable page 38 (Word Slide).

PREPARATION

Prepare an 8-page 'lift-the-flap' book for each child in Groups 1 and 2. Use copies of photocopiable page 38 (Word Slide) to make one CVC word slide per pair of children in Group 3.

Introduction

Introduce *Where's Spot?* to the children; some may already be familiar with the story. Establish the question that is being asked in the title on the front cover and ask the children what they think the book is about. Then read the story aloud, involving the children in lifting the flaps and reading the text, reinforcing the notion of searching for Spot.

After the reading, ask the children if they can think of any other books with a similar theme of looking for someone or something. Show them some similar books (see Resources) and quickly show them the 'looking for' storyline in a simple book such as *Here* and *Home*.

Finally, return to *Where's Spot* and talk about the question and answer language. Ask the children where the questions and answers are found. Discuss all the interesting places that Sally looks for Spot, and how the children knew that he was in the basket.

Whole-class skills work

Ask the children to listen carefully as you say the word 'Spot', then engage them in spelling this, writing the beginning, final and medial sounds on the board as the spelling is established. Say the o sound together. Next, ask the children for words that rhyme with 'Spot' and, again, establish the spelling by extending the sound of the words when saying them aloud, for example: d/o/t, p/o/t. Write the word 'pot' on the board again and use it as a starting point for making other words by changing the vowel sound. Establish the sounding out of these words as follows: p/a/t, p/e/t, p/i/t, p/u/t.

Differentiated group activities
1*: The teacher works with this group first. The children will need the story book selection used in the Introduction to support them in writing their own story on a similar theme with a question and answer format. They should use the syntactic frames in these books as a model. Each child writes his or her story in a blank lift-the-flap book in order to fit the question and answer format appropriately.
2*: The teacher also supports this group. The children work independently to write their own lift-the-flap book using a syntactic frame provided by you. Some suggestions for frames could include:
■ Is this my home?
■ Where's ...?
■ Are you my...?
3: The children work in pairs using a CVC word slide from page 38 (see Preparation), reading and saying aloud the words they make.

Conclusion
Select a child from Groups 1 and 2 to read their stories, checking with the children that what they have written makes sense. Reinforce the skill of blending phonemes as you do so. If you wish, give everyone an opportunity later in the day to read the books with a partner to make sure that what has been written makes sense.

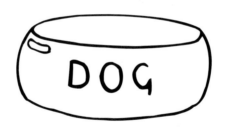

WORD SLIDE

■ Cut out the box and three strips below.

■ Cut out the slots in the box and insert each strip.

■ Make sure the vowel strip is placed in the middle slot.

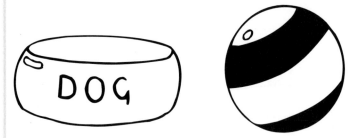

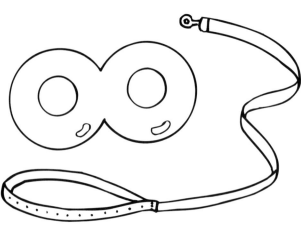

b
c
d
f
g
h
j
k
l
m
n
p
qu
r
s
t
v
w

b
c
d
f
g
k
l
m
n
p
s
t

a
e
i
o
u

HAVE YOU SEEN THE CROCODILE?

OBJECTIVES

UNIT	SPELLING/ VOCABULARY	GRAMMAR/ PUNCTUATION	COMPREHENSION/ COMPOSITION
READING AND WRITING FICTION *Have You Seen the Crocodile?* by Colin West.	Discover new words from shared reading and investigate their phonemic structure. Word recognition of high frequency words from list 1.	Use awareness of the grammar of a sentence in order to predict text.	Use a patterned story as a model for their own writing. Make simple 'lift-the-flap' picture books with sentences, modelling them on basic text conventions.

ORGANIZATION (2 HOURS)

	INTRODUCTION	WHOLE-CLASS SKILLS WORK	DIFFERENTIATED GROUP ACTIVITIES	CONCLUSION
HOUR 1	Make predictions about *Have You Seen the Crocodile?* from the cover and blurb. Shared reading of the story.	Develop recognition of some high frequency words. Put words in correct sentence order. Extend phonemic understanding using new words in story.	1: Match words from story to pictures. 2: Construct a 'lift-the-flap' book using writing frame and story as a model. 3*: Pupils read the story in pairs.	Selected pupil from Group 2 reads own story. Reinforce sight recognition of high frequency words.
HOUR 2	Discuss alternative stories using syntactic frame from *Have You Seen the Crocodile?* as a model.	Investigate alternative words to 'said'. Investigate phonemic structures of some new words.	1: Construct own story in a lift-the-flap book format using syntactic frame from story as a model. 2: Make sentences using given words and syntax from book. 3*: Guided reading of the story, with pupils suggesting alternative words to 'said'.	Selected pupil from Group 3 reads own story to class with teacher's assistance. Group 1 completes books later for other children to read.

RESOURCES

Copies of *Have You Seen the Crocodile?* by Colin West (Walker, ISBN 0-7445-1065-1)), writing and drawing materials, materials for making small books (see main Introduction, page 12 for guidance), photocopiable pages 42 (Name the Animals) and 43 (Animal Talk), cards with single words from the story written on (see Preparation), sheet of A1 card, laminator or sticky-backed plastic, cloth (for wiping away felt-tipped writing).

PREPARATION

Write each of these words on a separate card: Have/ you/ seen/ the/ crocodile?/ No/ said/ the/ parrot/ dragonfly/ bumble-bee/ butterfly/ humming bird/ frog. Make one set per child in Group 1. Prepare an 8-page blank 'lift-the-flap' book for each child in Groups 1 and 2 (see main Introduction, page 12 for guidance). Make one copy of photocopiable page 42 (Name the Animals) for each child in Group 1 and one copy of page 43 (Animal Talk) for each child in Group 2.

Finally, create a large laminated 'question and answer' writing frame on A1 card, reproducing the following text in large print:

> Have you seen the _____ ?
>
> No, said the _____ .

Introduction

Show the children *Have You Seen the Crocodile?*, selecting individuals to read the title and to identify the author. Then turn to the back cover and read the 'blurb'.

Ask the children to predict what they think the story is about and what other animals might feature in the book. Now read the story and engage the children in spotting the crocodile in the illustrations.

Whole-class skills work

Show the children the cards with the words '*Have you seen the crocodile?*' written separately on each one. Read them aloud in turn, then jumble them up. Select children to choose and read each word and to stand at the front displaying each card. When all the words have been chosen, ask the children to sort themselves out so that the words are in the correct order. Highlight the syntactic structure of the book by asking the class what we use when we want to ask or know something, such as a question.

Repeat the activity above for the '*No said the*' cards, with the children selecting the animal names on the rest of the cards. Encourage them to use their phonic knowledge when choosing the names and draw their attention to some of the phonemic structures as well as initial sounds, for example: *b* sounds in 'bumble-bee', *tt* sound in 'butterfly', *mm* in 'humming bird', *og* sound in 'frog' and so on.

Differentiated group activities

For these activities, children in all groups will need to have access to the text of *Have You Seen the Crocodile?*

1: Children work independently on photocopiable page 42 (Name the Animals). They then re-write the animal names in the order they occur in the story and produce accompanying drawings.

2: Children work independently, using the question and answer writing frame to create their 'lift-the-flap' books. They copy the text onto each page of their books, and draw an accompanying picture of the appropriate animal under each flap using the same order as in the story.

Provide the six animal name cards used in the Whole-class skills section to choose from.

3*: Pairs of children share in reading the book together. They should be encouraged to persist in their reading, drawing on the repeated syntactic frame and the picture clues indicating which animal is speaking.

Conclusion

Select a child from Group 2 to read from his/her 'lift-the-flap' book. Select children to read the words from the cards used in the Whole-class skills section, including the animal words.

Introduction

Display the laminated writing frame used in the previous session. Ask the children if they recognize some of the words and encourage them to suggest things/animals/people other than the crocodile which they might want to find – for example:

> Have you seen the caretaker?
> Have you seen the tiger?
> and so on.

Then follow through one of their suggestions by asking them to think of appropriate replies. Allow individuals to write their suggestions onto the frame and engage everyone in constructing the words from their knowledge of phonemes.

Whole-class skills work

Clear the writing from the frame. Tell the children you are going to read the story, but want them to find better words for the word 'said'. Ask them what sound a parrot might make – for example, squawk, croak – and engage them in adapting the word so that it fits the frame: *'No, squawked the parrot'*. As you read the story again, write the animal who says 'no' in the appropriate place on the frame each time. Ask the children to suggest appropriate alternatives to 'said' and to write these on the frame.

Now sound out and draw the children's attention to specific phonemic structures. For instance, if they suggest *'buzzed the bumble-bee'*, pick out the initial letter and *zz,* or, for *'hummed the humming bird'*, pick out *h* and *mm* ('buzzed' and 'hummed' might also serve for the dragonfly and butterfly, but do encourage the children to be inventive).

Differentiated group activities

1: Children work independently using the writing frame as a model to create a 'lift-the-flap book' based on their own ideas, as in the Introduction session.
2: Children work independently to complete photocopiable page 43 (Animal Talk).
3*: Children work with a copy of the book, reading through it and suggesting alternative words for 'said'. The teacher should write some of these words on the board to show their phonemic structure.

Conclusion

A child from Group 3 reads the story with your assistance, using some of the suggestions for 'said' covered in the group work. The books made by Group 1 can be illustrated and completed later for other children to read.

NAME THE ANIMALS

■ Match the correct animal names to the pictures.

parrot

dragonfly

bumble-bee

butterfly

humming bird

frog

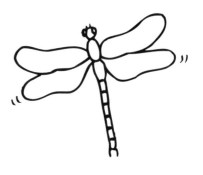

ANIMAL TALK

■ Fill the gaps with words from the boxes below.
You will have to think of some words yourself.

No _____ the _____

No _____ the _____

No _____ the _____

No _____ the _____

No _____ the _____

croaked	dragonfly
hummed	humming bird
buzzed	butterfly
squawked	frog
	parrot
	bumble-bee

HANDA'S SURPRISE

OBJECTIVES

UNIT	SPELLING/ VOCABULARY	GRAMMAR/ PUNCTUATION	COMPREHENSION/ COMPOSITION
READING AND WRITING FICTION *Handa's Surprise* by Eileen Browne.	Recognize new words from reading. Recognize critical features of words in order to predict the whole word.	Recognize full stops and capital letters when reading and name them correctly. Begin to use the term 'sentence' and identify sentences in text. Begin to use capital letters and full stops in writing.	Use phonological, contextual, grammatical and graphic knowledge to work out, predict and check meanings of unfamiliar words. Describe a story setting. Make simple books with sentences, modelled on basic text conventions.

ORGANIZATION (5 HOURS)

	INTRODUCTION	WHOLE-CLASS SKILLS WORK	DIFFERENTIATED GROUP ACTIVITIES	CONCLUSION
HOUR 1	Discuss cover of *Handa's Surprise*. Shared reading of story. Collect ideas for class story modelled on story just read.	Use phonological, contextual and graphic knowledge to identify unfamiliar words.	1: Design a front cover for their own story. 2: Work in pairs to make lists of gifts. Construct sentences from a given syntactic frame. 3*: Guided reading.	Selected pupils from Group 1 explain their designs for front covers. Teacher asks questions about chosen settings.
HOUR 2	Model writing of story using opening pages of *Handa's Surprise*.	Draw on children's phonological knowledge in order to spell new words.	1: Create their own story using *Handa's Surprise* as a model. 2*: Guided writing. 3: Match words to pictures.	Selected pupils from Group 2 recount the class story. Compare work done by Groups 1 and 2.
HOUR 3	Describe making of class story so far. Decide with pupils what the surprise ending should be after shared reading of *Handa's Surprise*.	Explore punctuation and the way some words are written at the end of *Handa's Surprise* to convey the surprise in the ending.	1: Write endings using syntactic frames from *Handa's Surprise*. 2: Create own simple stories using given syntactic frames. 3*: Guided writing.	Selected pupils from Group 3 explain how the ending has been written and discuss the punctuation used.
HOUR 4	Discuss ending of class story. Compare with endings of stories written by pupils in Group 1. Read from the above texts.	Write suggested words for describing gifts, drawing on pupil's phonological knowledge to assist spelling.	1*: Add words to further describe the gifts in own story. 2: As for Group 1, plus design a front cover for story books. 3*: Create own simple stories using syntactic frames.	Selected pupils from Group 3 read aloud their books and discuss their pictures for the final page.
HOUR 5	Shared reading of *Handa's Surprise*.	Identify use of punctuation in the story, i.e. capital letters and full stops, and how it affects reading aloud.	1: Read their own stories to each other with expression. 2: Reinforce understanding of descriptive words. 3*: Assemble Big Book.	Shared reading of class Big Book.

RESOURCES

Copies of *Handa's Surprise* by Eileen Browne (Walker, Big Book: ISBN 0-7445-3634-0, Small book: ISBN 0-7445-3660-X), materials for making a class Big Book and small books (see main Introduction, page 12, for guidance), writing, drawing and painting materials, card, Blu-Tack, board or flip chart, photocopiable pages 50 (Words and Pictures), 51 (Tasty Sweets) and 52 (Handa's Questions), a basket.

PREPARATION

Hour 1

Make a set of cards containing drawings of fruit featured in *Handa's Surprise* (such as tangerine, pineapple, avocado pear, banana, guava, mango, passion fruit and orange). Write the name of each fruit on a separate set of cards. Prepare an enlarged copy of the writing frame 'Will she/he like _____ or the _____?' for Group 2 to use as a model for writing.

Hour 2

Make enough copies of photocopiable page 50 (Words and Pictures) for one per child in Group 3. Create the following writing frames on cards for Group 1:

_____ put seven _____ _____ in a basket for her friend _____.

I wonder which fruit _____ like best?

Will _____ like the _____ or the _____ ?

Hour 3

Use photocopiable page 52 (Handa's Questions) to make one simple 10-page book per child in Group 2 (see main Introduction, page 12 for guidance). Cut out and stick each sentence (taken from *Handa's Surprise*) on separate pages inside each book. You will also need to enlarge these sentences from the end of *Handa's Surprise* to use for shared reading:

"Hello, Akeyo," said Handa. "I've brought you a surprise."
"Tangerines!" said Akeyo. "My favourite fruit."
"TANGERINES?" said Handa. "That *is* a surprise".

Next, prepare a set of cards with the following syntactic frames for each pair in Group 1:

"Hello_____," said _____. "I've brought you a surprise."

"_____!" said _____. "My favourite _____."

"_____?" said _____. "That *is* a surprise."

Hour 4

Use photocopiable page 52 (Handa's Questions) to make one simple 10-page book per child in Group 3. Prepare a large-print version of the following syntactic frame taken from *Handa's Surprise*:

Will he like the _____ _____ (gift)?
or will he like the _____ _____ (gift)?

Hour 5

Finally, prepare one copy of photocopiable page 51 (Tasty Sweets) per child in Group 2.

Introduction

Show the children the cover of *Handa's Surprise* and ask if they think the story is set in this country. If not, why not? Can they tell from the picture if it is a hot or a cold country? What animals can they see? What fruit do they recognize? Could any of them carry fruit on their head like the girl on the cover? Why might she be doing that? Ask the children to point to the title and read it aloud. Ask who they think Handa might be, and what might be the surprise.

Mention the author and then begin to read the story, involving the children as the story unfolds through the pictures. Emphasize the recurring pattern *'Will she like the _____ or the _____?'*. Afterwards, ask the children for suggestions as to what gifts they would put in a basket for their friend. Ask questions to get them thinking about a class version of the story: Where would the story be set? Where would they have to walk to get to their friend's house?

Whole-class skills work

Tell the children that you would like them to try to remember the fruit Handa put into her basket. Show them a similar basket and place the picture cards of the fruit on a table close by, together with the corresponding words arranged in a separate pile. Invite individuals to suggest a fruit and ask them to find the corresponding picture card to show the rest of the class. Before placing the picture card in the basket, ask another child to try to choose the correct word card to correspond with each fruit. Use the sound of the initial letter to help them make the choice and other key sounds in the name, for example *b* and *n* in 'banana'; *gu* and *v* in 'guava' and so on. Emphasize the need for the children to use their skills when listening for and recognizing sounds in words to help them make a guess at the whole word.

Use Blu-Tack to allow the children to stick the word cards on the board to form a list. When completed, ask some children to read from the list and select others to take the corresponding picture out of the basket and stick it next to the word on the board.

Differentiated group activities

1: Children work independently to design a front cover for their own story about gifts which they will have the opportunity to write in the following sessions. They should include an illustration of the seven gifts they would put in a basket for their friend. They should think about the setting and include this as part of the design.

2: Children work in pairs (preferably girl/boy so that choices don't become gender stereotyped) to decide on and make a list of seven gifts they would want to give to their friends. They then work independently using the writing frame below to construct sentences:

Will she/he like the _____ or the _____?

3*: Each child should have a copy of *Handa's Surprise* to engage in guided reading. Ask the children to point to where the repeated *'Will she like the... or the...'* frame occurs.

Conclusion

Select children from Group 1 to explain the front covers they have designed for a story they are going to write. Ask questions about the settings they have chosen, for example: Where is the story going to happen? Could the story be set anywhere? Why is it important to have this particular setting?

Introduction and whole-class skills work

Modelling the writing of a class Big Book will require the whole half-hour and will include drawing upon the children's phonic skills. Therefore the introduction and skills sessions are combined in this instance.

Start by showing the class the cover designs made by Group 1 in the previous session and, together, choose one to develop into a class Big Book. Begin the writing of the story, modelling the opening page on the opening of *Handa's Surprise*. If the children wish, use the name of the child whose cover has been chosen and the friend for whom the gifts are intended (try to use a girl and a boy if possible). Point out the capital letter at the beginning of the sentence and the full stop at the end, for example:

Emma put seven _____ in a basket for her friend Edward**.**

Ask the children to suggest a word that describes each gift, just as in the book. For example, if the gifts were sweets, they could use words such as 'chewy', 'sticky', 'tasty', 'crunchy' and so on. Draw on the children's phonic skills in order to spell the words.

Read the next page of the book and use the same language to progress the class story, changing the names and destination. Continue using the next page as a model: '*I wonder which fruit she'll like best?*' Ask the children what the mark at the end of the sentence might mean. Ask what part of the sentence will need changing if the person receiving the gifts is a boy rather than a girl. Then ask them to predict the next line for the next page and conclude the lesson at this point.

Differentiated group activities

1: Children should begin to construct their own story using the writing frames in *Handa's Surprise* as a model for their own ideas. They should also have access to the writing frames on cards for reference (see Preparation).

2*: Guided writing to continue constructing the class Big Book. Work out who or what is going to come along and take the gifts and delegate these as painting tasks later in the day. Also delegate two children to create a painting that captures the story setting as a cover for the book. Work on the repeated frames which constitute the middle section of the story, deciding on two words (as in the book) to describe the gift, for example: *Will he like the _____ gift or the _____ gift?*

3: Children read *Handa's Surprise* in pairs and then complete photocopiable page 50 (Words and Pictures).

Conclusion

Choose some children from Group 2 to explain to the class what is going to happen in the class story. Encourage them to talk about the order in which the items are taken. Ask children from Group 1 if they have been working in a similar way, engaging them in explaining what they have done.

Introduction

Show the children the class Big Book so far. Ask the children from Group 2 who worked with you in the previous session to remind everyone of who or what is going to take the gifts out of the basket in the story, then show the class the paintings that are being developed for the story. Say that now everyone has to decide together on what the surprise will be at the end of the story. Re-read *Handa's Surprise* with the children, then return to the discussion of the surprise in the class story. Make a joint decision as to the ending and delegate a series of paintings that depict the concluding events for children to do later.

Whole-class skills work

Show the enlarged sentences used at the end of *Handa's Surprise* (see Preparation) and explain how some of the marks enable the reader to interpret how to read the text, i.e. exclamation marks to show surprise, question marks to express a question and speech marks to denote words spoken. Point out how 'TANGERINES' is written in capital letters to show that Handa's surprise was even greater than Akeyo's. Also point out the '*is*' printed in italics and relate this to how you express and emphasize the word when reading aloud.

Differentiated group activities

1: Children should begin to construct the ending of their story started in the previous session. Give them the syntactic frame cards based on the ending of *Handa's Surprise* (see Preparation) to support them. They can complete the accompanying pictures later to show the resolution of the story.

2: Children work independently, using the simple books containing syntactic frames based on *Handa's Surprise* (see Preparation) to create their own story. Page 10 should be a picture of the surprise at the end of the story.

3*: In this guided writing session, children should work with the syntactic frames used at the end of *Handa's Surprise* in order to conclude the class Big Book story. Support them in making decisions on how to write some words in a particularly expressive way to help the reader, such as '*TANGERINE*' and '*is*' in *Handa's Surprise*. Discuss the use of other punctuation, i.e. capital letters and full stops.

Conclusion

Select children from Group 3 to read out the ending of the class story. Ask the children why certain words have been written/spoken differently to others. Point out how punctuation is used to denote a sentence and ask the children where and why capital letters have been used in the story, comparing it with the text in *Handa's Surprise*.

Introduction
Tell the children how the class story is developing by showing them the paintings done by selected children to depict the story ending, and the writing in the class Big Book modelled on the ending in *Handa's Surprise*. Select children to read the Big Book ending, encouraging them to use the way that some words are written as clues for reading with expression. Ask them if they think the class ending is as good as that in *Handa's Surprise*. Select a child from Group 1 to share his/her story with the class. Ask this child how difficult it was to think of an ending that caused such a surprise, and encourage him/her to talk about how the ending was arrived at.

Whole-class skills work
Remind the children that not all of the class Big Book is complete yet; work still needs to be done on the middle section. Ask those children who undertook the art work for this section to hold up their paintings in the order that the gifts are taken out of the basket in the story. This will help to remind everyone of the basic story sequence.

Next, display on the board the large-print syntactic frame:

Will he like the _____ (gift)? or will he like the _____ (gift)?

Ask the children to suggest a gift, then think of a word to describe it. Point out any words containing similar sounds, encouraging them to spot the same sounding phonemes orally and then seeing how this corresponds to the written form, for example:

sw**ee**t	tr**ea**cle	toff**ee**
ch**ew**y	fr**ui**ty	ch**ew**s
squish**y**	squash**y**	jell**y** babies.

Differentiated group activities
1*: The teacher works with this group after helping Group 3. Children re-read their own stories and add words that might further describe the gifts. They should use a different coloured pen so that it enhances the text rather than looking like a correction.
2: Children re-read their stories and add words to the frames to describe the gifts. They then design a cover picture that tells the reader where the story is set.
3*: Work with this group first. Children use the simple books containing syntactic frames to create their own stories. Page 10 should be a picture of the surprise ending.

Conclusion
Select children from Group 3 to read their books aloud and discuss the pictures they have produced for the final page of their story.

Introduction and whole-class skills work
Highlight to the children the fact that during the week, you have been using the word 'sentence' to describe pieces of writing. Tell them that you are now going to re-read *Handa's Surprise*, this time looking carefully at the sentences and some of the marks on the page that tell you how to read the story properly.

Look at the first page of the book and read the sentence aloud. Ask the children what is special about the word at the beginning (such as the use of a capital letter). What would happen if you put the full stop somewhere else, for example after 'delicious'? (Illustrate this for the children by re-reading the sentence, stopping at 'delicious'.) Turn the page and look at the next sentence: *She will be surprised, thought Handa as she set off for Akeyo's village'*. Ask what is special about the word at the beginning. Point out that 'She' is not a name like Handa (in the first sentence) but it still has a capital letter because it occurs at the start of a sentence. Compare this example with the beginnings of other sentences in the book.

Now go back to the second sentence again and experiment with moving the full stop again, for example stopping at 'as' instead of 'village'. Ask the children to explain what the full stop does and where it should be used. Finally, read the whole story aloud, pointing out to the children how you are using the different punctuation to help you read with expression.

Differentiated group activities

1: Children work in pairs, taking it in turns to read their own stories to each other and making any small alterations that enhance these. They should be encouraged to read their stories with expression.

2: The children reinforce their understanding of choosing appropriate descriptive words by completing photocopiable page 51 (Tasty Sweets). They should rely on their phonological and graphic knowledge when trying to spell the descriptive words. The results can then be used to assess each child's strengths and weaknesses. If assessment is not the priority, however, let the children work in pairs.

3*: Children work on the last stage of assembling the class Big Book, matching paintings to the text and arranging everything in sequence. They do this by drawing upon phonic and graphic knowledge, and their understanding of story structure.

Conclusion

Finish with a shared reading of the class Big Book. Encourage the children to express their opinions on the success of the book compared with *Handa's Surprise*.

WORDS AND PICTURES

■ Match each word to the correct picture.
The first one has been done for you.

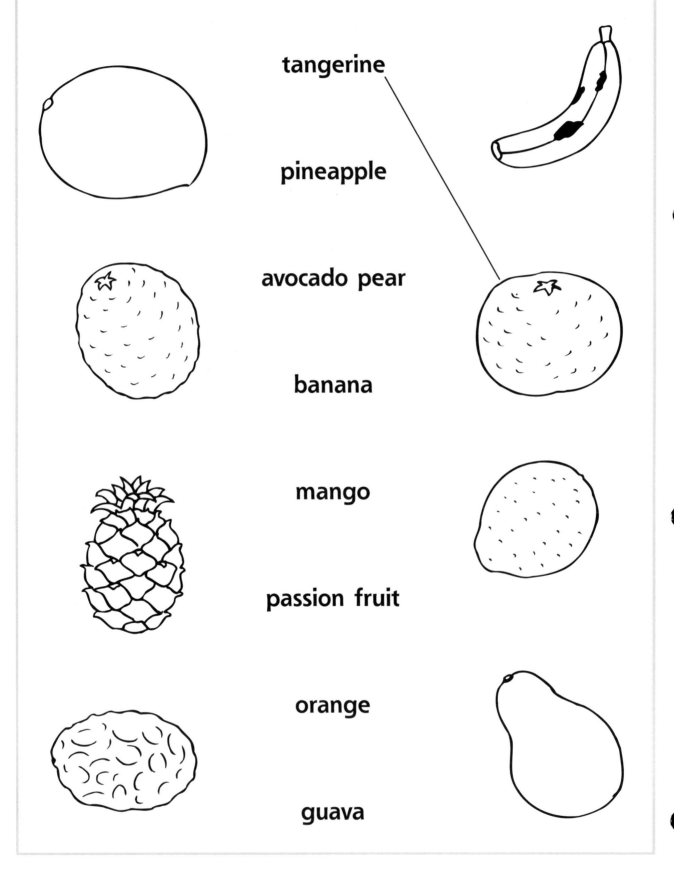

tangerine

pineapple

avocado pear

banana

mango

passion fruit

orange

guava

TASTY SWEETS

■ Think of a different word to describe each sweet below. Write it in the space provided.

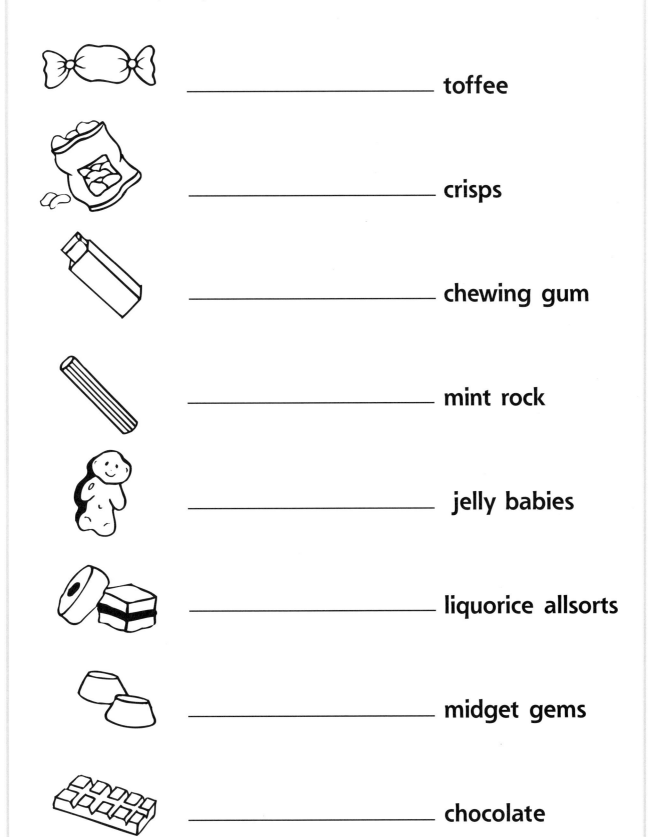

_____ toffee

_____ crisps

_____ chewing gum

_____ mint rock

_____ jelly babies

_____ liquorice allsorts

_____ midget gems

_____ chocolate

HANDA'S QUESTIONS

1. _____ put seven _____

   in the basket for her friend _____.

2. I wonder which _____ like best?

3. Will _____ like the _____

4. or the _____ ?

5. Will _____ like the _____

6. or the _____ ?

7. Will _____ like the _____

8. or the _____ ?

9. Which _____ will _____ like best?

THE LITTLE RED HEN AND FARMER DUCK

OBJECTIVES

UNIT	SPELLING/ VOCABULARY	GRAMMAR/ PUNCTUATION	COMPREHENSION/ COMPOSITION
READING FICTION *The Little Red Hen* (Traditional), and *Farmer Duck* by Martin Waddell and Helen Oxenbury.	Read on sight high frequency words including: said, the, who, will, help, this. Spell these words correctly.	Use a capital letter for the personal pronoun 'I'. Write captions and simple sentences, and re-read for sense. Predict text from grammar. Predict story from cover. Compare with other stories.	Identify main features in stories. Re-enact stories in a variety of ways. Raise an awareness of the difference between spoken and written forms through retelling known stories – compare oral version with written text.

ORGANIZATION (5 HOURS)

	INTRODUCTION	WHOLE-CLASS SKILLS WORK	DIFFERENTIATED GROUP ACTIVITIES	CONCLUSION
HOUR 1	Shared reading of *The Little Red Hen*. Use oral cloze to help pupils predict text.	Introduce pupils to key words ('said' and 'the') in story text for recognition and spelling.	1: Re-enact story through role play and felt story board. 2*: Re-order jumbled sentences. 3*: Guided reading: focus on 'the' and 'said'.	Four pupils from Group 1 re-enact the story.
HOUR 2	Re-telling of *The Little Red Hen*, with pupils contributing spoken language.	Introduce further key words in text for recognition and spelling.	1: Re-order jumbled sentences. 2: Retell story using speech bubbles as prompts. 3*: Plan a wall frieze of story; write speech bubbles for it.	Play part of Group 2's recording and make improvements. Selected pupil from Group 3 explains what he/she has been doing.
HOUR 3	Tell the story of *The Little Red Hen* in role.	Discuss differences between spoken and written form of the story.	1: Retell familiar story in role. 2*: Retell *Little Red Hen* in role. 3*: Read *Little Red Hen* from text and wall frieze.	Selected pupil from Group 1 retells the story in role. Listen to Group 2's recording and comment on expression.
HOUR 4	Predict story from cover of *Farmer Duck* Big Book. Shared reading of story.	Discuss characters in story. Write brief phrases and simple sentences about characters.	1*: Write phrases/simple sentences describing characters. 2*: Guided reading: find out about characters. 3: Re-enact story through role play.	Selected pupils from Group 1 talk about how they formed their opinions of characters in the story.
HOUR 5	Identify main features of story using *Farmer Duck*.	Relate main features to text and illustrations.	1*: Add to and sort previous comments on characters. 2: Identify main features of a story in another similar text. 3*: Guided reading reinforcing skills work.	Selected pupils from Group 2 talk about main features of stories in other books.

RESOURCES

Farmer Duck Big Book by Martin Waddell and Helen Oxenbury (Walker, ISBN 0-7445-5473-X), plus enough smaller copies of the book (ISBN 0-7445-3660-X) for group work, reading books with high frequency of 'the' and 'said', reading scheme books, a selection of traditional and contemporary stories such as *Alfie Gives a Hand* and *An Evening at Alfie's* by Shirley Hughes, *Little Red Riding Hood*, *Cinderella* (for identifying basic story features in Hour 5), Big Book stand, board or flip chart, two sheets of A1 card, laminator or sticky-backed plastic, an OHP and acetate (optional), smaller sheets of card, A3 paper, writing, drawing and painting materials, materials for making simple masks (see Preparation), stapler or glue, Post-its, felt board and easel, sandpaper, tape recorder and blank tape
   Photocopiable pages 59 (The Little Red Hen), 60 (Speech Bubbles) and 61 (Characters).
   Props for role-play of *Farmer Duck* such as cap and pyjama bottoms (for the farmer), a blanket (to represent a bed), an empty chocolate box, a newspaper, hay or straw (to represent a barn, etc.

PREPARATION

Hour 1

Make a copy of *The Little Red Hen* story on photocopiable page 59. Create a set of four simple masks from card to represent the cat, dog, pig and hen in the story (these are also used in Hour 2). Make these to either fit around the head using shearing elastic, or create them using paper plates on sticks for the children to hold up to their faces.
   Draw and cut a set of these same characters from cardboard and staple or glue a small piece of sandpaper to the back of each one so that they can be stuck onto a felt board. Copy onto separate cards each of these jumbled-up sentences for every child in Group 2:
■ I Not cat the said
■ said dog Not I the
■ the Not pig I said

Hour 2

Copy and stick onto card the text from Part B of photocopiable page 60 (Speech Bubbles). Cut into separate strips for the children to reassemble in the correct order. Make enough sets for each child in Group 1. Repeat this to make a single set of the speech bubbles in Part A of the photocopiable sheet. Attach small strips of sandpaper as above so that they can be stuck onto a felt board. Prepare enough blank speech bubbles cut from card for each child in Group 3 to write on a question and response from the story.

Hour 3

You will need to choose carefully some suitable reading scheme books for each pair of children in Group 1 to retell the story 'in role'. Each child in Group 3 can either use a copy of the photocopied story of The Little Red Hen as it stands, or you could prepare some blank eight-page books for them to stick the text into (the story divides neatly into six sections).

Hour 4

Use photocopiable page 61 (Characters) to prepare two large (A1) laminated cards, one showing the picture of the cat, dog, and pig from the *Little Red Hen*, and the other card the cows, sheep and hens from *Farmer Duck*. Enlarge them so that they are clear enough for the whole class to see, and place each one centrally on the card. You will also need to prepare enough copies of the Farmer Duck and Red Hen characters for one picture per child in Group 1. Enlarge each picture and stick it at the centre of an A3 sheet, leaving plenty of room for the children to stick Post its around the picture. Make enough simple card masks of sheep, cows, hens and a duck for the children in Group 3 to role play the story of *Farmer Duck*. Set up the role-play area to represent the farm, and provide some simple props (see Resources).

Introduction

Begin this session by telling the children the story of *The Little Red Hen* on photocopiable page 59, but do not display the text at this point. As the children become more familiar with the repetition in the story, encourage them to predict the familiar parts such as 'Not

I' said the cat or *Who will help me plant this wheat?* by stopping before each one.

You could give masks for the cat, dog, and pig to three children and ask them to say '*Not I*' and '*I will*' at the appropriate points in the story.

Whole-class skills work

Ask the children what the animals say when The Little Red Hen asks for help. Write '*Not I*' in large print on the board, engaging the children in the spelling of 'not' and asking what sort of 'I' should be used, such as a capital. Then ask them who says '*Not I*' first to engage them in spelling '*said the cat*'. They may well offer 'sed' for 'said', but show them the correct spelling and emphasize that they need to remember this.

Now write the word 'say' and relate it to 'said', asking the children which parts of the words are the same. Try to establish the *sa-* spelling at the beginning of 'said'. Another important word for the children to learn is 'the', so help them to learn the spelling for this by using the 'look, say, write, cover, check' strategy.

Having established the spelling of 'said' and 'the' on the board, cover these words with 'Post-its' so that the children have to draw on memory to help you spell them again for the following phrases:

Not I, said the dog.
Not I, said the pig.

The children should help with the spelling of '*Not I*' and, if appropriate, with the words '*dog*' and '*pig*' by sounding out the words carefully beforehand.

Differentiated group activities

1: A group of four children use the masks to act out the story of *The Little Red Hen* in the role-play area. They should prepare to present it at the end of the session. The rest of the group use the cardboard characters to re-tell the story on a felt board.

2*: The teacher supports this group after working with Group 3. Children work independently to solve the three jumbled sentences and re-write them correctly.

3*: The teacher works with this group first in a guided reading session. For this, carefully choose a reading book at the children's level where 'said' and 'the' feature heavily. Children should read the text independently, hunting for both these words.

Conclusion

Ask the four children in Group 1 to re-enact their story of *The Little Red Hen* for the rest of the class to see.

Introduction

Say to the children that you are going to re-tell the story of *The Little Red Hen* from the previous session but this time, you will need more help from them to do this. Before starting the story, ask the class what the animals say when the hen requests their help with the work, and how they reply when the hen wants some help in eating the bread. Now go through the story again with the children contributing the speeches by the animal characters from memory. Choose four children to play each of the story characters, with each wearing the appropriate mask. Choose a different child to represent The Little Red Hen each time she asks a question so that there are repeated opportunities to learn the language used and the sequence of events.

Whole-class skills work

Remind the children that in the previous session, you looked at how to write '*Not I*' said *the cat*. Ask them which of these words were actually spoken by the cat. Refer back to the reading in the introduction, reminding the children how the cat didn't have to say '*said the cat*', but only the words '*Not I*'.

Say you are now going to look at other words that are spoken in the story. Ask the children what the Little Red Hen's first request is ('*Who will help me plant this wheat?*'), and ask for their help as you scribe this question on the board, drawing on their phonic, graphic and contextual knowledge. Once this first question is established, help the children to see that most of the hen's words stay the same each time she asks another question. Demonstrate this by asking the children the sequence of the Little Red Hen's questions and inviting their help as you scribe the text on the board. (As many of these words are phonemically difficult, encourage the children to rely on the initial letter sounds together with contextual clues at this stage.)

Finally, ask the children what the animals say when the Little Red Hen wants their help in eating the bread. Invite two children to write *'I will'* on the board, helping them to remember the spelling by asking where they have seen the word 'will' before.

Differentiated group activities

1: Give each child the questions cut from photocopiable page 60 (Speech Bubbles) and ask them to reassemble these in the correct sequence as in the story, working from memory. They could either glue the questions on a sheet of paper or simply arrange them on the table top. They should then take turns to read the questions aloud. If time allows, they could draw a picture to accompany one of the questions and then write the appropriate words beneath.

2: Half the group should use the felt board to re-tell the story of *The Little Red Hen*. They should use cardboard cut-out characters and the speech bubbles from photocopiable page 60 containing the appropriate spoken language from the story. The other half of the group should use a tape recorder to record their own re-telling of the story. They can use card speech bubbles containing the spoken language from the story as prompts to help them.

3*: Tell children in this group that they are going to produce a wall frieze of the story which will be displayed for others to see during the next week or so. Start by inviting each child to write one question asked by the Little Red Hen (refer them to the text on the board from the skills session) on a cardboard speech bubble, together with the appropriate responses *'Not I'* and *'I will'* from the animals. (Make sure that all the questions in the story are covered. Some questions can be repeated if necessary to suit group numbers.)

Later in the day, give them an opportunity to paint an appropriate picture to accompany their chosen question. If appropriate, let other children contribute paintings of different elements of the wall frieze, such as background images and pictures of the cat, dog and pig. Compile all the materials together into the final frieze which tells the story in sequence through the speech bubbles.

Conclusion

Play back part of the recording done by children in Group 2 and discuss with the children what improvements could be made and how these could be done. Ask a child from Group 3 to explain what their group has been doing, and select children to read from their cardboard speech bubbles.

Introduction

The difference between spoken and written forms is not an easy concept to convey to young children. However, re-telling fairy stories in role can give children a general idea of some of the key language differences between the two forms, which is all that is required at this level. In this session, you can provide an oral version of the story of *The Little Red Hen* by taking on the hen's role, for example:

"Do you know who I am?
I'm the Little Red Hen and I'm not very happy. Do you know, no-one will help me plant this wheat. I've asked my friend the cat - well, I thought he was my friend but he wouldn't help me...", and so on.

Now ask the children what is different about this telling of The Little Red Hen. Encourage them to think about whose story it is – who is telling it? How do they know? What might the cat say if he was telling the story?

Whole-class skills work

Refer to the wall frieze of the story and read together what is being spoken by the characters. How do the children know who is saying what? (They will be able to see the connection between the animals and speech bubbles.) How would they know who was speaking if the pictures of the characters were taken away?

Next, choose one of the phrases from the speech bubbles, such as 'Not I', and write it on the board. Can the children tell which character is saying this (without looking at the frieze)? Is something else needed to help them? Now write *'said the cat'*, next to the phrase. Ask the children if they can now tell which character has spoken these words? In this way, you can help them begin to see the need to identify who is speaking in written story forms.

Differentiated group activities

1: Children work in pairs with a copy of a familiar book, such as a reading scheme book, which they read together. They then practise re-telling it in the role of the main character.

2*: The teacher supports this group after working with Group 3. Children work in pairs using a tape recorder to record each others' retelling of *The Little Red Hen* story in role as the red hen. They should be encouraged to tell their stories at a reasonably quick pace to sustain the listeners' interest. Explain that these oral story versions will be played back and commented on in the plenary session, especially regarding the expression of the red hen's feelings.

3*: The teacher works with this group first, doing a guided reading of the photocopiable story of *The Little Red Hen*. (This could be assembled into small books for the children to illustrate later.) This should be followed by a guided reading of the story from the speech bubbles on the wall frieze. This offers the opportunity to reinforce the idea of the differences between the spoken and written versions by discussing the language that is missing, for example: *said the cat*.

Conclusion

Select a child from Group 1 to tell their story in the role of the main character. Play one of the recordings made by a pair of children in Group 2 and discuss how well they expressed how the Little Red Hen was feeling.

Introduction

HOUR 4

Display the Big Book version of *Farmer Duck* on a stand. Ask the children to point to and read out the title on the cover. Can they see the author's name? Do they know who the author is? Why are there two names? Identify one name as the illustrator, then ask questions about the picture:
■ What is the duck doing?
■ Do you think it might be Farmer Duck?
■ Does he look happy with what he is doing?
■ Does it remind you of another story? Which one? (*The Little Red Hen*)
■ Do you think there will be friends to help Farmer Duck?
   Now read the story aloud. Then ask the children if they were right to think it reminded them of the story of *The Little Red Hen*. Discuss some similarities and differences between the two stories.

Whole-class skills work

Focus on making comparisons between Farmer Duck's friends – the cows, sheep and hens, and the Little Red Hen's friends – the cat, the dog and the pig. Place the two laminated cards showing the friends (see Preparation) side by side on the stand and ask the children to tell you things about them that help to describe their character. Don't tie them to providing single adjectives as this is difficult for them and may bring them to a standstill. Instead, encourage them to describe the actions of the animals in *Farmer Duck* in planning to overthrow the farmer, and the actions of the animals in *The Little Red Hen* in refusing to help her. Ask them to compare what the animals say or what they might be thinking. Explain that exploring what characters do, say and think in a story provides the reader with an idea of what the characters are like. Write the children's suggestions on the picture cards using simple phrases.

Differentiated group activities

1*: The teacher supports this group after working with Group 2. Give each pair a picture of one of either Farmer Duck or the Little Red Hen from photocopiable page 61 (Characters) glued in the centre of a sheet of A3 paper. Each pair then works together to describe their allotted character. Encourage them to do this by drawing on what the characters do, say and think in the stories. Let them write their ideas on Post-its and stick these onto their sheet. (These can then be pulled off for sorting in the next session).

2*: The teacher works with this group first, doing a guided reading of *Farmer Duck*, with each child following the story using their own small copy. Ask the children to point to words being read at intervals in the reading. Then reinforce the skills work by inviting them to read some parts independently in response to questions such as:
■ How do we know what the animals are thinking?
■ What does the farmer do to make us not like him?

■ Why do we think Farmer Duck is so unhappy?

3: Provide masks and props in the role-play area for a group of children to re-enact the story of *Farmer Duck*.

Conclusion

Display one picture from Group 1 and ask the relevant pair of children to read out some of their ideas and describe how they formed their opinions.

Introduction

The purpose of this introduction is to identify the main features of many traditional stories by using five simple questions. Display *Farmer Duck* on the stand to remind the children of the story. Ask them what they know about heroes and heroines and refer to familiar traditional and contemporary stories in order to help them, for example: *Cinderella*, *Little Red Riding Hood*, *The Three Billy Goats Gruff*, *Snow White and The Seven Dwarfs*, *The Lion King*, *Alfie Gives a Hand*, *Dogger*, and so on). Then ask the following questions:

■ Who is the hero/ heroine in *Farmer Duck*?
■ Who is the villain? Do they know of other villains in other stories?
■ What is the story really about? (For example, heroes versus villains, 'rags-to-riches', good outwitting evil, and so on.)
■ Who are the helpers in the story?
■ What is achieved or what 'good' happens at the end of the story?

Whole-class skills work

Read *Farmer Duck* to the children again, this time making direct links to the questions you asked in the introduction by referring to the text and pictures. Draw attention to all the hard work done by Farmer Duck (hero) and the laziness of the farmer (villain) who stayed in bed all day. Ask the children to pick out further examples which point to who is a 'hero' or 'villain' in both the text and illustrations. Draw attention to the way in which the hens are the helpers, in that they look after Farmer Duck when he is *'sleepy, weepy and tired'* and how they try to plan with the other animals to save duck from the miserable work on the farm. Finally, relate the story's ending to the question about what good eventually comes of the situation.

Differentiated group activities

1*: The teacher supports this group after working with Group 1. Children should add to the comments they made about their allotted character in the previous session in the light of the extended reading above. They should then sort their 'Post its' on the A3 sheet into all those that show what the characters did, what they said, what they thought and anything else that has made the children form an idea or opinion of the character.

2: Children work in pairs with a copy of *Farmer Duck* and a traditional or contemporary story with which they are familiar. They should identify heroes/heroines, villains and helpers and be able to explain what each story is about and what good occurs at the end. They should prepare to present their findings at the end of the session.

3*: The teacher works with this group first, in a guided reading of *Farmer Duck*, with each child following the story using their own small copy. Ask the children to point to words being read at intervals during the reading. Invite them to read some parts independently in response to questions such as those asked in the Introduction session above. They should have the opportunity to read independently in relation to the questions discussed in the introduction and skills sessions.

Conclusion

Select children from Group 2 and guide them in talking about the heroes and villains in the other stories they have looked at. Encourage them to talk about the main point/s in the story, who helped the hero/heroine and what good occurred in the end.

THE LITTLE RED HEN

Once upon a time, there was a Little Red Hen. She had some grains of wheat which she wanted to plant.

'Who will help me plant this wheat?' she asked.

   'Not I,' said the cat.

   'Not I,' said the dog.

   'Not I,' said the pig.

'Then I will,' said the Little Red Hen.

The wheat started to grow.

'Who will help me hoe this wheat?' asked the Little Red Hen.

   'Not I,' said the cat.

   'Not I,' said the dog.

   'Not I,' said the pig.

'Then I will,' said the Little Red Hen.

The wheat was ready to cut.

'Who will help me cut this wheat?' asked the Little Red Hen.

   'Not I,' said the cat.

   'Not I,' said the dog.

   'Not I,' said the pig.

'Then I will,' said the Little Red Hen.

The wheat needed grinding into flour.

'Who will help me grind this wheat?' asked the Little Red Hen.

   'Not I,' said the cat.

   'Not I,' said the dog.

   'Not I,' said the pig.

'Then I will,' said the Little Red Hen.

The flour needed making into bread.

'Who will help me bake this bread?' asked the Little Red Hen.

   'Not I,' said the cat.

   'Not I,' said the dog.

   'Not I,' said the pig.

'Then I will,' said the Little Red Hen.

The bread was ready to eat.

'Who will help me eat this bread?' asked the Little Red Hen.

   'I will,' said the cat.

   'I will,' said the dog.

   'I will,' said the pig.

'No you will not!' said the Little Red Hen. 'I will!'

SPEECH BUBBLES

Who will help me plant this wheat?

Who will help me hoe this wheat?

Who will help me eat this bread?

Who will help me cut this wheat?

Not I.

Who will help me grind this wheat?

Who will help me bake this bread?

I will.

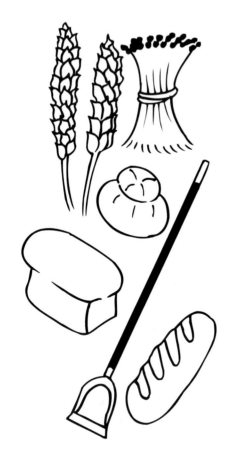

✂- -

Who will help me plant this wheat?

Who will help me hoe this wheat?

Who will help me cut this wheat?

Who will help me grind this wheat?

Who will help me bake this bread?

Who will help me eat this bread?

Not I.

I will.

CHARACTERS

PEACE AT LAST

OBJECTIVES

UNIT	SPELLING/ VOCABULARY	GRAMMAR/ PUNCTUATION	COMPREHENSION/ COMPOSITION
READING AND WRITING FICTION *Peace at Last* by Jill Murphy.	Reinforce key words for sight vocabulary by putting words into sentences to fit into the story. Begin to locate middle sounds in words.	Be able to join in and predict words from overall sense. Write simple sentences. Use capital letters for names, for the start of a sentence and for the personal pronoun 'I'.	Predict story pattern. Recognize features, eg use of capital letters, for expression.

ORGANIZATION (3 HOURS)

	INTRODUCTION	WHOLE-CLASS SKILLS WORK	DIFFERENTIATED GROUP ACTIVITIES	CONCLUSION
HOUR 1	Shared reading of *Peace at Last*. Pupils join in with repetitive phrases and predict what comes next.	Read repetitive sentences and reinforce recognition and spelling of key words 'went', and 'the'. Recognize features such as capital letters for assisting reading.	1*: Make sentences from a selection of given words. 2: Record what sounds Mr Bear heard in each room. 3*: Locate and read repetitive language from the story.	One or two children from each group read sentences from the story.
HOUR 2	Shared reading of *Peace at Last* with oral cloze.	Read repetitive sentences and reinforce recognition and spelling of further key high frequency words.	1: Re-order jumbled sentences to match sequence in story. 2*: Locate and read repetitive language. Write it in correct story sequence. 3*: Rearrange a given sentence from story.	A selected pupil from Group 2 reads from his/her story strips and relates this to work undertaken by other groups. Selected pupils spell high frequency words from memory.
HOUR 3	Discuss how to identify and convey to others what a story is about.	Relate story to pupils' own experiences. Write simple sentences to describe these.	1*: Write simple sentences about what they do when they can't go to sleep. 2: Select some favourite books and tell each other what the books are about. 3*: Guided writing: simple sentences.	Pupils from Group 2 tell others what their favourite book is about. Share sentences from Groups 1 and 3.

RESOURCES

Enough copies of *Peace at Last* by Jill Murphy (Macmillan ISBN 0-333-63198-6) for group work, a selection of the children's favourite stories from the class collection, board or flip chart, drawing and writing materials, card, approximately five large yoghurt pots or similar, photocopiable pages 66 (It's Too Noisy!) and 67 (Sort the Sentences).

PREPARATION

Hour 1

For Group 1, you will need one yoghurt pot or similar per pair of children, each containing two of the following sentences written on card and then cut up as shown below:

SNORE/ went/ Mrs Bear
NYAAOW/ went/ Baby Bear

TICK TOCK/ went/ the/ living-room clock
DRIP DRIP/ went /the/ leaky kitchen tap
Hmmmmm/ went/ the/ refrigerator
TOO-WHIT TOO-WHOO/ went/ the/ owl
SNUFFLE SNUFFLE/ went/ the/ hedgehog
MIAAAOW/ went/ the/ cats
TWEET TWEET/ went/ the/ birds
SHINE SHINE/ went/ the/ sun

Make one copy of photocopiable page 66 (It's Too Noisy!) per pair of children in Group 2.

Hour 2

For Group 1, make one copy per pair of photocopiable page 67 (Sort the Sentences). Cut out the sentences and jumble up each set for the children to sort into the correct order. For Group 3, prepare one sentence from the story written on separate cards, for example: So/ he/ got/ up/ and/ went/ to/ the/ living-room, for the children to help you unjumble in Hour 3. Prepare another similar sentence from the story in this way for the children to rearrange by themselves.

Hour 3

For Group 2, gather a selection of books that the children are familiar with and enjoy reading.

Introduction

Read the story *Peace at Last* to the children. Involve them in making the different sounds, predicting what comes next and saying with you the refrain from the story: *'I can't stand THIS'*.

Whole-class skills work

Now ask the children what happened when Mr Bear first tried to get to sleep. Then choose a child to check in the book and read what it says (*'Mrs Bear began to snore. SNORE went Mrs. Bear'*). As you write *'SNORE went Mrs Bear'* on the board, ask why *'SNORE'* is written in capital letters. Let the children give their suggestions, then sum up by explaining that the capital letters are a way of telling the reader to make the sound of a loud snore. Then ask the children to help with spelling the word *'went'*. The hardest sound for them to hear will be *'n'*, so help them to hear it by emphasizing it at the end of the word and showing how this relates to the written version.

Continue by involving the children in explaining what happened next to stop Mr. Bear from going to sleep. Encourage them to guess this in the correct sequence and select someone to check in the book each time to see if they are correct. Write a couple of these examples on the board (note *'sang'* instead of *'went'* on page 14 of the book) focusing on the spellings of *'went'* and *'the'*.

Differentiated group activities

1*: The teacher works with this group after helping Group 3. Give each pair of children a pot containing two of the cut-up sentences from the story (see Preparation). Let them pick out the words and arrange them to make complete sentences. Each child could then write down one of these sentences if time permits.

2: Children work in pairs with a copy of the book to write in the 'Noise' column on the grid on photocopiable page 66, writing down the sounds that stopped Mr Bear from going to sleep. Explain to them that they should list each sound in the column which relates to the room where Mr Bear heard the noise.

3*: The teacher works with this group first. Ask the children to locate the different settings in the story, finding out the place in which each different noise occurs. They should read aloud the repetitive parts as they do this, for example *'Oh no I can't stand this'*; *'So he got up to sleep in the living room'*, etc. Let the children continue to read together in pairs while you join Group 1.

Conclusion

Choose children to read repetitive phrases/sentences from the story that they encountered in the group activities.

HOUR 2

Introduction

Re-read *Peace at Last* to the children but stop regularly before certain words to encourage children to use their awareness of grammar to predict the text. For example:

Mr Bear was tired
Mrs Bear ___ tired
and Baby Bear ___ tired,
so they all ___ to bed.

Mrs Bear began __ snore
'SNORE', _____ Mrs Bear.

Whole-class skills work

Ask the children where Mr Bear first went when Mrs Bear woke him with her snoring. When they have given some suggestions, ask a child to check in the book, then write on the board what the text says: *'So he got up and went to sleep in Baby Bear's room'*. Select children to read the words aloud as you write them. Ask what happened in Baby Bear's room and where Mr Bear went next.

Repeat this activity with the rest of the story, asking the children to continue guessing the sequence. Again, check in the book each time to see if they are right and write the story text on the board. As the children predict each word in the repetitive phrase, write it on the board for them. For example, the children say 'So' and you write it, they then say 'he' and you write it, and so on. Encourage them to spot and point to the same words – 'so', 'he', 'got', and so on – repeated in the previous sentences written on the board. Encourage them to recognize the patterns of repeated words in *'So he got up and went to sleep'*, *'So he went off to sleep'*. Finally, cover the board and ask them to spell some of the high frequency words they have used.

Differentiated group activities

1: Children work in pairs with a copy of the book to unjumble the list of sentences from photocopiable sheet 67 (Sort the Sentences) in order to locate each one in the book and rearrange the list so that the sentences are in the sequence in which they occur in the book.

2*: The teacher works with this group after helping Group 3. Pairs should use the photocopiable grid from Hour 1, adding in each column the sentence from the book saying where Mr. Bear went each time he was disturbed. For example, in the first column they should write *'So he got up and went into Baby Bear's room'*. Give them a copy of the book so that they can locate the appropriate section and read it before writing.

3*: The teacher works with this group first. Children should work on rearranging the words from one jumbled sentence from the story written on separate cards, for example: So/ he/ got/ up/ and/ went/ to/ the/ living-room. Follow this by giving them a similar sentence to rearrange by themselves while you join Group 2.

Conclusion

Choose a child from Group 2 to read from his or her photocopiable sheet. Read the sentences together, pointing to each word as you say it with the children. Select children to spell high frequency words.

HOUR 3

Introduction

Show the children a book they know well and model how to describe what a story is about. Next, show them *Peace at Last* and, after discussing the different scenes, ask the children how they would tell someone else about the book. Emphasize that they should say in their own words what the book is about rather than trying to repeat the language used in the book.

Whole-class skills work

Ask the children if they have experienced disturbed nights or nights when they just could not get to sleep. What do they do to try and overcome this? As they make suggestions, write them on the board, for example:

I read my book.
I jump up and down on my bed.

I play on my computer.
I giggle with my sister.

Point out the need to always use a capital 'I' when they are writing about themselves, and to use a capital 'I' if beginning a sentence with a word that starts with 'i'. Remind them of the need to use a full stop at the end of the sentence.

Now ask the children to point to high frequency words used more than once in the sentences on the board, for example 'on' and 'my'. Involve them in contributing to the spelling of these, asking some children to spell whole words.

Differentiated group activities

1*: The teacher works with this group after helping Group 3. Children work independently to write simple sentences about the things they do when they can't get to sleep. Later, they could draw a picture of themselves in their bedroom and attach the sentences.

2: Children work in pairs, looking through a selection of books they know well and choosing their favourites. They then tell each other what the book is about.

3*: The teacher works with this group first. Children continue to say what they do when they can't get to sleep, while you model the writing of some simple sentences. They should then write a sentence of their own, drawing on key words already covered while you join Group 1.

Conclusion

Ask children from Group 2 to tell the rest of the class about their favourite stories. Choose children from Groups 1 and 3 to read some of the sentences they have written and also invite other children to read some of these sentences.

IT'S TOO NOISY!

■ Write the noise that Mr Bear hears in each of the places listed below.
■ Write the sentence from the book which tells you where Mr Bear goes next.
The first example has been done for you.

	Noise	Sentence
Mr and Mrs Bear's bedroom	Snore	So he got up and went into Baby Bear's room.
Baby Bear's room		
Living room		
Kitchen		
Garden		
Car		

SORT THE SENTENCES

So he got up and went to
sleep in the garden.

So he got up and went to
sleep in the living room.

So he got up and went to
sleep in the kitchen.

So he got up and went to
sleep in the house.

So he got up and went to
sleep in the car.

So he got up and went to
sleep in Baby Bear's room.

ANOTHER DAY

OBJECTIVES

UNIT	SPELLING/ VOCABULARY	GRAMMAR/ PUNCTUATION	COMPREHENSION/ COMPOSITION
READING POETRY 'Another Day' by John Cunliffe.	Identify rhyming words, and rhyming phonemic elements. Generate new words from reading and discussion.	Use awareness of grammar to decipher new or unfamiliar words.	Read independently and point to written word, making correspondence between this and spoken version. Recite small sections of the poem.

ORGANIZATION (3 HOURS)

	INTRODUCTION	WHOLE-CLASS SKILLS WORK	DIFFERENTIATED GROUP ACTIVITIES	CONCLUSION
HOUR 1	Shared reading of the poem 'Another Day' by John Cunliffe. Discuss what it is about.	Identify and predict rhyming words in poem. Make rhyming words using onsets and the rime -ap.	1: Read and pick favourite lines of the poem. 2*: Re-read poem with expression in order to recite small sections to rest of class. 3: Explore and invent rhyming words using the rime -ap.	Selected pupils from Group 2 recite parts of the poem they have learned. Pupils from Group 1 talk about why they have chosen particular lines. Make a display.
HOUR 2	Read poem in wrong order to develop listening skills and appreciation of rhyme.	Generate words for a given phrase, and explore some phonemic structures.	1: Read and sequence text from poem. 2*: Generate words for a given phrase using 'Look, say, cover, write, check' strategy. Add words to own word book. 3*: Read and sequence small sections of text.	Pupils from Group 2 read their work; other pupils also read Group 2's work. Plan a class poem from the work.
HOUR 3	Discuss how to read second part of poem with expression.	Make words using onsets and the rime -ip.	1: Read sections of second part of poem with expression. 2*: Read and pick out favourite lines of poem. 3*: Explore and invent rhyming words using the rime -ip.	Listen to pupils from Group 1 recite sections of poem. Discuss how to complete a display of the work.

RESOURCES

Writing and drawing materials, board or flip chart, two large (A3) sheets of card, smaller sheets of card and scissors (optional for Hour 1), laminator or sticky-backed plastic, painting materials or pastels, glue, Blu-Tack, brass split pins, a Big Book stand (for displaying enlarged version of poem).
  Photocopiable pages 72 ('Another Day'), 73 (What do they do?) and 74 (Word Wheel).

PREPARATION

Make one copy of the poem 'Another Day' on photocopiable page 72 per pair of children. Make an enlarged laminated version of the first part (from 'Boys shout' to 'All in!') and second part of the poem, large enough for whole-class work. Enlarge the first verse of the poem and cut it up into separate lines. Arrange these lines in the jumbled-up order listed in the Introduction for Hour 2, fixing them onto a single sheet of card with Blu-Tack.

For each pair of children in Group 1, provide a copy of the poem (or a section, depending on the children's ability) with the phrases in the wrong order, as in the Introduction for Hour 2. Repeat this for each pair of children in Group 3, but use only small sections of the poem. Copy photocopiable page 73 (What do they do?) and cut up to provide one section for each pair of children in Group 2. Make enough copies of photocopiable page 74 (Word Wheel) for each child in Group 3. Stick onto card, cut out and assemble, using a brass split pin to combine the separate parts.

Introduction

Read to the children the poem 'Another Day' by John Cunliffe, but do not display the text at this point. Together, discuss what the poem was about, asking questions such as:

- What setting does the poem take place in?
- What is the poem about?
- Has anything described in the poem also happened to you?
- Do any phrases or words remind you of either yourself or other children in the class?
- Which phrases or words do you particularly like or dislike?
- When you heard the poem, did you use your imagination to picture what was happening?
- What pictures did you see in your imagination?

Whole-class skills work

Re-read the poem, but this time ask the children for their help. As you read, pause before the second rhyming word in each couplet and let the children predict the word.

Now display the enlarged laminated version of the first part of the poem from '*Boys shout*' to '*All in!*', and encourage the children to identify, point to and read out the rhyming words. Select the word 'clap' ('*Hands clap*') and ask the children if they can think of other things hands do that rhyme with 'clap', for example: snap, slap, tap, flap. Make a list on the board, initially focusing on the onset and rime in each word, for example: sn/ap, sl/ap, t/ap, and so on. Then sound out and spell each word phonemically to encourage the children to hear each sound separately, for example: s/n/a/p, s/l/a/p, and so on. Tell the children that each of the sounds in these words is called a 'phoneme'.

Differentiated group activities

1: Children work in pairs to read the first part of the poem, up to '*All in!*' and decide on which phrases they like best. Each child should then independently choose three of these phrases and draw pictures to show what they imagine when they hear or read them.
2*: Guide the children through a further reading of the poem to help them read aloud with expression. Ask pairs of children to work together to learn small sections of the poem that they can present to the rest of the class at the end of the session. Then move on to help another group if necessary.
3: Children work in pairs to make a list of words that rhyme with 'clap'. They then choose those words from the list which describe actions that hands can do. Each child could write these words on a cardboard cut-out of their hand, or simply make a list on a sheet of paper.

Conclusion

Ask children from Group 2 to recite parts of the poem they have learned. Relate this to Group 1's work by asking if they chose as their favourites any of the lines featuring in Group 2's presentations. Encourage the children to talk about the pictures that the lines and phrases create in their imaginations. Plan to make a display of the work including the rhyming work done by Group 3.

Introduction

Display the first verse of the poem 'Another Day' arranged in the wrong order (see Preparation) and read it to the children as follows:

giggle girls
shout boys
write pencils
squiggle squiggle

Look to see if some of the children have noticed, then continue:

> out cross it
> wrong it get
> out all
> gone bell's

When the children have begun to point out that the poem sounds wrong, ask them how they know this (because the words are mixed up and it no longer rhymes). Discuss the importance of where the rhyme occurs and how this can make the poem sound right or wrong. Now see if the children can use their knowledge of both word order and the rhyme structure in this poem to help you re-arrange the lines in the correct order.

Whole-class skills work

Display the enlarged version of the first part of the poem used in Hour 1. Establish with the children that the first verse is set in the classroom. Now explain that you want them to look at the second verse which is set in the playground. Read this verse together, then ask the children if they can think of things that balls do other than bounce, for example: roll, fly, spin and so on. (You can demonstrate this for the children, using a ball and making it spin, roll and so on.) Write these words on the board, drawing on the children's phonic knowledge to sound out and spell them, and using the word 'phoneme' to describe the units of sound.

Now repeat this activity with some other words not contained in the poem, encouraging the children to suggest ones they might include in a poem of their own. Choose words with a similar potential to previous examples, such as 'mouth'. Ask the children what mouths do, demonstrating as necessary, then write their suggestions on the board, for example: shout, scream, whisper, chat.

Differentiated group activities

1: Children work in pairs to read and re-sequence the first part (or a smaller section) of the poem that you have jumbled up (see Preparation). The children will need to look closely at the rhyming words as they re-order the text.

2*: The teacher works with this group first. Give each pair of children one of the sections from photocopiable page 73 (What do they do?) to complete by suggesting and writing associated words. Encourage them to use the 'Look, say, cover, write, check' strategy for learning the new spellings. These could be included in the children's personal word book for future reference.

3*: Children work in pairs with small sections of the poem to unjumble the phrases placed in the wrong order (see Preparation).

Conclusion

Encourage children from Group 2 to read their work with expression as if they were reading a poem. Ask children from other groups to join in with the readings and discuss how to put all Group 2's sections together to make a class poem. Illustrate this using paints or pastels.

Introduction

Display the laminated version of the second part of the poem. Read from 'All quiet' to 'Boy sleeps' using a quiet voice. Ask the children why you are reading it like this. Then read from 'Home time' to 'Watch telly' in a louder, more excited voice, but don't shout out any of the lines. To help the children understand why your voice/expression has changed, ask them to think about how they feel when school is over and they're going home. What words would they use to describe this – excited, happy, glad?

Now read the final part of the poem, again using a quiet voice and appropriate expression for each line. Ask the children how your voice sounds (tired, sleepy, drowsy). Can they explain why you are reading it in this way?

Whole-class skills work

Remind the children of the rime -ap as in 'clap' that they explored in Hour 1. Now move on to look at the rime -ip as in 'chip' (from verse four of the poem). Ask the children to suggest words that rhyme with 'chip' and sound each one out orally by onset and rime, for example: sh/ip, p/ip, cl/ip, l/ip.

Now write each word on the board and sound it out by phonemes. Finish by stretching out the words as you say them, blending the sounds together, for example: sh/i/p, p/i/p, c/l/i/p, l/i/p.

Differentiated group activities

1: Children work in pairs to learn small sections of the second part of the poem, ready to present to the rest of the class at the end of the session. Ask them to practise reading aloud with the appropriate expression.

2*: The teacher works with this group first. Children work in pairs to read the second part of the poem, deciding which phrases they like best. Each child should then independently choose three of these phrases and draw pictures to show what they imagine when they hear or read them.

3*: The teacher works with this group after helping Group 2. Give each child a blank word wheel for the rime -ip (from photocopiable page 74) and ask them to write onsets in the spaces to make new words (see below).

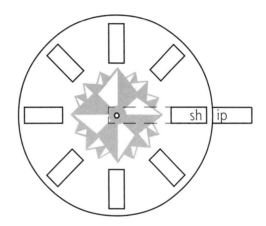

Conclusion

Listen to children from Group 1 reciting sections of the poem they have learned. Discuss completing the display of the work started in Hour 1. Provide a table where children can continue to make words using word wheels for -ap and -ip. Extend to include -op and -up.

ANOTHER DAY

Boys shout,
Girls giggle,
Pencils write,
Squiggle squiggle.
Get it wrong,
Cross it out,
Bell's gone,
All out!

Balls bounce,
Hands clap,
Skipping ropes,
Slap slap.
Hand-stands,
By the wall,
Sara Williams,
Best of all.
Boys fight,
Girls flee,
Teacher's gone
And spilt
His tea.
Clatter bang!
Big din,
Whistle goes,
All in!

All quiet,
No sound,
Hear worms,
Underground.
Chalk squeaks,
Clock creeps,
Head on desk,
Boy sleeps.

Home time,
Glory be,
Mum's got,
Chips for tea.
Warm fire,
Full belly,
Sit down,
Watch telly.

Bed time,
Creep away,
Dream until,
Another day.

John Cunliffe

WHAT DO THEY DO?

What do balls do?

Balls _____

What do skipping ropes do?

Skipping ropes _____

What do hoops do?

Hoops _____
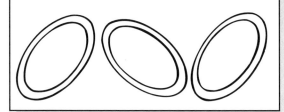

What do hands do?

Hands _____
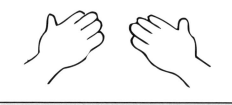

What do feet do?

Feet _____
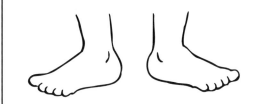

What do mouths do?

Mouths _____

WORD WHEEL

■ Cut out the wheel and the rectangular strip.
■ Fix the end of the strip to the back of the centre of the circle using a split paper fastener, making sure that the strip rotates.

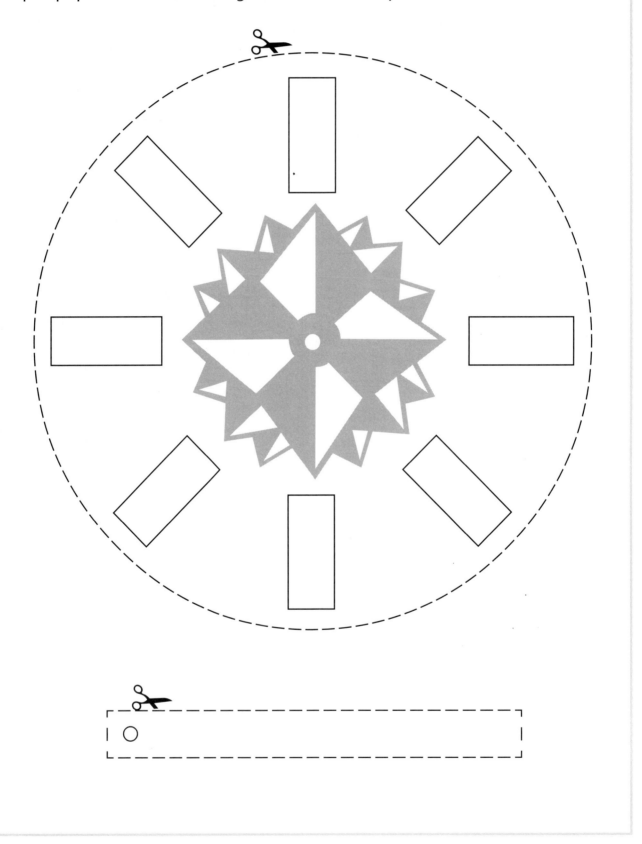

WHAT'S COOKING?

OBJECTIVES

UNIT	SPELLING/ VOCABULARY	GRAMMAR/ PUNCTUATION	COMPREHENSION/ COMPOSITION
READING AND WRITING FICTION AND NON-FICTION Recipe.	Explore new words from reading and shared experiences. Distinguish between 'onsets' and 'rimes' and invent new words using the rime -ake.	Write one-word instructions and simple sentences. Re-read for sense or to make improvements. Reinforce using capital letters at the start of names.	Read and use captions/ labels. Write captions/one word instructions. Write and draw simple instructions.

ORGANIZATION (3 HOURS)

	INTRODUCTION	WHOLE-CLASS SKILLS WORK	DIFFERENTIATED GROUP ACTIVITIES	CONCLUSION
HOUR 1	Shared reading of non-fiction text: recipe. Follow picture/word instructions to bake cake.	Learn simple rhyme to reinforce capital letters at the start of names.	1*: Follow picture/word recipe for making a cake. 2: Order picture/word instructions for making a cake. 3: Role play making a cake using recipe board.	Selected pupils from Group 1 explain how they would improve the recipe instructions.
HOUR 2	Shared reading of *Spot Bakes a Cake* by Eric Hill.	Use a writing frame to construct an invitation.	1: Using lift-the-flaps, recount how to make a cake. 2: Re-arrange jumbled words to write an invitation. Use capital letters. 3*: Construct picture/word instructions for decorating a cake.	Selected pupil from Group 1 reads his/her lift-the-flap book. Other children read and distribute invitations.
HOUR 3	Explore new words to instruct on how to decorate a cake.	Distinguish onset and rime using the rime -ake. Shared reading of *Spot Bakes a Cake*.	1: Make cover for lift-the-flaps books. 2: Provide onsets for the rime -ake using a word wheel. 3*: Improve instructions for how to decorate a cake.	Selected pupil from Group 1 reads from his/her completed lift-the-flap book. Look at improved instructions in 'How To Decorate a Cake' book. Display pupils' books.

RESOURCES

Multiple copies of *Spot Bakes a Cake* by Eric Hill (Puffin, ISBN 0-14-05-55137) for group work, big book stand (for displaying enlarged text), two felt boards, a laminator or sticky-backed plastic, sheets of card (A3 and A4), glue, Blu-Tack, board or flip chart, writing materials, OHP and acetate sheets (optional).

Photocopiable pages 79 and 80 (Bake a Cake: 1 and 2), 81 (Pat-a-Cake) and 82 (Word Wheel).

Utensils and ingredients for cake-baking, including a balance scale, as listed on the photocopiable recipes (Bake a Cake: 1 and 2), items for cake-decoration (icing, small sweets and so on), access to an oven, sandpaper, playdough, envelopes (for sending class invitations), class post box.

PREPARATION

Teach the rhyme 'Pat-a-Cake' on photocopiable page 81 to those children who are unfamiliar with it.

Make an enlarged laminated version of both the picture and word cake recipes on photocopiable pages 79 and 80 (Bake a Cake: 1 and 2). Repeat for photocopiable page 81 (Pat-a-Cake), but blank out the letter 'B' and the word 'Baby'. Make another enlarged copy (or OHT) of this sheet, this time with the full text. Collect together enough of the necessary utensils and ingredients to demonstrate making the cake in the introduction, and to allow each pair of children in Group 1 to make the cake. Place the enlarged photocopiable recipe sheets on a big book stand and arrange the ingredients and utensils for the demonstration on a table close by. Set out the necessary items for Group 1 to make their cake. (You may also wish to provide each pair in this group with a copy of both recipe sheets – see Hour 1.)

For each group of four children in Group 2, stick one copy of the photocopiable recipe sheet (Bake a Cake: 1) onto cardboard, cut into six sections and laminate. Stick small pieces of sandpaper on the back of each section so that they can be used on a felt board.

Set up the role play area as a kitchen, with the utensils needed for the cake recipe and some Playdough. Make a recipe board by enlarging each section of the recipe sheet (Bake a Cake: 1) separately and sticking onto card. Laminate, then attach Blu-Tack on the back of each section. Laminate a sheet of A1 card, then attach the recipe pictures to this, arranging them in the correct sequence.

Prepare a blank lift-the-flap book with eight pages for each child in Group 1 and an ordinary blank book large enough to contain Group 3's cake-decorating instructions (see main Introduction, pages 10 and 12 for guidance). Make enough blank invitation cards for each child in the class. Set up a class post box, and prepare a large (A3) laminated 'invitation' writing frame as follows, leaving enough space in the middle for information on date and time to be added in later:

Make two sets of the following words, each word written on a separate card: place, drop, sprinkle, spread, scatter, squeeze, swirl, blob, arrange. Finally, make one word wheel for each child in Group 2 using photocopiable page 82 (Word Wheel).

Introduction
Display the enlarged version of the photocopiable recipes (pages 79 and 80) next to the table containing the necessary utensils and ingredients. Explain to the children that you would like them to help you bake a cake. Encourage them to look at the pictures on the Bake a Cake: 1 sheet. Then point to the word recipe (Bake a Cake: 2) and explain that it contains instructions on how to make a cake. Ask them to help you read it. Go through both sheets again, with the children looking at the pictures and reading the words to help instruct you in how to make the cake. Finally, place the cake in the oven. Once it is baked, freeze it until you are ready to decorate it in a later session.

Whole-class skills work
Together, read the enlarged full version or OHT of the rhyme 'Pat-a-Cake' on photocopiable page 81. Then re-read it and substitute the letter 'B' and the word 'Baby' with the initial letter of one child's name and his/her full name (instead of 'Baby'). Make sure you involve the child in saying his or her initial and name, and focus on the need to use a capital letter for each one. Next, display the enlarged incomplete version of the rhyme with spaces replacing 'B' and 'Baby'. Invite individual children to come up and write both their initial and full name, using capitals in the appropriate places.

Differentiated group activities
1*: Children work in pairs, following the recipe to make a cake (the assistance of an

additional adult helper would be helpful here). They can refer to the large laminated versions of the recipe, or use a normal photocopied version if necessary.

2: Children work in groups of four to arrange their laminated set of recipe pictures in the correct sequence on the felt boards. They should read the written recipe instructions on their copies of photocopiable page 80 (Bake a Cake: 2) to help them.

3: Children work in the role-play area to act out making the cakes. They can use the Playdough to act out mixing the cake and placing it in a tin. Display the recipe board for the children to remove the appropriate section as they make their cake. They should then place them back in the correct sequence ready for other children to use. (Continue to let the children use the role-play area throughout this unit.)

Conclusion

Ask children from Group 1 how helpful they found the recipe instructions. What recommendations do they have for improving the instructions? Finally, encourage everyone to think about how they might decorate the cakes in the next session.

Introduction

Display the book *Spot Bakes a Cake* and choose a child to read the title and the author. Then read the story aloud, choosing children to come out to lift the flaps and read the text beneath. Ask the children what they think about Spot's attempts to make and decorate a cake. Look carefully at all the things Spot uses to decorate the cake. Can the children guess who the cake is for? Who guessed correctly that it is for Dad's birthday?

Whole-class skills work

Announce to the children that you would like to hold a class party. First, however, you need their help in preparing the invitations. Remind them of the previous session in which they looked at how to use capital letters in names. Explain how knowing about capital letters is important and will help them when writing the invitations.

Display the large writing frame showing the basic structure of an invitation (see Preparation). Read out the word 'invitation' and ask the children what the other two words on the card say ('To' and 'From'). Ask a child to pick a friend in the class who they would like to send an invitation to. Let the 'sender' write both names in the appropriate places using capital letters correctly.

Now explain that more information needs to be added to the middle of the invitation. Can the children think what this might be? Once they have made some decisions, ask them to help you write the additional text, drawing on their phonic and graphic knowledge. It could read something like this:

Differentiated group activities

1: Children work independently, each using a ready-made lift-the-flap book to recount how they made a cake in the previous session. Give them copies of *Spot Bakes a Cake* to use as a writing model. Explain that they should not work on the cover of their book until the next session.

2: Children write the invitation cards (and envelopes) for the class party. Remind them of the need to use capital letters in the appropriate places. Give them the laminated writing frame to refer to, but add on to this a jumbled-up version of the additional sentence from the skills session for the children to rearrange. Let the children use the class post box to send off their invitations.

3*: Working independently but with teacher/assistant guidance, the children construct picture and word instructions for decorating a cake. Before the end of the session, assemble each child's instructions into a ready-made book. Delegate the writing and drawing tasks for making a front cover modelled on the 'How to Decorate a Cake' book illustrated in *Spot Bakes a Cake*.

Conclusion

Begin by asking a child from Group 1 to read his/her lift-the-flap book aloud to the class. Talk about the need for this group to make a cover for their books and ask them to think about this for tomorrow. Finally, ask a child to empty the post box and, with help from other children, read the names on the envelopes and hand out the invitations. (If necessary, continue writing the invitations in the writing area.)

Introduction

Show the children the 'How to Decorate a Cake' book made in the previous session. Ask a child who was not involved in the book to come out and interpret one of the instructions, helped by the child who wrote them if necessary. Decide with the class if any other words could be added to make the instructions clearer.

Move on to briefly explore ways of making the instructions more detailed and varied in their use of language. The word 'put' is often heavily over-used by many children at this stage, for example: 'put chocolate on', 'put sweets on' and so on. Encourage them to think of alternatives by asking *how* they are going to put on the chocolate (pour or spread), or the sweets (place, sprinkle, drop), or the hundreds and thousands (sprinkle, scatter, shake). How are they going to ice the cake? Will they *spread* it on with a knife or *squeeze* it on from a bag. Is the icing going to be smooth or spiky, swirly or in blobs, and so on?

Whole-class skills work

Display the enlarged version of the Pat-a-Cake rhyme and the *Spot Bakes a Cake* Big Book. Draw the children's attention to the rime *-ake* recurring in *make*, *cake* and *bake*. Ask the children if they can see this pattern anywhere else in the rhyme (*Baker's*).

Ask them to suggest other words that rhyme with *make* and *cake*. Tell them that the part of the word that rhymes (*-ake*) is called the 'rime' and the beginning of the word is called the 'onset'. Let the children hear what it sounds like to separate words by onset and rime by saying 'b/ake', 'm/ake', 'c/ake' and so on.

Explain that by changing the onset of a word, lots of new words can be made. Sound out their suggested rhyming words containing *-ake* by using onset and rime, for example: l/ake, fl/ake, t/ake.

Finish by reading to the children *Spot Bakes a Cake*.

Differentiated group activities

1: Each child makes a front cover for their lift-the-flap book. To do this, they draw a picture of how they would decorate their cake and use appropriate words to create short, simple instructions, such as 'spread the jam', 'sprinkle the sweets' to place around the picture. Provide them with a set of cards containing words covered in the Introduction (see Preparation) to help them, but encourage a 'look, say, cover, write, check' approach so that they get into the habit of remembering.

2: Give each child a ready-made word wheel (see Preparation) and ask them to provide further onsets for the rime *-ake* to make new words. On completion, let them work in pairs to compare their new words.

3*: Children work in pairs to improve their instructions for the jointly-combined 'How to Decorate a Cake' book, supported by you as necessary. Provide them with a set of cards containing words covered in the Introduction (see Preparation) and encourage them to use these to improve their instructions.

Conclusion

Ask a child from Group 1 to read from his/her completed lift-the-flap book. Make a display of the lift-the-flap books alongside a copy of *Spot Bakes a Cake* for the children to continue to read. Look at the improvements made to a couple of the cake-decorating instructions from Group 3 and discuss the appropriateness of the new words they have included. Display their book with Group 1's lift-the-flap books, and Group 2's word wheels for everyone to read and use. All that needs to be done now is to decorate the cakes and hold the party!

BAKE A CAKE: 1

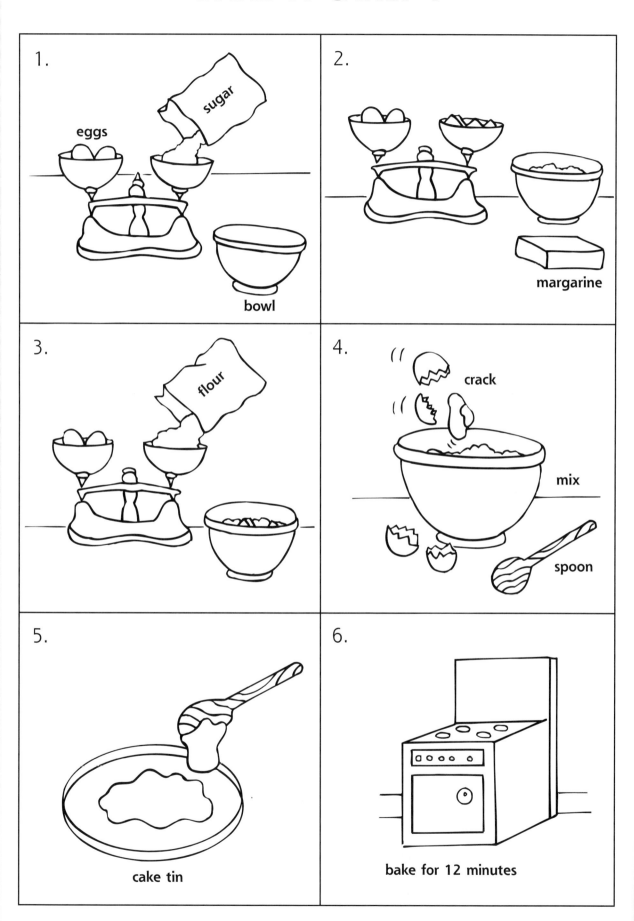

1.

eggs

sugar

bowl

2.

margarine

3.

flour

4.

crack

mix

spoon

5.

cake tin

6.

bake for 12 minutes

BAKE A CAKE: 2

- Put two eggs in one side of the scales.

- Balance the eggs with the sugar.

- Put the sugar in a bowl.

- Balance the eggs with the margarine.

- Mix margarine and sugar together until creamy.

- Balance the eggs with the flour.

- Put the flour into the mixture.

- Crack the eggs and whisk until frothy.

- Add the eggs to the mixture.

- Mix together until creamy again.

- Grease a small round cake tin.

- Spoon in the mixture.

- Place in a hot oven (190°C/375°F).

- Bake for 12 minutes until golden brown.

PAT-A-CAKE

Pat-a-cake, Pat-a-cake
Baker's man
Bake me a cake
As fast as you can
Prick it and pat it
And mark it with B
Put it in the oven
For baby and me.

Traditional

WORD WHEEL

■ Cut out the wheel and the rectangular strip below.
■ Fix the end of the strip to the centre of the back of the circle using a split paper fastener, making sure that the strip rotates.

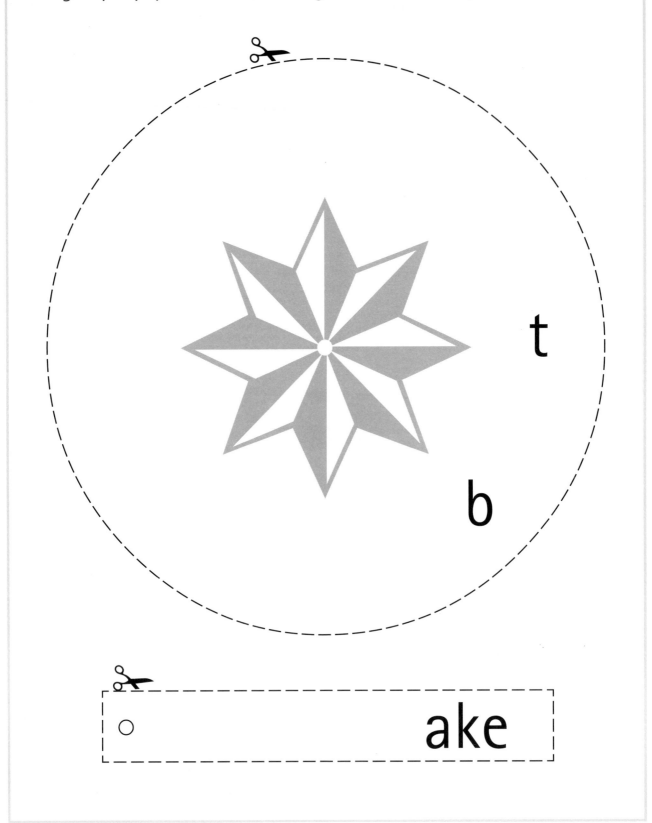

t

b

ake

SCHOOL DAY

OBJECTIVES

UNIT	SPELLING/ VOCABULARY	GRAMMAR/ PUNCTUATION	COMPREHENSION/ COMPOSITION
NON-FICTION READING AND WRITING Our School Day.	Use 'Look, say, cover, write, check' routine for learning spellings and putting words into personal word books.	Read captions and simple sentences. Check meaning by using grammatical awareness. Use lines to indicate relationship between word and items.	Use a selection of non-fiction books to read captions and pictures. Read and write captions. Read, follow and devise simple instructions.

ORGANIZATION (5 HOURS)

	INTRODUCTION	WHOLE-CLASS SKILLS WORK	DIFFERENTIATED GROUP ACTIVITIES	CONCLUSION
HOUR 1	Sequence photographs of a typical school day and match simple sentences to them.	Introduce 'Look, say, cover, write, check' strategy for spelling.	1: Prepare a plan of the school day. 2*: Sequence sentences about the school day. 3*: Match sentences to photographs.	Selected pupils from Groups 1 and 2 explain how they have used 'Look, say, cover, write, check' strategy for spelling. Use photos to make wall frieze.
HOUR 2	Shared reading of School by Carol Watson. Demonstrate finding information.	Construct sentences.	1: Construct a book about the school day. 2*: Read for information. Make comparisons. 3*: Guided writing: simple sentences.	Pupils from Group 2 report on their findings. Read out some of Group 3's work and discuss where to place it on wall frieze. Display Group 1's books.
HOUR 3	Shared writing of captions for lunchtime routines.	Demonstrate how to use and construct labels.	1: List things to remember for lunchtime. 2: Draw and label favourite food. 3*: Guided writing: captions.	Compare lists and captions and discuss.
HOUR 4	Shared writing of captions for happy playtimes.	Interpret some signs around school.	1*: Guided writing of captions; draw signs. 2*: Find and interpret signs. Prepare to present findings. 3: Draw sign for a given caption.	Pupils in Group 2 present their findings. Others interpret the signs found. Decide on best signs for happy playtimes.
HOUR 5	Share familiar playground songs and rhymes. Teach a clapping game/rhyme.	Model writing instructions for a playground game.	1: Write instructions in words/symbols. 2*: Rehearse and record playground rhymes/songs. 3*: Guided writing: game instructions.	Listen to Group 2's recorded rhymes and ask pupils to demonstrate the playground games.

RESOURCES

Copies of School by Carol Watson (Franklin Watts, ISBN 07496-2792-1) for group work, a selection of other non-fiction books about the school day, Blu-Tack, 'Post-its', clipboards (one for each pair in Group 2), laminator or sticky-backed plastic, a board or flip chart, writing and drawing materials, OHP and acetate sheets (optional), card (including an A1 sheet), materials for making small books, a tape recorder and blank tapes, a camera, photocopiable pages 88 (Playground Clapping Rhyme) and 159 (Story Map - from 'Polar Bear, Polar Bear' unit, Term 3), a lunchbox and typical contents, a collection of signs (from around the school), string (cut into lengths of about 15cm).

PREPARATION

Hour 1
Write the sentences below in the order shown. Use large print on a sheet of A1 card, then laminate.

Our School Day
We learn to read.
We play with our friends.
We go to assembly.
We go home.
We eat lunch.
We come to school.
We listen to stories.
We learn about number.

Take photographs of a typical day at your school, cover the activities in the list above. Enlarge the photographs on the photocopier for whole-class use. Make a word bank (pockets) set out alphabetically in which words associated with this topic are written on card strips.

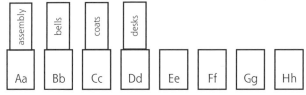

You will also need one copy of the blank story strip from photocopiable page159 (Story Map from 'Polar Bear, Polar Bear' unit in Term 3), for each child in Group 1. Make each child in this group a book with the letters of the alphabet on separate pages.

Hour 2
Collect together several non-fiction books about school for Group 2.

Hour 3
Prepare a packed lunch box with typical contents such as sandwiches, crisps, a chocolate bar, fruit, juice and so on. Make a blank card label for each item in the box.

Hour 4
Gather a selection of familiar signs from around the school.

Hour 5
Make an OHT of the clapping rhyme on photocopiable page 88 or enlarge to A3 size. Familiarize yourself with the instructions for this:

Two children face one another and prepare to start clapping each other's hands in time to the rhyme.
For 'sea sea sea' - make waves with hands.
For 'see see see' - stop clapping and put hands to eyes as if looking out to sea, beating the three beats on their forehead.
For 'chop chop chop' - use hand as if chopping for three beats.
For 'knee knee knee' - use three beats on knee.
Last verse - one beat on forehead, one beat for a chop, one beat on knee.

Introduction
Begin by sitting the children in a circle on the floor. In the middle, place the enlarged photographs showing a typical day at your school.
　　Look at each picture with the children, discussing where and when it was taken, and what is happening. Then ask the children to identify the theme of the pictures (such as the school day). How could they use the pictures to show someone what happens in a typical school day? Let the children establish the need to sequence the pictures and then invite their help in doing this.

Now announce that you have some sentences about these pictures (see Preparation). Hold up one of the sentence cards and read it together, for example 'We come to school'. Ask a child to place the card beneath the corresponding picture. Repeat this with one more sentence.

Whole-class skills work

Tell the children that to write about their school day, they will need to spell lots of different words, so you are going to show them a special way to remember spellings. Introduce them to the 'Look, say, cover, write, check' strategy using the word 'school' as an example. Take them through the process of looking at the word, saying it, then covering it up, emphasizing the need to remember what it looks and sounds like before writing and checking it. Next, choose someone to write the word from memory on the board. Ask the other children to say if they think it is correct, then check.

Tell the children that you have placed other useful words in the word bank (see Preparation). Using another word, such as 'lunch', go through the process of finding the 'l' pocket, and then recap on the 'look, say, cover, write, check' strategy.

Differentiated group activities

1: Give each child a copy of the story strip from photocopiable page 159 (Story Map - the 'Polar Bear, Polar Bear' unit in Term 3), together with a word book. They should use the story strip to make a picture and word plan of what they do in a school day. They should use the word bank for unfamiliar words, writing these in their book and using the spelling strategy you have shown them to write the word on their plan.

2*: The teacher supports this group first. Children work independently to make a zigzag book called 'Our School Day' (see main Introduction, page 12 for general guidance). Provide them with the large laminated list of sentences (see Preparation) for them to choose from and place in the correct order in their book. Alternatively, they can try constructing their own sentences.

3*: Children continue to match the sentence cards to the enlarged photographs as in the Introduction. Look at some new words, such as 'friends', and help the children to find them in the word bank, then use the 'Look, say, cover, write, check' process.

Conclusion

Choose children from Groups 1 and 2 to show what they have drawn and written about the school day. Ask them if and how they used the word bank to reinforce the 'Look, say, cover, write, check' strategy you showed them.

Display the enlarged versions of the photographs as a wall frieze using Blu-Tack to enable further ordering activities. (Do not display the sentence cards as children will provide their own captions in the next session.)

HOUR 2

Introduction

Just before the start of this session, quickly put one of the 'school day' photographs in the wrong order on the wall frieze. Then begin by asking the children to look at the wall frieze. Ask if they like the photographs and wait to see if anyone spots that one picture is in the wrong order. Put the photograph back in the correct order, then announce that what is needed now is a sentence saying something about each picture.

To help them gather some ideas for this, show the children the non-fiction book *School* by Carol Watson (see Resources). Emphasize that, as you are looking for bits of information, you do not need to start at the beginning of the book and can 'dip' into it in any order. Find pictures in the book that are similar to the class photographs and read what the text says. List some sample sentences or ideas on the board.

Whole-class skills work

Choose one of the class pictures and invite suggestions for a sentence about it. Ask the children to help you write the sentence, prompting them as follows:

■ Ask them what type of letter begins a sentence.
■ Ask them to suggest spellings drawing on their phonic knowledge.
■ Use the word bank and 'Look, say, cover, write, check' strategy.
■ Write the sentence over two lines to make it clear that it doesn't finish at the end of the board or flip chart – emphasize that the end of a line isn't the end of a sentence!
■ Do the children think the words are in the right order?

- Do they need to make any changes?
- What goes at the end of a sentence?

Differentiated group activities

1: Children use their plans from the previous session to help them construct a simple book about the school day (see main Introduction, page 12 for general guidance). They use *School* as a model for the layout. (This task may need to be continued outside the literacy hour.)

2*: The teacher supports this group after working with Group 3. Give each pair of children a selection of books about the school day, including *School*. They should look for similarities between their school day and those represented in the books. Let them use 'Post-its' to identify additional photographs that would be interesting to include in the class wall frieze.

3*: The teacher works with this group first in a guided writing session. Continue to compose sentences with the children to accompany the photographs in the frieze, reinforcing the teaching points made in the skills session and using ideas from the Introduction.

Conclusion

Children from Group 2 talk about the books they have been looking at, and what suggestions they have for including more photographs in the wall frieze. Choose children to read some of the work done by Group 3 and make joint decisions about where to place the sentences on the frieze. Display Group 1's books for the children to read at other times.

Introduction

Talk to the children about the lunchtime routine at school. Ask them what things they must always remember to do at this time, and model the writing of some captions to place in the classroom as reminders, for example:

- Wash your hands before lunch.
- Keep lunch boxes here.
- Remember to screw on any lids.

Whole-class skills work

Ask the children about their favourite packed lunch or hot dinner. Show them a packed lunch box and ask them to guess what might be inside. Show them the contents, then choose children to help you write a card label for each one. Draw on their phonic knowledge and use the 'look, say, cover, write, check' strategy when spelling the words. Then ask the children to read the labels and tie them to each item using string.

Differentiated group activities

1: In pairs children write a list of important things to remember to do at lunchtime.

2: Children work independently to draw their favourite lunch – either in a lunch box or on a dinner tray – and write labels with lines pointing to the appropriate item.

3*: Guided writing, with the children composing captions as reminders of important things to do at lunchtime.

Conclusion

Children in Group 3 should compare and discuss the captions they have made with the lists of reminders compiled by Group 1. Involve all the children in deciding where to place the captions so they will be helpful reminders.

Introduction

Together, discuss playtimes and consider what rules could help to make these breaks even more enjoyable. Model writing some suitable captions containing rules or instructions, for example:

- Play games together.
- Stay in the playground.
- Take turns to go on the tyres.
- Fasten your coat.

Write these on the board or flip chart for the children to refer to in the group activities.

Whole-class skills work

Show the children a number of signs they will have seen in school and ask them to interpret their meaning. Then ask them to suggest some signs they could draw to go with the captions for happy playtimes written in the Introduction.

Differentiated group activities

1*: The teacher works with this group first in a guided writing session, with children working in pairs to write captions for making playtimes enjoyable and draw signs to accompany them.

2*: The teacher supports this group after working with Group 1. Children work in pairs to go on an indoor search for signs in school. Each pair should use a clipboard to draw the sign, record where it is and suggest what it means. They then work with the teacher, preparing to present their findings.

3: Children work in pairs with a given caption from the Introduction which they read and say aloud. They then draw a suitable sign to go with the caption. Give other captions to the pairs as they finish.

Conclusion

Ask a pair of children from Group 2 to report on their findings. Have they found any signs that the other children didn't know about? Who can work out what the signs mean? Finally, invite the children to select the most important captions and signs for 'Happy Playtimes' and use these to make a wall display.

Introduction

Look again at the 'Happy Playtime' wall display from the previous session. Briefly discuss what playtime games the children enjoy and ask them what playground rhymes or chants they know, encouraging them to demonstrate if appropriate.

Now show the children the easy clapping rhyme on photocopiable page 88 (displayed as an OHT or enlargement). Read it through together first of all, then teach them using two children to demonstrate the actions.

Whole-class skills work

Tell the children that giving instructions can be difficult, especially if they are quite complicated. Explain that this is why signs are often used for displaying instructions, because signs can convey ideas quickly and clearly.

Now remind the children of the clapping game they have just learned and model writing instructions for it using symbols and signs.

Differentiated group activities

1: Work in friendship groups to devise a set of instructions, using words and symbols (as in the skills session), for a game they play in the playground.

2*: The teacher supports this group after working with Group 3. Children work in pairs or threes to rehearse some of the songs and rhymes they use in the playground. They record these onto tape for others to hear.

3*: The teacher works with this group first in a guided writing session, where children are helped to devise a set of instructions using words and symbols for a familiar playground game.

Conclusion

Play back some of the rhymes recorded by Group 2 and ask who else knows these playground games. Choose children to demonstrate the actions to accompany the rhymes for others to learn.

PLAYGROUND CLAPPING RHYME

A sailor went to sea sea sea
To see what he could see see see
And all that he could see see see
Was the bottom of the deep blue sea sea sea

A sailor went to chop chop chop
To see what he could chop chop chop
And all that he could chop chop chop
Was the bottom of the deep blue chop chop chop

A sailor went to knee knee knee
To see what he could knee knee knee
And all that he could knee knee knee
Was the bottom of the deep blue knee knee knee

A sailor went to sea chop knee
To see what he could see chop knee
And all that he could see chop knee
Was the bottom of the deep blue sea chop knee

THE THREE LITTLE PIGS: READING

OBJECTIVES

UNIT	SPELLING/ VOCABULARY	GRAMMAR/ PUNCTUATION	COMPREHENSION/ COMPOSITION
READING FICTION *The Three Little Pigs* (Traditional story).	Use onset, rime and analogy to read unknown words. Extend initial consonant clusters.	Identify sentences and order/re-order them. Introduce speech bubbles.	Listen to and re-tell a traditional story. Identify and discuss characters and speculate about their behaviour. Compare *The Three Little Pigs* with other stories.

ORGANIZATION (5 HOURS)

INTRODUCTION	WHOLE-CLASS SKILLS WORK	DIFFERENTIATED GROUP ACTIVITIES	CONCLUSION
HOUR 1 Tell the story of *The Three Little Pigs*. Discuss the sequence of events.	Distinguish between onset and rime using the word 'chin' from the story. Make new words using the rime -in.	1: Practise re-telling the story in pairs. 2: Build words using -in. Devise a game. 3*: Compose a Big Book of the story together.	Selected pair from Group 1 re-tells the story. Selected pupils from Group 2 show their game. Teacher shows Group 3's Big Book.
HOUR 2 Read *The Three Little Pigs* using Group 3's Big Book. Discuss characters' behaviour.	Re-read the story and reinforce the sequence of events.	1: Find parts of the story which illustrate points about the main characters. 2: Re-order sentences from the story. 3*: Guided reading and sequencing of story text.	Selected pupil from Group 1 reports on his/her opinion of the story characters. Selected pupil from Group 2 reads aloud to rest of class.
HOUR 3 Re-read class Big Book on *The Three Little Pigs*. Identify main events of plot.	Distinguish between onset and rime using 'brick' and 'stick' from the story.	1: Read and re-order main features of the story plot. 2*: Role-play story. Discuss plot features. 3: Build new words using -ick.	Group 2 enacts through role play the story of *The Three Little Pigs*. Discuss use of props and key features. Extend Group 3's activity using different rimes.
HOUR 4 Compare *The Three Little Pigs* with other stories that have similar beginnings.	Mask words and encourage pupils to read back or read on to guess the word.	1*: Read and compare a selection of books. 2: Reassemble words into sentences. 3: Spell familiar words in the text using picture clues.	Pair of pupils from Group 1 discusses findings, referring to books read. Reinforce spelling work.
HOUR 5 Add speech bubbles to illustrations in class Big Book and read story through what is said.	Mask various connectives so pupils can predict words.	1*: Re-enact story through reading what is said. 2: Read speech bubbles and match to appropriate place in story. 3: Cloze activity using connectives.	Group 1 presents a re-enactment of the story.

RESOURCES

A version of *The Three Little Pigs*, a version of *The Three Billy Goats Gruff*, examples of modern stories with similar thematic links (for example, *Alfie Gives a Hand,* Red Fox, ISBN 0-09-925607-X and *Moving Molly,* Red Fox, ISBN 0-09-991650-9, both by Shirley

Hughes), large wedge-tipped black felt pen for scribing, board or flip chart, writing materials, materials for making a class Big Book and smaller books (see main Introduction, page 10 for guidance), Big Book stand, a pointer, sheets of card, sheets of paper (A3), stapler, Blu-Tack, glue, laminator or sticky-backed plastic, materials for making masks (see Preparation), photocopiable pages 95 (Story Sentences), 96 (Character Portrait), 97 (Tell the Tale), 98 (Spell the Words) and 99 (Speech Bubbles), props including bundles of straw, sticks, bricks, a pot, an imaginary fire (made from coloured foil), 12 small envelopes.

PREPARATION

Hour 1
Write this repeated rhyming phrase in large text on A1 card for whole-class use:

Little pig, Little pig,
Let me come in!

Not by the hair on my chinny-chin-chin,
I will not let you in!

Then I'll huff and I'll puff and I'll blow your house in!

Prepare one small card with the rime -in written on for each child in Group 3. Next, write the following initial consonant clusters in large text on A1 card and laminate:

br bl ch cl cr dr fl fr gl gr pl pr
sc sk sl sm sn sp st tr tw

Hour 2
Make one copy of photocopiable page 96 (Character Portrait) for each child in Group 1. Create one word-processed small version of the class Big Book of The Three Little Pigs (made in Hour 1) for each pair in Group 1. Make one copy of photocopiable page 96 (Story Sentences) for each child in Groups 2 and 3. Cut up the sentences into separate strips, differentiating for Group 3 by varying the number of sentences on one strip, for example using three strips of four sentences to simplify it. Also make one 12-page 'little book' (see main Introduction, page 10 for guidance) for each child in Group 2.

Hour 3
Write the words 'brick' and 'stick' in large print on separate cards. Make one copy of photocopiable page 97 (Tell the Tale) for each child in Group 1. Set up the role-play area for Group 2 with a selection of simple props (see Resources). Prepare some simple card masks of the pigs and wolf, either to fit around the children's heads (use shearing elastic) or to hold in front of their faces (use paper plates on sticks). For each child in Group 3, prepare a small card containing the rime -ick, and approximately six blank cards for writing single words on (optional).

Hour 4
Collect together some modern stories with similar beginnings to The Three Little Pigs (see Resources). Make one copy of photocopiable page 95 (Story Sentences) per pair in Group 2. Cut up each sentence into its component words and place each one in an envelope (you could number these discreetly so you know which sentence is inside). You will also need 12 pre-cut strips of paper for each pair to stick the complete sentences on. For each child in Group 3 make one copy of photocopiable page 98 (Spell the Words). Take the class Big Book of The Three Little Pigs and mask all the words listed on this photocopiable page using Blu-Tack (also see main Introduction, page 12).

Hour 5
Prepare a blank speech bubble for each illustration in the class Big Book. Mask some of the connective words ('and', 'but', 'then', 'next', 'so', 'because', and so on) in this book. Photocopy a section of the text with the masked words for each child in Group 3 to fill in the blank spaces. Make one copy of photocopiable page 99 (Speech Bubbles) per child in Groups 1 and 2.

Introduction

Display the enlarged version of the repeated rhyming phrase from the traditional story of *The Three Little Pigs* (see Preparation). Now begin to tell the children the story, asking them to join in by repeating the rhyming phrase in the appropriate places. Use all your story-telling skills, such as exaggeration, inference and so on, to support the children and help them become more expressive readers.

At the end of the story, ask a few open-ended questions, for example:
- Were there any parts you particularly liked or disliked?
- How would you describe the story to someone else?

Then encourage the children to focus on the plot, discussing the key events and the order they occur in (use the word 'sequence' with the children). Record their responses on a flip chart. Your list of events might include:

- The pigs leave home.
- They separate to lead their own lives.
- The wicked wolf appears.
- The first pig is threatened by the wolf and seeks help.
- The second pig is threatened by the wolf and seeks help.
- The third pig is threatened but outwits the wolf.

Explain that some children are going to use the list on the flip chart to help them re-tell the story to the class.

Whole-class skills work

Now refer again to the enlarged version of the repetitive rhyming phrase. Using a pointer, encourage the children to match the words said to those read. Ask them to suggest words that rhyme with *chin* and, each time, pick out the rhyming sound *in*. Then point to the word *chin*, and distinguish between the onset *ch-* and the rime *-in*. Ask the children to suggest other onsets for the rime *-in*, for example p/in, th/in, b/in, etc.

Next, distinguish between single consonant onsets and double consonant onsets by writing the children's suggestions in two separate columns on the flip chart or board. Explain that one column is for one letter before the rime and the other is for two letters before the rime. Choose children to make new words by writing an onset in front of the rime *-in* using the appropriate columns. Explain that some children are going to use what they have just learned to invent word guessing games.

Differentiated group activities

1: Children work in pairs, practising telling the story to one another using lots of expression. Let them use the prompts on the flip chart to remind them of the story sequence. Explain that one pair will tell the story to the class later.

2: Children find alternative onsets for the rime *-in* to make a list of new words. They use the list of consonant blends to support them (see Preparation). Based on their list, they devise a guessing game for others to play by drawing a picture next to the rime as a clue to what the onset/word might be.

3*: Guided writing, with you acting as scribe to help children construct the whole story text as a class Big Book. (Later, they should paint pictures to illustrate the book ready for Hour 2.) Be sure to include connectives in this text for use in Hour 5, for example: '*but* the third pig built his house of bricks. *So* he climbed down the chimney', and so on.

Conclusion

One pair of children from Group 1 tell their story of *The Three Little Pigs* to the whole class (at story-telling time, if necessary). Talk about the skills they have used in doing this, such as facial expression, gesture, loud/soft voice and vocal expression. Show the children the game that Group 2 have made and allow some time for them to play this. Briefly refer to the class Big Book made with Group 3 and say that you will be using this in the next session.

Introduction

Read the story of *The Three Little Pigs*, using the Big Book made by Group 3. Afterwards, ask the children what sort of characters the three little pigs are. Point out that there is no description of the pigs in the story, but can the children guess what these characters are like from their actions and behaviour?

Encourage them to define the character of each little pig and the wolf. Write their character descriptions on a flip chart, for example:

■ I think that the first little pig is frightened/ scared/ weak because...
■ The wolf is wicked/crafty because...

Talk about how the children came to these conclusions. Which part of the story made them think that way about the characters? Help them locate the supporting text.

Whole-class skills work

Re-read the story and involve the children in predicting what happens next as a way of reinforcing the sequence of events.

Differentiated group activities

1: Children work individually on photocopiable page 96 (Character Portrait) together using the class Big Book and small copies of the story (see Preparation) for reference. Encourage them to try and capture the nature of the character when drawing the portrait. Emphasize that they should use a maximum of three words to describe their chosen character and write text below to support their opinion.

2: Children work in pairs to sequence the 12 sentences from photocopiable page 95 (Story Sentences), placing one on each page of their their 'little books' (see Preparation).

3*: Children work individually to read and re-arrange the cut-up sentences from photocopiable page 95 (Story Sentences). They place one section behind the other in the correct sequence for stapling together.

Conclusion

Examine Group 1's portraits and ask if the appropriate characteristics have been captured – for example, does the wolf look mean enough? Does the first little pig look friendly? Ask one child from Group 1 to explain how he/she supported his/her opinion of the character using the story text. Finally, ask one child from Group 2 to read aloud the re-assembled sentences in his/her little book, with the other children listening carefully to check the sequence.

Introduction

Re-read *The Three Little Pigs* story from the class Big Book, raising questions as you go along to alert the children to the plot. Help them to identify the main events of the plot as follows: the pigs leave home, the wolf (villain) appears, the pigs seek help, the third pig (hero) outwits the wolf and justice is done with good finally triumphing over bad.

Whole-class skills work

Show the children the word cards (see Preparation) and ask them to identify the words 'stick' and 'brick'. Ask them to identify the rime (*-ick*) and the onsets (*st-* and *br-*). Now invite them to suggest other onsets with two letters blended together (double consonant blends) and write their responses on the flip chart. Some words the children suggest will make sense while others may not, for example 'bl/ick'. Discuss the meaning of the words to check whether or not they make sense.

Differentiated group activities

1: Children work individually to complete photocopiable page 97 (Tell the Tale).

2*: Children discuss features of the plot and role play the story of *The Three Little Pigs* using props and masks.

3: Children choose from a list of onsets which they match with the rime *-ick* to create new words (see Preparation, Hour 1). They can either list them on paper or put each word on a blank card. This activity can be easily extended by providing other rimes such as *-ack*, *-uck*, *-eck*, *-ock*.

Conclusion

Children from Group 2 re-enact the story. Discuss how they have incorporated the props into their story and reinforce the key events of the plot. Briefly conclude the lesson by extending Group 3's work using different rimes such as *-ock*, *-ack*, etc.

Introduction

Ask the children how the story of *The Three Little Pigs* begins (the pigs leave home and set off to make a new life). Then read the opening of *The Three Billy Goats Gruff* and ask them if they can spot any similarities. Help them to make connections between the two beginnings and ask if they know of any other stories that begin like this, for example 'Little Red Riding Hood', where the main character leaves home to go to the woods.

Now talk about some modern stories which have similar links, such as *Alfie Gives A Hand* by Shirley Hughes. In this book, Alfie experiences his first time away from home when he attends a friend's birthday party. Discuss how Alfie takes his comfort blanket to the party. What might the three little pigs have taken to their new homes?

Explore the feelings involved when doing something new. Relate them to how the three little pigs might have felt. Another suitable book to look at is *Moving Molly*, also by Shirley Hughes.

Whole-class skills work
Now show the children the class Big Book of *The Three Little Pigs*, with the words from photocopiable page 98 (Spell the Words) masked off (see Preparation). Ask them to guess the words, uncovering the first letter if necessary, or help them with other strategies such as read back (looking back on previous words in the text to help with meaning) or read on (looking at the rest of the sentence to solve the problem).

Differentiated group activities
1*: In pairs, let the children choose a book (from the selection in the Introduction) to read and compare its beginning with *The Three Little Pigs*. They should then discuss what the characters might feel about their situation.
2: Children work individually to reassemble the sentences from photocopiable page 95 (Story Sentences) by sticking the words onto pre-cut strips of paper (see Preparation). They then sequence the sentences to make a whole story script.
3: Children work in pairs to spell some simple words from picture clues linked with the story using photocopiable page 98 (Spell the Words). Encourage them to use the 'Look, say, cover, write, check' strategy.

Conclusion
One pair of children from Group 1 talk about their findings. Encourage them to support their ideas by reference to the texts. Reinforce Group 3's spelling work by referring to the masked words in the class Big Book and assess other children's abilities to spell these.

Introduction
Use the illustrations in the class Big Book to prompt the children to suggest what the characters might be saying. Write their suggestions on pre-cut speech bubbles and Blu-Tack them onto the illustrations. Now read the story together using just the speech bubbles, inviting children to be the characters as they read. Remember to include the repetitive rhyming phrase (see Introduction, Hour 1). Encourage the children to read expressively by asking them how the pigs might have felt when running for help. Let them try making their voice sound powerful and wicked like the wolf's!

Whole-class skills work
Display the class Big Book with the connectives masked off (see Preparation). Go through the story, asking the children to guess the words as you go along. Use read back and read on strategies to help them.

Differentiated group activities
1*: Half the group work with the teacher, reading the speech bubbles in the class Big Book. They take on the characters in the story and act out what is being said in preparation for a class presentation. The other children should work on photocopiable page 99 (Speech Bubbles). Change over half way through.
2: Children work individually to complete photocopiable page 99 (Speech Bubbles).
3: Children work individually to complete photocopies of the class Big Book text with the connectives missing, filling in the blank spaces with the correct words.

Conclusion
Group 1 perform their re-enactment of the Big Book story, then the other children comment on this work. Draw attention to the spoken form represented by the speech bubbles in the Big Book.

STORY SENTENCES

Once upon a time there were three little pigs.

The first little pig made his house of straw.

The second little pig made his house of sticks.

The third little pig made his house of bricks.

Then a big bad wolf came along.

He blew down the house of straw.

He blew down the house of sticks.

He couldn't blow down the house of bricks.

He climbed down the chimney.

He tumbled into a pot of boiling water.

That was the end of the wolf.

The three little pigs lived happily ever after.

CHARACTER PORTRAIT

■ Choose a character from the story. Write the character's name and draw a picture in the frame provided.

■ Write three words to describe this character, one word in each of the 'description' boxes.

■ Now write the story text that supports your opinion.

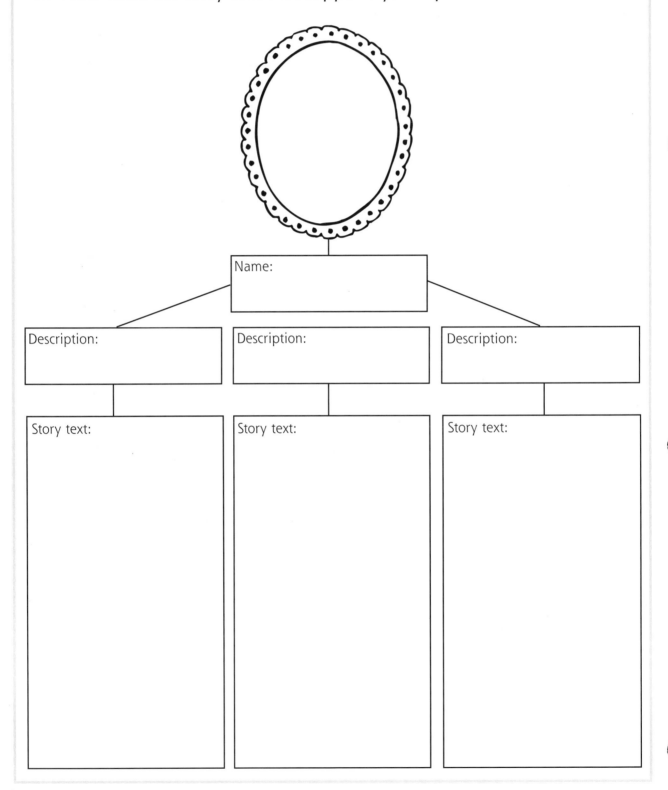

Name:

Description:

Description:

Description:

Story text:

Story text:

Story text:

TELL THE TALE

- Cut out the pictures below and put them in the correct order.
- Cut out each section of the story and put it below the correct picture.

Once upon a time there were three little pigs. They built three houses from straw, sticks and bricks.	He tumbled into a pot of boiling water. That was the end of the wolf.
The big bad wolf blew down the house of straw. And blew down the house of sticks.	He couldn't blow down the house of bricks. So he climbed down the chimney.

SPELL THE WORDS

■ Look at the pictures below.
■ Write the name of each item three times below its picture.

      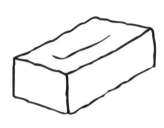

_____   _____   _____

_____   _____   _____

_____   _____   _____

_____   _____   _____

_____   _____   _____

_____   _____   _____

SPEECH BUBBLES

- Cut out the pictures and the speech bubbles.
- Put each speech bubble next to the correct picture.
- Stick down the bubbles and pictures in the correct order on some paper.

I need some straw to build my house.

Arrgh! Arrgh!

I need some sticks to build my house.

I need some bricks to build my house.

THE THREE LITTLE PIGS: WRITING

OBJECTIVES

UNIT	SPELLING/ VOCABULARY	GRAMMAR/ PUNCTUATION	COMPREHENSION/ COMPOSITION
WRITING FICTION *The Three Little Pigs* (Traditional story).	Practise and reinforce discrimination, spelling and reading of beginning, middle and final letter sounds in simple words.	Identify and compare basic story elements using appropriate story language. Recognize appropriate punctuation.	Shared writing of class story. Identify key features in plots, especially beginnings and endings. Extend rhyming and alliterative patterns.

ORGANIZATION (5 HOURS)

	INTRODUCTION	WHOLE-CLASS SKILLS WORK	DIFFERENTIATED GROUP ACTIVITIES	CONCLUSION
HOUR 1	Shared reading of similar beginnings from stories, including class Big Book of *The Three Little Pigs*. Teacher scribes key words.	Construct sentences from key words describing pupils' feelings, linking them to pupils' personal experiences.	1*: Write beginning of a story from personal experience. 2: Write simple sentences about feelings. 3*: Shared writing of beginning of story for a class Big Book.	Discuss and compare opening sentences written by all three groups.
HOUR 2	Shared reading of selected Group 1 pupil's story. Discuss and record plot development.	Shared reading of rhyming frame in *The Three Little Pigs*.	1: Write a story beginning, developing the plot through a series of questions. 2: Collect repeated rhymes from other traditional stories. 3*: Continue shared writing of class story.	Focus on story development by referring to work of Groups 1 and 3. Play guessing game.
HOUR 3	Read class story so far and develop plot for it. Write pupil's suggestions and highlight how to write what is said.	Use word endings to develop understanding of rhyme and spelling.	1: Select story beginning from Hour 2 and develop plot. 2*: Use word endings to form rhyming words and phrases. 3*: Continue shared writing of class story.	Pupils help to create a classroom display about developing a story. Vote on rhyme for class story. Discuss development of class story.
HOUR 4	Shared reading of class story so far. Discuss ideas for a suitable ending and record suggestions.	Refer to Group 2's work from Hour 1 and, together, compose some possible rhymes for use in the class story.	1: Write ending for own story. 2: Use word endings for rhyming words and phrases. 3*: Shared writing of class story ending.	Discuss completion of class story. Pupils from Group 1 tell their stories.
HOUR 5	Shared reading of completed class story, focusing on grammar and punctuation.	Use word endings to develop understanding of rhyme and spelling.	1: Make short rhymes using different word endings. 2*: Write stories from a given structure. 3*: Guided reading, focusing on grammatical features.	A confident pupil from each of Groups 1 and 2 shares what he/she has done in order to encourage others. Selected pupil from Group 3 discusses punctuation.

RESOURCES

The Three Little Pigs class Big Book (made in previous unit), a selection of books with openings on the theme of going somewhere or doing something for the first time, such as *The Three Billy Goats Gruff* (for example, by Jonathan Langley, Picture Lions, ISBN 0-00-664250-0), *Alfie Gives a Hand* (Red Fox, ISBN 0-09-925607-X) and *Moving Molly* (Red Fox, ISBN 0-09-991650-9), both by Shirley Hughes), versions of fairy stories with repeated rhyming phrases (such as *Goldilocks*, *Red Riding Hood*, *The Little Red Hen*, *Chicken Licken*, *The Gingerbread Man*, *The Runaway Pancake*), board or flip chart, materials for making a class Big Book (see main Introduction, page 10 for guidance), Big Book stand, writing materials, card, including sheet of A3, laminator or sticky-backed plastic.

Photocopiable pages 105 (How Did You Feel?) and 106 ('Write a Story' Game).

Enlarged version of the repeated rhyming phrase used in Hour 1 of the previous unit (The Three Little Pigs: Reading).

PREPARATION

Hour 1

Make one copy of the writing frame on photocopiable page 105 (How Did You Feel?) for any child in Group 2 requiring this support. Make a blank Big Book for a class story.

Hour 2

Choose a story opening written by a child in Group 1 (Hour 1) which demonstrates the appropriate use of capital letters, full stops and other punctuation. Ask the child's permission to use it with the whole-class, then enlarge it. Make one copy of photocopiable page 106 ('Write a Story' Game) for each child in Group 1. For Group 2, collect some traditional fairy stories with repeated rhyming phrases (see Resources).

Hour 3

For Group 2, write these word endings (rimes) on separate cards in large print and laminate: *-at*, *-it*, *-un*, *-p*, *-et*, *-en*. Make at least two sets as children in Group 1 will need two cards per individual or pair for Hour 5. For each pair of the more able Group 2 children, make one copy of the class story so far. Photocopy the story beginnings written by Group 1 in Hour 1 for each child in this group to choose from.

Hour 4

Photocopy the extended stories written by Group 1 in Hour 3 for each child in this group to choose from.

Hour 5

Write the 'Story Structure' points below on A3 card using large print (for Group 2 to refer to). Laminate or cover in sticky-backed plastic.

Story Structure
- A first-time event
- Danger, or threat
- Seeking help
- Overcoming danger
- A satisfying end to the story

Introduction

Read the beginning of *The Three Little Pigs* using the class Big Book made in the previous unit. Remind the children of other stories with similar openings (*The Three Billy Goats Gruff*, *Alfie Gives a Hand*, *Moving Molly* – see Resources) and encourage them to describe the main similarities between them (see Introduction to Hour 4 in previous unit), ie they all feature a character doing something new, or going somewhere new for the first time.

Encourage the children to talk about similar situations from personal experience, shaping questions to help them explain their feelings in that situation, for example:
- How does being scared make you feel?
- Do your knees shake or do you feel as if butterflies are in your tummy?
- Can you feel excited at the same time as feeling scared?

Write on the board some key words that convey the feelings being described, for example: scared, anxious, excited, worried, frightened, wobbly, and so on.

Whole-class skills work

Use the collection of words about feelings and link them to the children's experiences using simple sentences, for example:
■ Ben was scared when he went to stay with his cousin.
■ Sunita felt trembly when she had to read to the class.
■ Emily's legs felt wobbly when she went swimming for the first time.
As you compose the sentences, ask individual children to re-read them with your help. This exercise will help the children to start thinking about how to construct simple sentences which express their own experiences and feelings.

Differentiated group activities

1*: Each child writes the beginning of a story based on personal experience or experiences discussed in the Introduction. They should consider carefully how to convey their feelings in the story clearly.

2: Children work individually, selecting words from the collection on the board (see Introduction) to describe in one or two written sentences how they felt when doing something for the first time. Give a copy of photocopiable page 105 (How Did You Feel?) to children who need support and let them choose a writing frame.

3*: The group works with the teacher for ten minutes to plan the opening of a story for a class Big Book, on the theme of 'doing something new'. Let the children draw on their own experiences for ideas. You will also need to make decisions about which characters will be included. By watching how you scribe and transpose what they say into writing, the children will begin to learn what skills and thinking processes are involved in constructing story texts. (Hours 2–4 will continue to build on this work as the story writing progresses.) Then when you move to Group 1, the children should draw a picture and write a sentence about doing something new.

Conclusion

Look at some of the opening sentences written by Groups 1 and 3. Discuss, compare and ask the children what alternative opening sentences might have been used. Ask Group 2 children if some of their own sentences would make good beginnings for stories.

Introduction

Display the enlarged version of the story opening written by a child in Group 1 (see Preparation). Read this with the children, demonstrating how features such as capital letters and full stops and other punctuation help the reader to make sense of the text.

Next, refer back to the class Big Book of *The Three Little Pigs*, showing the children that just after the beginning of the story a threat appears in the form of the big bad wolf. Ask how they might include a similar event in the child's story you have just read. Write their ideas on the board, discussing the appropriateness of their suggestions to the story.

Whole-class skills work

Now ask the children if they could include a repetitive rhyme in the child's story, as in *The Three Little Pigs*. Place the enlarged version of *The Three Little Pigs* rhyme (see Resources) on a stand and ask the children to read it. Encourage them to discuss the sounds of the words and draw their attention to the rhyme at the end of words such as *chin/in*, *huff/puff*. Tell the children that some of them are going to find rhymes from other fairy stories.

Differentiated group activities

1: This activity aims to show children how using a series of questions can be a useful way of developing a story plot. At the end of the session, each child will end up with a 'story beginning' which can be read out in the conclusion and used in Hours 3 and 4.

Give everyone a copy of photocopiable page 106 ('Write a Story' Game) and use this to play a game similar to 'consequences'. Everyone answers the first question on their sheet, then folds it over and passes it on, without the next person looking at the answer. They repeat this for all the other questions. Encourage them to write their responses in sentences using capital letters and full stops.

2: Children make a collection of the repeated rhyming phrases from various fairy stories. Explain that their collection will be used as a guessing game, with other children having to guess which story each rhyme belongs to.

3*: Children continue to work on the class story, with the teacher scribing as in Hour 1.

This time, discuss what form of threat can be built into the story and include a suitable episode to introduce this.

Conclusion

Read out some of the 'story beginnings' from the photocopiable sheets written by Group 1 – some of the results will be quite amusing! Have fun, but emphasize the serious point that when writing a story, using questions like those on the photocopiable sheet is a useful way of developing the plot. Discuss the work Group 3 have done on the class story. Finish by guessing which stories Group 2's collection of rhymes have come from.

HOUR 3

Introduction

Start by reading aloud what has been written so far in the class story. Involve the children as much as possible by encouraging them to predict words, especially the high-frequency, non-picture words such as 'here', 'said', 'went', 'was', etc. Point out how you use the punctuation to help you read the text, especially the speech marks which show those words that are spoken. Ask a couple of children to run through the story so far and invite suggestions about what might happen next in the class story, using questions to prompt them, for example:
■ How might the threat be developed further?
■ Where would help against the threat come from?
■ How could the threat be overcome?
Use the *The Three Little Pigs* as a model by making direct reference to where and how these events occurred in that story, for example the threat of the wolf was developed further by him climbing onto the roof to come down the chimney; the third pig outwitted the wolf by putting a pot of water to boil on the fire, and the threat was finally overcome by the wolf tumbling into the pot of boiling water. Write some appropriate suggestions on the board and encourage the children to notice how you are transforming what they say into writing, for example a child might say 'I think he should run for help', which you then transpose into 'He ran for help'.

Whole-class skills work

Begin by emphasizing that when writing a rhyming phrase, you have to select words especially carefully for their sound and rhyme. Choose one of the word ending cards (see Preparation) and ask the children to suggest rhyming words for this. Record their words on the board, encouraging them to sound out and spell the words as you write.

Differentiated group activities

1: Each child selects one of the photocopied story beginnings completed in Hour 1 and plans how to extend it, writing the middle part. (The children should think about the process you demonstrated for this in the Introduction.)
2*: Using photocopies of the story so far, the more able children work in pairs to compose a repeated rhyme for the class story. Other children work in pairs using a rime card (see Preparation), saying and writing words that share the same word ending, such as rhyming words.
3*: Children continue working on the class story with the teacher scribing. They discuss the suggestions made in the Introduction and plan how to develop the plot further by focusing on the threat aspect and building this up. After ten minutes, the teacher moves to Group 2 and children practise reading story aloud in turns.

Conclusion

Ask Group 1 how they might display their work so that other children can see the process of developing a story. Share Group 2's rhymes and hold a class vote on which one to include in the class story. Finally, show the children how the class story is developing through Group 3's work on it.

HOUR 4

Introduction

Once again, read aloud what has been written so far in the class story. Take every opportunity to involve the children in predicting the grammar and recognizing punctuation and its effect.
Now ask the children to think about how the story is going to end. Help them to generate ideas by referring to the endings of other stories such as *The Three Little Pigs*, *Three Billy Goats Gruff*, *Alfie Gives a Hand* and *Moving Molly*. Ask them to think about:

■ How satisfactory do they find these story endings?
■ What would be a a satisfactory ending to the class story?
■ What would have to happen to bring about this ending?
Collect their suggestions on the board, again emphasizing the writing process.

Whole-class skills work

Remind the children of the repeated story rhymes collected by Group 2 in the previous session, and ask them to recite some examples. Display an enlarged version of the rhyme from 'The Three Little Pigs' and, together, pick out the main rhymes *in* and *chin*. Ask the children if they can hear the *i* sound of *in* in other words, for example in *pig* and *little*. Can they hear other sounds that are repeated, such as the *ch* in *chinny chin chin*?

Now discuss the possibility of including a rhyme in the class story and record the children's ideas for this on the board. Work together on some possible rhymes, pointing out where the rhyme might occur (i.e. not always at the end of a line). Make comparisons with rhymes from the fairy stories; for instance, if a child's suggestion includes short vowel sounds, refer directly to the short vowel sounds in *'little pig, little pig, let me come in'* or *'run, run as fast as you can'*.

Differentiated group activities

1: Children choose a photocopy of one of the extended stories from this group in Hour 3, and work in pairs to construct and write a suitable ending to the chosen piece.
2: Each pair of children use a word ending card (see Hour 3), saying and writing words that rhyme. They then use these words to compose a simple two- or four-line rhyme (as covered in the skills sessions for Hours 3 and 4).
3*: Children discuss how to end the story for the class Big Book, using the ideas from the Introduction. Once an ending has been agreed upon, the teacher scribes it.

Conclusion

Ask two pairs of children from Group 1 to tell their stories, encouraging them to discuss the decisions they had to make in the story-writing process. Next, announce that the class story is completed and if time allows, share the rhyme that has been included.

Introduction

Read aloud the completed story in the class Big Book and enjoy it! Then use this as a basis to discuss and raise questions about story structure, for example is the beginning of the class story as good as that in *The Three Little Pigs*? Why/why not? What other threats or dangers could have been introduced? Finish by talking about the ending to the class story – how satisfying is it? How else might it have ended?

Whole-class skills work

It is important for young children to develop an awareness of rhyme, and this activity will help to reinforce essential skills. Start by referring to Group 2's work in Hour 3, then choose one of the word ending cards (see Preparation) and ask the children to suggest rhyming words for this. Record their suggestions on the board, encouraging them to sound out and spell the words as you write.

Differentiated group activities

1: Children work in pairs or individually. They use two of the word-ending cards to make a four-line rhyme.
2: Children work individually to compose their own story using the 'Story Structure' card (see Preparation) as a reference. This activity can be continued outside the literacy hour as a sustained writing activity.
3*: Children re-read the finished version of the class Big Book, focusing on grammatical features, especially sentences (capital letters, full stops) and features of expression (exclamation marks and words in capitals) and how they affect the way in which a story is read. They continue with their reading when the teacher moves to Group 2.

Conclusion

Choose a child from Group 1 and Group 2 to talk about their work in a way that will encourage others to write. Ask a child from Group 3 to talk about what he/she understands about punctuation and how it assists reading.

HOW DID YOU FEEL?

■ Use some of the sentences below to help you begin your story.

When I went to _____ for the first time,

I felt _____.

When I was doing _____ for the first

time, I felt _____.

I felt _____ when I had to

_____ for the first time.

I was _____ when I went to

_____ for the first time.

The first time I went to _____ I felt

_____.

The first time I had to _____

I felt _____.

'WRITE A STORY' GAME

fold

■ Who or what is the main character?

■ Where is the main character going?

■ Why is the main character going there?

■ Who does the main character meet at this place?

■ What do both characters say?

■ What do both characters do?

■ How do both characters feel?

THE GRASS HOUSE

OBJECTIVES

UNIT	SPELLING/ VOCABULARY	GRAMMAR/ PUNCTUATION	COMPREHENSION/ COMPOSITION
READING AND WRITING POETRY 'The Grass House' by Shirley Hughes.	Identify 's' sounds in text.	Recognize features in text that assist reading with expression.	Become aware of meanings contained in phrases of a poem. Use poem as a model for creating own poems.

ORGANIZATION (1 HOUR)

INTRODUCTION	WHOLE-CLASS SKILLS WORK	DIFFERENTIATED GROUP ACTIVITIES	CONCLUSION
Recite the poem 'The Grass House', then read it from the text. Discuss the meaning of poem and relate to pupils' own experiences.	Identify 's' sounds in the poem.	1: Use 'The Grass House' as a model for writing a poem about their own private place. 2*: Guided reading: listening and looking for s sounds in the poem. 3: Make words ending in -ss and use them in a sentence.	Pupils learn 'The Grass House' by heart.

HOUR 1

RESOURCES

Photocopiable pages 109 ('The Grass House') and 110 (My Private Place), writing materials, board or flip chart, OHP and acetate sheets (optional), laminator or sticky-backed plastic, card, materials to create a grass house in the classroom, including: playhouse, large sheets of strong, thick paper, green and brown hessian (cut into strips), large sheets of green paper, staple gun, green-coloured matting, corrugated cardboard tubes and dried grasses/flowers (optional).

PREPARATION

Make an OHT of the poem on photocopiable page 109 ('The Grass House'), or enlarge it (for whole-class use) and laminate or cover with sticky-backed plastic. Prepare enough copies of the poem for one between two in Groups 1 and 2. Learn the poem by heart ready to recite it to the children in the Introduction. Prepare enough copies of photocopiable page 110 (My Private Place) for those children in Group 1 who need the support of a writing frame. Then, prepare a sliding 'word maker' for the letters -ss (see diagram opposite) for each pair of children in Group 3.

Finally, create a 'grass house' in the classroom by placing a paper roof over a play house and hanging strips of green and brown hessian from it to resemble long grass. Pin green paper to the walls, and provide green matting for the floor. Corrugated cardboard tubes holding dried grasses and flowers add to the effect. The children can use this as a private place for quiet reading, or a place where friends 'come for tea'.

WORD MAKER
Letter strip made from card

gra
pre
me
cre
gla
dre
pa
le
cla
bra

—— ss

Card with slits cut for strip to pass through and match up with -ss letters

Introduction

Begin the session by reciting 'The Grass House' from memory, as a way of encouraging the children to learn the poem by heart. Then display the OHT or enlarged version of the poem and read from the text.

Now begin to look at the meaning of the poem by asking the children what they think is meant by 'the grass house'. Do they have a 'private place' where they like to go to be alone? Ask further questions about the text, for example: what is meant by *'Feathery plumes/Meet over my head'*? You may have to explain this, but encourage the children to offer their ideas. Next, ask them:

■ What does *'Down here/ In the green'* mean?
■ In the poem, who else knows where the grass house is?

Then ask the children if anyone else knows about their private places.

Conclude by re-reading the poem from the text, drawing the childen's attention to the way that the layout assists reading, for example the effect of listing *'Seeds/ Weeds/ Stalks/ Pods'* which causes the reader to dwell on the words, and the gap between *'And tiny little flowers'* and *'Only the cat'* which also causes the reader to pause and dwell again on what is being said.

Whole-class skills work

Select children to find and point to where the words *'grass house'* occur in the poem. Ask them to identify the sound at the end of each of these words. Now tell them to read and say together *'Seeds/ Weeds/ Stalks/ Pods'* and ask what letter sounds they can hear. Draw their attention to the strong s sound and ask the children to point to where this sound occurs in the four words. Point to the words *'grass house'* again, asking the children to read them, and repeat with *'Seeds/ Weeds/ Stalks/ Pods'* to reinforce the effect of the final repetitive s sounds.

Next, look at the -ss ending of the *'grass'* and compare with the single -s ending in *'Seeds/ Weeds/ Stalks/ Pods'* and the -se ending of *'house'*. Tell the children that in the group activities some of them are going to investigate more words with the -ss ending.

Differentiated group activities

1: Children work independently to create their own poem about a private place, using 'The Grass House' as a model. If necessary, give individuals a copy of the writing frame on photocopiable page 110 (My Private Place) to complete.

2*: Guided reading of 'The Grass House'. Ask the children to listen to and look for the s sounds in the poem. Draw their attention to the final s sounds, such as *'gra<u>ss</u>'*, *'hou<u>se</u>'*, *'pla<u>ce</u>'*, *'plum<u>es</u>'*, *'seed<u>s</u>'*.

3: Children work in pairs using a sliding 'word maker' to create words ending in -ss (see Preparation). They take turns to read each new word and then write a sentence together containing this word.

Conclusion

Remind the children how you recited the poem at the beginning of the session. Tell them that they too are going to learn the poem and begin by learning the opening together. Help them to continue learning the rest of the poem at suitable opportunities during the week.

THE GRASS HOUSE

The grass house
Is my private place.
Nobody can see me
In the grass house.
Feathery plumes
Meet over my head.
Down here,
In the green, there are:
Seeds
Weeds
Stalks
Pods
And tiny little flowers.

Only the cat
And some busy, hurrying ants
Know where my grass house is.

Shirley Hughes

MY PRIVATE PLACE

The _____

Is my private place

Nobody can see me

In the _____

_____

_____

_____

_____

Only the _____

And _____

Know where my _____ is.

A BUSY DAY

OBJECTIVES

UNIT	SPELLING/ VOCABULARY	GRAMMAR/ PUNCTUATION	COMPREHENSION/ COMPOSITION
READING AND WRITING POETRY 'A Busy Day' by Michael Rosen.	Recognize by sight and spell some high frequency words. Spell using onset and rime.	Recognize how punctuation affects the way a poem is read, especially question marks. Predict text from grammar (prepositions).	Learn and recite a poem. Extend language patterns in the poem.

ORGANIZATION (3 HOURS)

	INTRODUCTION	WHOLE-CLASS SKILLS WORK	DIFFERENTIATED GROUP ACTIVITIES	CONCLUSION
HOUR 1	Shared reading and discussion of the poem 'A Busy Day'.	Relate punctuation to the way in which the poem is read.	1: Learn to recite part of the poem. 2*: Punctuate the poem. 3: Extend the poem's opening lines by writing about own experience.	Pupil from Group 1 recites the poem. All pupils read and begin to learn the poem by heart.
HOUR 2	Pupils predict prepositions. Continue discussion about the meaning of the poem.	Recognize and spell high frequency words included in the poem.	1: Develop a poem using the patterned language in 'A Busy Day' as a model. 2: Cloze procedure using prepositions. 3*: Guided reading: high frequency words.	Two selected pupils from Group 1 read their poems. Reinforce sight recognition of high frequency words.
HOUR 3	Pupils share a reading of 'A Busy Day', underlining high frequency words. Talk about the school day in relation to the poem.	Provide onsets to the rimes -op, -in and -ot.	1*: Extend opening lines of poem by writing about own experience of the school day. 2: Make words by suggesting onsets to a given rime. 3*: Suggest rhyming words for rime -op.	Selected pupil from Group 1 reads his/her poem. Read out words using onsets and rimes from Group 3.

RESOURCES

Board or flip chart, OHP and acetate sheets (optional), writing and drawing materials, card, laminator or sticky-backed plastic (optional), 'Post-its', tape recorder (optional), laminated card showing consonant letter blends (see page 91, Three Little Pigs: Reading unit, Preparation for Hour 1), photocopiable pages 114 ('A Busy Day'), 115 (Popping Where?) and 116 (Out and About).

PREPARATION

Hour 1

Prepare an OHT or enlarged laminated version of 'A Busy Day' on photocopiable page 114. Provide enough copies of the poem for each pair in Groups 1 and 3, and one copy of photocopiable page 115 (Popping Where?) for each child in Group 3.

Hour 2

Cover all the prepositions in the OHT or enlarged version of 'A Busy Day' with 'Post its', for example: *'pop _____ the road, pop _____ for a walk, pop _____ to the shop'* and so on. Now make a set of flash cards with the *'over'*, *'out'*, *'down'*, *'up'* and *'in'* (all high frequency words from List 1 of the *National Literacy Framework*) written on in large print for whole-class use. Repeat this for the other high frequency words in the poem, 'got', 'to', 'for', 'what' and 'where'. For each child in Group 1, prepare two cards with the phrases 'pop in' and 'pop out' written on. Make one copy of photocopiable page 116 (Out and About) per child in Group 2.

Hour 3

For each child in Group 1, provide a sheet based on the first five lines of 'A Busy Day' as shown:

For each pair of children in Group 2, make a set of cards with the word endings (rimes) -op, -in and -ot written on. You will also need to prepare an A1 laminated card showing consonant letter blends in large print if you have not already done so (see Resources). Next, prepare a card showing the rime -op in large letters for use with Group 3. You will also need to make two or three blank cards for each child in this group to write down some onsets.

pop in _____
pop out _____
pop over _____
pop out _____
pop down _____

Introduction

Display an OHT or enlarged version of the poem 'A Busy Day' and read it to the children at a fairly brisk pace to capture the 'busy' feel. Ask the children what they think the poem is about. What does the frequently repeated phrase 'pop in/ pop out' mean? Relate it to the children's own experience by asking if their parents sometimes say they are 'popping out'. What do they mean by this? Have the children ever 'popped out' to their friends or to the shop, perhaps? Where else might they 'to pop'? Write their ideas on the flip chart. Keep the list for tomorrow's session.

Whole-class skills work

Together, look again at the text of 'A Busy Day'. Do the children notice anything unusual or different about the punctuation? Can they see any full stops or capital letters? Now demonstrate how the lack of punctuation and the layout of the poem encourage the reader to read it quickly. Why would the writer want the poem to be read in this way? Make the link between the poem's pace and meaning. Next, ask what effect the question marks have. Say the line 'got to pop' first as a statement, then as a question. Repeat for 'pop where?' and 'pop what?'. Encourage the children to see that the questioning tone has the effect of drawing them into a conversation with the writer.

Differentiated group activities

1: Children work in pairs reading the poem together, then learning the first verse by heart (down to line 7: 'got to pop').
2*: Display the enlarged version of the poem having masked the question marks. Together, decide where the question marks will go, then add them in and do a guided reading of the poem using appropriate expression.
3: Children work independently, drawing on their own experience (as discussed in the Introduction) to write the first five lines of their own poem using the structure of 'A Busy Day' and extending it, for example: 'Pop in to see my Gran/ Pop out to walk our dog'. They should use the grid on photocopiable page 115 (Popping Where?) to help plan their ideas.

Conclusion

Ask a child from Group 1 to recite the opening of 'A Busy Day', then display the poem again and encourage the class to read it together with expression. Cover parts of the text to encourage the children to use their memory.

Introduction

Display the OHT or enlarged version of 'A Busy Day' with the prepositions covered up (see Preparation). Read the text together, selecting children to predict the covered words. Next, remind them of some of the things they 'pop' in and out for and add more ideas to the flip chart list begun in Hour 1.

Whole-class skills work

Show the children the cards containing the high frequency words 'over', 'out', 'down', and 'in', which are also the missing prepositions from the poem (see Preparation). Select

a word and ask a child to read it. Repeat this with the cards containing the other high frequency words from the poem ('got', 'to', 'for', 'where' and 'what'). Now invite the children to write the words on the board from memory, to help them learn the spellings.

Differentiated group activities

1: Give each child the cards with 'pop in' and 'pop out' written on to help them construct simple sentences about the people and places they 'pop' to see. Ask them to set out their sentences in a list form as in the poem, and to prepare to read their text.

2: Children work individually to fill in the missing words from the phrases on photocopiable page 116 (Out and About). They use these as a model for writing their own phrases about people and places they 'pop' to see.

3*: Do a guided reading of 'A Busy Day', with the children pointing to and reading the high frequency words explored in the skills section. Ask them to identify these words on the flash cards and then match them to the same words in the poem.

Conclusion

Select two children from Group 1 to read their 'list' poems aloud. Encourage other children to comment and make comparisons with the things they do. Finish by reinforcing their sight recognition of high frequency words using the flash cards.

Introduction

Display the poem again and select children to read it aloud. Ask them to find, read and underline high frequency words as you say them. Then move quickly into the content of the poem by reminding the children of the previous session in which they talked about the sort of 'pop in' and 'pop out' things they do. Encourage them to think about this in the context of their school day, for example, 'popping' into a classroom, 'popping' up the stairs, 'popping' down the corridor.

Now choose a child to extend the poem's opening line ('*Pop in*'), perhaps: 'Pop in to Mrs Wilson's classroom'. Write this on the board (or on the OHT or laminated version of the poem). Then take the next line ('*pop out*') and add a phrase such as 'to play'. Continue this with the rest of the poem, drawing on the children's experiences of the school day. Ask the children to sound out and spell the words as you scribe them.

Whole-class skills work

The children's pleasure on hearing the poem lies in the repetition of the phrases and words, especially '*pop*', so savour the sound of this word together. Write the rime *-op* on the board and ask the children to make other words by using different onsets. Choose other rimes from the poem (for example *-in, -ot*) and let the children continue to make new words, drawing on their knowledge of initial consonant letter blends.

Differentiated group activities

1*: The teacher supports this group after working with Group 3. Children work independently, using their sheet based on the opening lines of 'A Busy Day' (see Preparation) to write their own poem about the school day. They should extend each line drawing on their own experiences and the ideas discussed in the Introduction.

2: Children work in pairs with the word-endings *-op, -in* and *-ot*. One child chooses a card, then both take it in turns to suggest onsets to make a word. This activity can be recorded by children writing words as they say them, or by using a tape recorder. Provide a card showing initial consonant letter blends as a reference (see Resources).

3*: Guide the children through 'A Busy Day', pointing to individual words and reading together. Show the rime *-op* (written on a card) and go round, asking each child to suggest a new rhyming word. The children should write their suggested onset on a blank card and then match it to the rime so they can see the spelling and read the word. Refer to the consonants letter blend chart if appropriate.

Conclusion

Ask one Group 1 child from to read his/her poem, encouraging him/her to reflect the 'busy' theme by reading at a suitable pace. Next, show the cards worked on by Group 3. Ask one child to hold up a rime card and another to match it with the Group 3 onset cards. Then ask another child to read the word.

A BUSY DAY

Pop in
pop out
pop over the road
pop out for a walk
pop down to the shop
can't stop
got to pop

got to pop?
pop where?
pop what?

well
I've got to
pop round
pop up
pop into town
pop out and see
pop in for tea
pop down to the shop
can't stop
got to pop

got to pop?
pop where?
pop what?

well
I've got to
pop in
pop out
pop over the road
pop out for a walk
pop in for a talk...

Michael Rosen

114

POPPING WHERE?

- Use this grid to help you plan your writing.
- Fill in your ideas for the phrases in each column.

pop in	pop out	pop over	pop down

OUT AND ABOUT

■ Read the phrases below carefully.
■ Choose a word from the box below to fit each phrase.
■ Write the word in the space provided.

out	in	over	down

pop _____ the road

pop _____ for a walk

pop _____ to the shop

pop _____ to town

pop _____ and see

pop _____ for tea

pop _____ for a talk

BEAR HUNT

OBJECTIVES

UNIT	SPELLING/ VOCABUALRY	GRAMMAR/ PUNCTUATION	COMPREHENSION/ COMPOSITION
READING AND WRITING FICTION *We're Going on a Bear Hunt* by Michael Rosen and Helen Oxenbury.	Investigate spelling, recognizing critical features of some words and sounding out.	Predict words from preceding sentences. Recognize the effects of different types of print.	Read, making links between texts and illustrations. Through shared and guided writing, apply phonological and graphic knowledge and sight vocabulary to spell words. Use grammatical structures as models for writing.

ORGANIZATION (5 HOURS)

	INTRODUCTION	WHOLE-CLASS SKILLS WORK	DIFFERENTIATED GROUP ACTIVITIES	CONCLUSION
HOUR 1	Introduce *We're Going on a Bear Hunt*. Make predictions using front cover. Appreciate the rhythm of the story. Sequence events.	Explore *sh* sound and words that include it.	1: Make story maps. 2*: Shared writing of a story to create a class Big Book. 3: Go on a *sh* hunt.	Selected pupil from Group 1 re-tells the story using the story map. Inform pupils about the class story.
HOUR 2	Predict prepositions in *We're Going on a Bear Hunt* using cloze procedure. Sequence events.	Recognize and use devices for conveying expression and meaning, including: capital letters, size and shape of type, exclamation marks.	1*: Continue shared writing of class story. 2: Sequence story in zigzag books using given words from text. 3: Change upper case to lower and vice versa.	Two pupils from Group 1 share the class story so far. Pupil from Group 3 explains his/her work. Share some of Group 2's zigzag books.
HOUR 3	Build profiles of the characters in *We're Going on a Bear Hunt* through exploring the illustrations.	Recognize and read new words. Recognize devices for enhancing meaning.	1: Work in pairs building character profiles from story. 2: Write words in a way that enhances meaning. 3*: Guided writing of class story, focusing on character and key words.	Share the class story so far. Selected pupils from Group 1 discuss work on characters.
HOUR 4	Continue to glean meaning from the illustrations in *We're Going on a Bear Hunt*. Develop vocabulary and understanding through exploring the word 'scared'.	Explore and recognize high frequency words in story text.	1: Continue work from Hour 3. 2*: Guided reading of high frequency words and shared writing of class story. 3: Cloze procedure for high frequency words.	Two pupils from Group 2 read the class story so far. Rest of class thinks of ideas for story ending ready for next session. Recap on high frequency words.
HOUR 5	Read and sequence events at end of *We're Going on a Bear Hunt*.	Spell by sounding out words associated with a particular sound.	1*: Read and sequence events at the end of the story. 2: Invent and spell words associated with a particular sound. 3*: Guided reading; shared writing of class story ending.	Selected pupils read the class story.

RESOURCES

We're Going on a Bear Hunt by Michael Rosen and Helen Oxenbury (Walker) – Big Book ISBN 0-7445-4781-4 and enough small copies for group work and guided reading ISBN 0-7445-2323-0 – materials for making a class Big Book and zigzag books (see main Introduction, pages 10 and 12 for guidance), Big Book stand, board or flip chart, writing and drawing materials, card, 'Post its', sheets of A3 and A4 paper, children's reading books (Group 2), a collection of twigs, dried grasses and wet clay.

PREPARATION

Hour 1

Make a blank Big Book for writing the class story in.

Hour 2

Before the session, mask the prepositions in the text so that in the shared reading children have to predict the words. For each child in Group 2 make a zigzag book of eight sides which will form a 'mini' version of the story *We're Going on a Bear Hunt* (see main Introduction, page 12 for guidance). Make two sets of cards with the following phrases/sentences written on:

> Swishy Swashy!
> Splash splosh!
> Squelch squerch!
> Stumble trip!
> Hoooo woooo!
> Tiptoe! Tiptoe!
> IT'S A BEAR!!!!
> We're not going on a bear hunt again.

For each child in Group 3, provide a set of cards with a selection of about five short extracts from the book, some entirely in lower case and some entirely in upper case, for example: we're going on a bear hunt; WHAT'S THAT?, IT'S A BEAR!

Hour 3

For each child in Group 2, provide a sheet with these phrases from the story: long wavy grass; deep cold river; thick oozy mud; big dark forest; swirling whirling snowstorm; narrow gloomy cave.

Hour 4

For Group 2, prepare a set of flash cards with high frequency words from the story, for example: *going, big, on, one, to, day, not, go, got, it*. For each child in Group 3, copy a passage from the story and omit various words, for example:

> We're _____ on a bear hunt.
> We're going to _____ a _____ one.
> _____ a beautiful day!
> We're _____ scared.

> Uh-uh! A river!
> A deep cold _____.
> We can't go _____ it.
> We can't go _____ it.
> Oh no!
> We've _____ to go _____ it.

Hour 5

Prepare a set of 'journey' cards (for whole-class use) based on the story as follows:

> Back through the grass.
> Back through the river.
> Back through the mud.

Back through the forest.
Back through the snowstorm.
Back through the cave.

For the skills session, provide a small bowl of water and towel (for demonstrating onomatopoeia). Write a jumbled list of the six stages of the family's return journey home (see above) and provide a copy for each child in Group 1. For the same group, prepare a sheet of A4 paper with three large blank boxes on each side for each child. Provide a collection of twigs, dried grasses and wet clay for Group 2. For each pair of children in this group, prepare a sheet of paper with associated 'sound' words from the story, i.e. *swishy swashy*, *squelch squerch* and *stumble trip* written in the middle.

Introduction

Introduce the children to the Big Book *We're Going on a Bear Hunt*. Ask them what they think the characters are doing on the front cover. They might suggest that the characters are going somewhere – show them the word *Going* in the title, and then focus on the whole title. Establish that the book is about some characters going on a bear hunt, then invite suggestions for other things they might be hunting (things, people, strange or unusual creatures, places and so on) and write these on the board.

Now read the story aloud, capitalizing on the rhythm and encouraging the children to join in, especially with the noises – *swishy swashy*, *squelch squerch*, etc. Afterwards, discuss the beginning of the story. What obstacles did the family encounter? Map the whole story in this way, letting children draw on the board a list of symbols to represent the various obstacles the family had to overcome. Keep this list for the group activities.

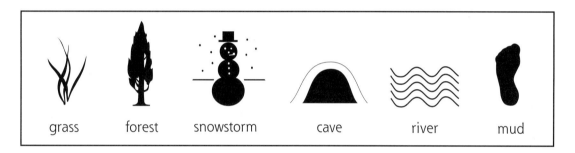

| grass | forest | snowstorm | cave | river | mud |

Whole-class skills work

Show the children the consonant blend *sh* in large print and make the sound. Can they remember some of the words in the story where they heard this sound? (For example: *splashy*, *sploshy*, *swishy*, *swashy*.) Select children to find these words in the book and ask them to point to the letters that make the *sh* sound. Alert them to the difference between the sound *sh* in *splishy sploshy* and the *ch* sound in *squelch squerch*. Together, look for other words in the book that contain a *sh* sound (look towards the end of the book: *shiny* and *shut*).

Differentiated group activities

1: Children work in pairs. Referring to a small copy of *We're Going on a Bear Hunt*, they devise a map of the story sequence on A3 paper. They use symbols and words from the story to denote the order of the events, referring to the list from the Introduction.
2*: In this and the following hours, the teacher guides the groups through the story composition process to create a class Big Book modelled on *We're Going on a Bear Hunt*. Decide on what kind of hunt the characters in the class story will go on, referring back to the suggestions made in the Introduction. Write the title and scribe the story beginning. Encourage the children to use syntactic frames from the story to hang their ideas on.
3: Children work in pairs to find words with the *sh* sound in their reading books and then list them. They sort their list into columns according to where the *sh* sound occurs in the words, ie the beginning, middle or end.

Conclusion

Ask a child from Group 1 to re-tell *We're going on a Bear Hunt* from their story map. Let one pair from Group 3 talk about *sh* words. Inform the children about the class story in progress.

Introduction

Display the Big Book of *We're Going on a Bear Hunt*, with all the prepositions masked out. Read the story together, encouraging the children to predict which word comes next. Afterwards, ask the children if they can remember the sequence of events. Write the following jumbled list on the board and ask them to help you re-write it in the correct order.

> Squelch squerch!
> Hoooo woooo!
> Tiptoe! Tiptoe!
> Swishy Swashy!
> IT'S A BEAR!!!!
> Splash splosh!
> We're not going on a bear hunt again.
> Stumble trip!

Whole-class skills work

Display the Big Book page which says: *Swishy Swashy! Swishy Swashy! Swishy Swashy!* Do the children notice anything about the size of these words? Why should the type get bigger? What does this mean? (The reader should say these words more loudly.) Ask if there is anything else on the page that might help the reader to know *how* to say something (the exclamation mark). Now go through the other pages in the book, looking for more exclamation marks and special uses of type that affect the way the text is expressed, such as the layout and use of bold type (**WHAT'S THAT? IT'S A BEAR!!!!**). Stress the difference between lower and upper case by asking the children what effect putting **WHAT'S THAT?** and **IT'S A BEAR!** in upper case and bold print have on the way we read it (we read it much more loudly.)

Differentiated group activities

1*: Continue to write the class story, scribing details of the first couple of obstacles the characters encounter. Again, let the children draw on the syntactic frames from the story.
2: Give each child a zigzag book and provide the cards with sentences from *We're Going on a Bear Hunt* (see Preparation). Ask the children to copy the sentences on the cards into their zigzag books in the same sequence as they occur in the story, using their memory of the events to guide them.
3: Give each child a selection of short extracts from the book in upper and lower case (see Preparation). They should re-write the lower case extracts in upper case and vice versa, referring to the story book.

Conclusion

Ask two children from Group 1 to share the class story so far. A child from Group 3 should explain their work, with the teacher emphasizing how using capitals for whole words or phrases affects expression. A child from Group 2 should read aloud his/her zigzag book.

Introduction

Explain that you are going to read *We're going on a Bear Hunt* again, but this time you want the children to think about the feelings of the family in the story, including the dog, by studying the illustrations. Show them the Big Book and point out that at the beginning, the family look happy. What other words might describe their feelings – for example, pleased, excited, glad, cheerful? Write the children's suggestions on 'Post its' and place them next to the characters in the book. Continue to use 'Post its' as you explore the book further (up to page 14), using the suggestions below.
■ Look at the backs of the family as they prepare to cross the river (pages 5 and 6). How might they be feeling? What are they thinking?
■ Look at the dog's face as he crosses the river and the way that the baby holds out its hand (page 8). What are the dog and baby thinking? Does the expression on the dog's face match the part of the text that says *'We're not scared'*?
■ What does dad think about the mud (pages 9 and 10)? Look how he carries the shoes. What is he thinking (page 12)?
■ As they approach the forest, it is obvious that the family are experiencing different feelings about it. Compare dad's face and the boy's body. What do these tell us about

how the characters are feeling? Finish by saying you are going to continue exploring the family's feelings in the next session when the characters enter the forest.

Whole-class skills work
Remind the children of yesterday's session about how print size and exclamation marks can help to convey meaning. Say that today you're going to look at some other ways of expressing meaning through print. Focus on important words in the story, for example 'scary', and ask the children what you could do to the letters to make them look scary, for example:

SCARY

Then write 'long wavy grass' on the board and choose a child to read it. Ask how the look of the letters in each of these words could be changed to bring out the meaning more, as they did with the word 'scary'. Repeat this for other suitable words or phrases in the story.

Differentiated group activities
1: Children work in pairs studying the pictures in their copy of *We're Going on a Bear Hunt* and discussing, then writing about the characters' thoughts and feelings. They should only go as far as page 14 in the book.
2: Give each child some phrases from the story (see Preparation) and ask them to rewrite the words, making the letters reflect their meanings.
3*: Continue scribing the class story, focusing on the way that illustrations can help to reveal the characters' feelings through showing their expressions and actions. Pick some key words and experiment with their typography, as in the skills session.

Conclusion
Share the class story so far, then ask Group 1 to talk about their work on characters.

Introduction
Note that this session continues from the work in the Introduction to Hour 3. Display the *We're Going on a Bear Hunt* Big Book again and continue to read the story from page 14, interpreting it through the illustrations and text. Discuss the way that phrases such as 'we're not scared' are contradicted by the illustrations. Encourage the children to draw on words such as *scared*, *frightened*, and *afraid* to explain the family's feelings and thoughts as their fear mounts.

Extend the children's vocabulary by writing *scared* in the middle of the board. Create a web diagram by adding other words or sentences the children suggest to describe the family's growing fears. If they find it difficult to think of alternative words, encourage them to think about their own experiences of being afraid to help stimulate some ideas.

Whole-class skills work
Emphasize how reading the story and writing about the characters' feelings is helping the children to learn lots of new words. Check if they recognize *over*, *under*, and *through*. Repeat for other high frequency words in the story: *going*, *big*, *on*, *one*, *to*, *day*, *not*, *go*, *got*, *it*. Identify shape and sound links in words such as:

go going   shape and sound: *go*
not got   shape and sound: *ot*

Differentiated group activities
1: As for Hour 3, but this time focusing on the second half of the book (from page 14) to explore the characters' feelings and thoughts.
2*: For the guided reading part of this session, provide cards with words from the skills session (*got*, *go*, *going*, etc) and encourage the children to identify these words as you read through the class story so far. Continue the shared writing of the story but don't yet write the ending.
3: Children work independently, supplying the missing words in extracts of text from the story (see Preparation) thereby reinforcing work initiated in skills session.

HOUR 5

Conclusion
Let two children from Group 2 read the class story so far. Next, ask everyone to start thinking about a suitable story ending ready for tomorrow's session. Finally, recap on some high frequency words from the story.

Introduction
In this session, focus on the ending of the story, especially the way in which the family has to quickly retrace their journey in order to get home. Show the children the set of 'journey' cards (see Preparation) and tell them that they are going to travel back through all the different places the family visited in the story, in the same sequence. Then invite individuals to read and select the appropriate cards and place them in order until the sequence is complete.

Whole-class skills work
Remind the children of their previous work on making words resemble their meaning by changing the appearance of the letters, for example:

SCARY

Now explain that some words *sound* like their meaning, and demonstrate this by asking a child to move their hand in a bowl of water. Can the children hear the 'splash splosh' sound? Engage the children in sounding out these two words as you write them on the board. Emphasize the *sp-l, -ash* and *-osh* sounds.

Listen to the sound of the water being moved around again, then encourage the children to think of other words that imitate the sound. Write the words on the board, sounding them out to assist spelling. Accept invented words, as the main objective is for children to connect the sound and meaning of the words.

Differentiated group activities
1*: The teacher supports this group after working with Group 3. Provide each children with the jumbled list of the six return journey stages in the story and the A4 sheets with six boxes drawn on (see Preparation). The children should write the correct journey stage in each box and illustrate appropriately.

2: Children should work in pairs using one of the resources from the collection to make sounds (see Preparation). They should record their new words on their sheets of paper with associated words from the story.

3*: The teacher works with this group first. Together, read the ending of *We're Going on a Bear Hunt* and use this as a model to write the ending of the class story. Encourage the children to suggest words that enhance the sound of actions in the story and add these in for extra effect!

Conclusion
Ask two children to read the class story. Encourage the children to reflect upon what they have learned during the last week by asking:
■ Do the illustrations add meaning to the story?
■ Do they tell us more about the characters?
■ What new words have been used?
■ Has writing words in a special way helped the reader to read with expression?

LITTLE BEAR

OBJECTIVES

UNIT	SPELLING/ VOCABULARY	GRAMMAR/ PUNCTUATION	COMPREHENSION/ COMPOSITION
READING AND WRITING FICTION Can't You Sleep, Little Bear? and Let's Go Home, Little Bear by Martin Waddell and Barbara Firth.	Discriminate, read and spell words with initial consonant clusters. Build words with different consonant clusters.	Use capital letters for proper nouns, and at the beginning of sentences.	Identify and discuss characters and speculate on behaviour in using text and illustrations.

ORGANIZATION (5 HOURS)

	INTRODUCTION	WHOLE-CLASS SKILLS WORK	DIFFERENTIATED GROUP ACTIVITIES	CONCLUSION
HOUR 1	Introduce and read Can't You Sleep, Little Bear? Make connections between text and illustrations.	Explore use of capital letters in names.	1: Make zigzag books. 2: Do cloze activity and draw Little Bear. 3*: Guided reading: capital letters.	Selected Group 1 pupil reads zigzag book. Reinforcement of use of capital letters referring to Group 3's work.
HOUR 2	Shared re-reading of Can't You Sleep, Little Bear? Discuss how Big Bear felt.	Focus on use of capital letters in sentences and names.	1*: Pairs stick 'Post its' on text describing the bears' feelings. 2: Place capital letters correctly in text extract. 3: Pairs search for capital letters around the school.	Pair of Group 1 pupils share opinions about bears' feelings. Reinforcement of teaching points on capital letters referring to work by Groups 2 and 3.
HOUR 3	Shared re-reading of Can't You Sleep, Little Bear?, adding thought bubbles.	Use repetitive grammatical structures to encourage prediction. Learn to recognize some new words.	1: Pairs write and stick text to thought bubbles. 2*: Cloze activity. 3: Children play Lotto game.	Use work of Group 2 pupil to reinforce recognition of new words. Display Lotto game.
HOUR 4	Introduce Let's Go Home, Little Bear. Compare with Can't You Sleep, Little Bear?	Build words using initial consonant clusters.	1*: Describe Big Bear's character. 2: Build words using initial consonant clusters. 3: Match sentences to appropriate pages in book.	Use Group 2's work to reinforce word-building. Ask Group 1 how their task helped them to read the story.
HOUR 5	Relate Let's Go Home, Little Bear to children's own experiences of feeling scared.	Think of alternative explanations for 'Plodders', 'Drippers' and 'Ploppers'.	1: Continue work begun in skills section. 2*: Children write about things that scare them. 3: Cloze activity.	Selected Group 1 pupils present their alternative explanations. Two Group 3 pupils share their work.

RESOURCES

Can't You Sleep, Little Bear? by Martin Waddell and Barbara Firth (Big Book: Walker, ISBN 0-7445-3691-X), smaller copies of the book for group work (Walker, ISBN 0-7445-1316-2), Let's Go Home, Little Bear by Martin Waddell and Barbara Firth (Big Book – see main Introduction, page 10 for guidance on making your own), smaller copies of the book for group (Walker, ISBN 0-7445-3169-1), board or flip chart, writing and drawing materials, 'Post-its', Big Book stand, clipboards (one for each pair in Group 3), laminator or sticky-backed plastic (optional), card (including large sheet of A3 or A1), glue, Blu-Tack, paper for making zigzag books (see main Introduction, page 12, for guidance).

Photocopiable pages 128 (Go to Sleep!), 129 (Lotto Game), 130 (Make a Word) and 96 (Character Portrait from 'The Three Little Pigs: Reading' unit).

PREPARATION
Hour 1
Make an 8-page zigzag book and prepare a copy of photocopiable page 128 (Go to Sleep!) for each child in Group 1. For each child in Group 2, prepare a sheet of sentences with missing words as follows:

Little Bear		to go to sleep.	
Little Bear	and	to go to sleep.	
Little Bear	and	and	to go to sleep.

Hour 2
Prepare a copy of the text from the first page of the story for each child in Group 2, substituting lower case letters for all the upper case ones.

Hour 3
Make 10–15 blank thought bubbles from paper. Prepare an enlarged version of the following repeating sections from the story, masking out the underlined words:

Extract 1
"I'm <u>scared</u>," said Little Bear.
"Why are you <u>scared</u>, Little Bear?" asked Big Bear.
"I don't like the <u>dark</u>," said Little Bear.
"What <u>dark</u>?" said Big Bear.
"The <u>dark</u> all around us," said Little Bear.

Extract 2
"Now go to <u>sleep</u>, Little Bear," said Big Bear, and he padded <u>back</u> to the Bear Chair and settled <u>down</u> to <u>read</u> the Bear Book, by the <u>light</u> of the <u>fire</u>.

For each child in Group 2, prepare two story extracts with words missing, particularly less familiar words. If appropriate, place the missing words at the bottom of the extract in the wrong order. For example, page 6, from *Big Bear looked...lantern that was there*. (Omit: looked, that, part, cave, dark, took, tiniest). Or page 8, from *Big Bear looked...put it beside the other one*. (Omit: saw, quite, still, went, out, bigger, beside.) Stick photocopiable page 129 (Lotto Game) onto card, then cut up the differently-arranged word tables to provide one for each child or pair in Group 3 (all tables contain the same words, but in a different order). Write a full set of the 20 different words used on the cards and place them in a cloth bag.

Hour 4
If possible, make a Big Book version of *Let's Go Home, Little Bear*. Prepare a large (A1 or A3) card chart of initial double letter blends (for whole-class use) as follows:

bl	br	cl	cr	dr	fl
fr	gl	gr	pl	sc	sk
sl	sm	sn	sp	st	tr

Write short pieces of the text from *Let's Go Home, Little Bear* on 'Post-its', for example:

They went for a walk in the woods.
"I think it's a Plodder!"
"Drip, drip, drip," said Little Bear.
"That was the ice as it dripped in the stream."
"I think it's a Plopper."
"That was the snow plopping down from a branch."
"Come on and be carried," said Big Bear.
WOO WOO WOO
CREAR CREAR CREAR
"Now tell me a story," Little Bear said.

Make enough 'Post-its' with the above text for each pair in Group 3. Make one copy of photocopiable page 130 (Make a Word) for each child in Group 2, and one copy of photocopiable page 96 (Character Portrait) from 'The Three Little Pigs: Reading' unit for each child in Group 1.

Hour 5

For each child in Group 2, prepare a list of beginnings of simple sentences, on the theme of being scared, for them to complete, for example:

I feel scared when _____.
It is scary when _____.
The thing that scares me most is_____.
I am scared by _____.
The _____ scares me.

Choose some short extracts from the story text which include repeating frames and mask out some of the words, particularly new ones. Make a copy for each child in Group 3.

Introduction

The purpose of this introduction is for the children to enjoy the story *Can't You Sleep, Little Bear?* and to recognize the relationship between the illustrations and text. Introduce the Big Book version to the class, mentioning the author's and illustrator's names, then read the story aloud.

Now talk about the children's experiences of feeling afraid of the dark. Turn to page 10 where Little Bear is doing handstands on the bed and read what it says: *Little Bear tried and tried to go to sleep.* Then examine the picture. Do the children really think that Little Bear tried to go to sleep? Do they sometimes play about when they can't get to sleep? What do they do? Turn to the double-page spread showing Little Bear doing further acrobatics and read the text. Ask: Is Little Bear really afraid of the dark?

Whole-class skills work

Draw the children's attention to the capital letters used at the beginning of the names 'Big Bear' and 'Little Bear'. Write out a child's name using only lower case letters and ask if it's written correctly. Next, invite a child to come out and write his or her name using capitals correctly. What effect do the capital letters have? (They make the name stand out more.) Explain that capital letters are used in everyone's names to show each person's importance. Now look at the use of capitals for names of things as well as people, referring to the story. For example, point out the capital letters in 'Bear Cave' on the first page and find some other examples, such as Bear Chair and Bear Book on page 2.

Differentiated group activities

Note that all groups will need access to small versions of *Can't You Sleep, Little Bear?*
1: Provide each child with a zigzag book and a copy of photocopiable page 128 (Go to Sleep!). Children should place the sentences in the correct order in their zigzag book (without referring to the book) and illustrate Little Bear's attempts to sleep.
2: The children complete the missing words in the sentences (see Preparation) and use them as captions for three drawings of Little Bear trying to go to sleep.
3*: During this guided reading session, draw the children's attention to where capital letters occur in the story, focusing on names of people and places. Ask each child to make a list of these names.

Conclusion

Choose one child from Group 1 to read the story from their zigzag book. Using the collection of names compiled by a child in Group 3, reinforce why capital letters are used (to denote a person or a special place or thing).

Introduction

Re-read *Can't You Sleep, Little Bear?*. Explain that you're now going to look at how Big Bear was feeling. Ask the children:
■ Would you like Big Bear to look after you?
■ Would you like Big Bear to put you to bed?

■ How do you think Big Bear felt when Little Bear wouldn't go to sleep? Encourage them to relate their comments to the text and illustrations, asking them to point to pictures that support what they say. Let them use the illustrations to suggest words to describe Big Bear at different points in the story (eg kind, fed up, puzzled). Write these words on 'Post-its' and stick them next to the appropriate text and pictures.

Whole-class skills work

Remind the children about the use of capital letters at the beginning of people's names. Turn to the beginning of the story book and together, point to where the capital letters occur. Explain that not all the words with capital letters are names of people. Can they see where else capitals have been used? Encourage them to notice how capitals are used at the beginning of a sentence as well as in names of people and places.

Differentiated group activities

1*: Sharing a copy of the book, children work in pairs sticking 'Post its' on the pictures which include words describing Little Bear and Big Bear's feelings.
2: In pairs children add capital letters correctly to the story extract (see Preparation).
3: Each pair shares a clipboard and paper to do a survey around the school listing any names, labels, etc they see which include capital letters.

Conclusion

Ask a pair of children from Group 1 to share their opinions about how the the bears were feeling at different points in the story. Reinforce the teaching points about the use of capital letters by asking children from Group 3 to report their findings.

Introduction

Having explored in previous sessions how Big Bear and Little Bear were feeling, the children are now going to focus on what these characters were thinking. Read the story again, but choose appropriate places to stop and ask for children's comments on what the bears might be thinking. Together, decide on the bears' thoughts and write them in a thought bubble, then attach it to the text using Blu-Tack. For example:

I'm still scared. (Little Bear)
Oh no, what does he want this time? (Big Bear)

Whole-class skills work

Show the children the enlarged version of extract 1 from the story (see Preparation). Read and point to the text, encouraging the children to predict the missing words *scared* and *dark*. Let them attempt to spell these words before you reveal them. Now repeat the exercise using extract 2, this time letting the children try spelling the words *sleep*, *back*, *down*, *read*, *light* and *fire*.

Differentiated group activities

1: Each pair of children reads the text and pictures in their copy of the book and sticks 'Post its' describing the bears' thoughts on the appropriate pages.
2*: Each child fills in the missing words in the two story extracts (see Preparation).
3: Children play the Lotto game as individuals or in pairs (see Preparation). One child picks a word from the cloth bag and reads it aloud. The children mark it on their card by colouring over it. The first one to complete a line (horizontal, vertical or diagonal) wins.

Conclusion

Reinforce word recognition of new words by going through one child's extract from Group 2. Display the Lotto game on a table for use at other times during the week.

Introduction

Display your homemade *Let's Go Home, Little Bear* Big Book (or smaller version) and ask the children if it reminds them of another book they have read. Can they think who the author and illustrator might be? Ask them to look at the front cover: can they tell what the book is about? Do they think Little Bear and Big Bear will behave in the same way as in the other story? What do they think Little Bear might be scared of in this book?

   Now read the story, and afterwards, compare both *Little Bear* stories, prompting the children with questions. For example, what scared Little Bear in *Can't You Sleep, Little*

Bear? Was it the same thing as in *Let's Go Home, Little Bear?* How did Big Bear help to calm Little Bear's fears in *Let's Go Home, Little Bear?* Refer directly to the text, ie when Little Bear thought Plodders were following him, Big Bear explained that the *plod* was his feet in the snow. Compare this with *Can't You Sleep, Little Bear?*, where Big Bear fetches a lantern to stop Little Bear being afraid of the dark. What does this show about Big Bear's personality?

Whole-class skills work
Encourage the children to enjoy the sound of the words *plopper*, *plodder* and *dripper* in the story. Ask them what they think a *plopper* might look like, encouraging them to make a link between the sound of the word and the picture it elicits. For example, what sort of eyes would a plopper have – would they be big and round or would they droop? What about ears – would these stick out or flop down? Write the root word of *plopper* on the board, ie *'plop'*. Together, sound out the word, encouraging the children to hear the initial letter blend, *pl*. Now write *-od* and ask a child to choose an initial letter blend from the large chart (see Preparation) to make a word. Let the children choose onsets and continue to make other words – both real and nonsense – in this way.

Differentiated group activities
1*: Children work independently, sharing a copy of *Let's Go Home, Little Bear*, and completing the Character Portrait sheet. They should find words to describe Big Bear and support these with references to the text.
2: Each child works on photocopiable page 130 (Make a Word).
3: Children work in pairs with a copy of *Let's Go Home, Little Bear* and the 'Post-its' containing sentences from the story (see Preparation). They stick each 'Post-it' on the appropriate page in the book.

Conclusion
Explore word building with Group 2 and plan to develop this work in the form of an ongoing word building 'game' or running task over a period of a week. Ask if Group 3 enjoyed their task and whether it helped them to read the book.

Introduction
Remind the children of what they discovered in previous sessions, drawing particular attention to Little Bear being scared in both stories and Big Bear being kind and thoughtful. Re-read *Let's Go Home, Little Bear* to the children, then ask how *they* felt when they were listening to the story. Were they scared? Discuss any similar experiences of being afraid that they may have had (eg have they ever been out late and wanted to get home; been in a strange place like a wood or a park when no-one else was around?).

Whole-class skills work
Remind the children how Big Bear was able to explain away Little Bear's fears by referring directly to the text (*plod* was the sound of his feet in the snow). Ask if they can think of a different explanation – what else might a *plodder* be? Could it be something like a *plopper* discussed in the previous hour, or perhaps bears or other animals plodding through the snow? Write their suggestions on the board or, if using your own Big Book, write these on paper and Blu-Tack them onto the appropriate page. Do the same for *drippers*. Encourage the children to read the words written on the board with you so that they can practise predicting and sounding out unfamiliar words.

Differentiated group activities
1: Pairs of children refer to Big Bear's explanations and offer alternative explanations for *ploppers*, *plodders* and *drippers* through drawing and writing.
2: Children work independently, completing simple sentences about things that scare them (see Preparation).
3*: Give each child various extracts of repeating frames from the text with words missing, particularly new words specific to the story.

Conclusion
Children from Group 1 offer their alternative explanations of *ploppers*, *plodders* and *drippers*. Select two children from Group 3 to share their sentences about what makes them feel scared.

GO TO SLEEP!

"I don't like the dark," said Little Bear.

Big Bear lit the tiniest lantern.

Little Bear tried to go to sleep.

Big Bear lit a bigger lantern.

Little Bear tried to go to sleep.

Big Bear lit the Biggest
Lantern of Them All.

Little Bear was still scared.

"I've brought you the moon,
Little Bear," said Big Bear.

LOTTO GAME

sleep	fire	chair	bear
look	dark	read	tried
over	safe	moon	book
back	stars	warm	light
lantern	down	cave	little

fire	chair	look	over
sleep	read	back	warm
bear	dark	stars	down
tried	moon	lantern	cave
safe	book	light	little

little	lantern	dark	sleep
light	moon	bear	over
book	tried	warm	look
safe	down	back	chair
cave	stars	read	fire

MAKE A WORD

■ The words below are not complete.
Choose from the double letters in the box below to start each word.
Then add one letter of your own choice to finish each word.

___ ___ o ___   ___ ___ o ___   ___ ___ o ___

___ ___ o ___   ___ ___ o ___   ___ ___ o ___

___ ___ i ___   ___ ___ i ___   ___ ___ i ___

___ ___ i ___   ___ ___ i ___   ___ ___ i ___

bl	br	cl	cr	dr	fl
fr	gl	gr	pl	sc	sk
sl	sm	sn	sp	st	tr

■ Now try to make some more words using the letters above.
Write them in the space below.

_____   _____   _____

_____   _____   _____

_____   _____   _____

SAY CHEESE!

OBJECTIVES

UNIT	SPELLING/ VOCABULARY	GRAMMAR/ PUNCTUATION	COMPREHENSION/ COMPOSITION
READING AND WRITING NON-FICTION Lists and recipes.	Explore and generate words with initial consonant cluster ch and identify it in words. Develop understanding of phonemic structures and critical features of words for spelling.	Use awareness of grammatical sense to decipher new or unfamiliar words.	Develop awareness of the different layout of non-fiction text as in lists and recipes.

ORGANIZATION (3 HOURS)

	INTRODUCTION	WHOLE-CLASS SKILLS WORK	DIFFERENTIATED GROUP ACTIVITIES	CONCLUSION
HOUR 1	Play Kim's Game.	Write a list. Identify separate phonemes and critical features of words.	1: Compose shopping lists. 2*: Create shopping list using given vocabulary. 3: Match text to pictures.	Selected pupil from Group 1 reads out their shopping list. Teacher comments on phonic/graphic features of words in list, as in skills session.
HOUR 2	Shared reading of the recipe on photocopiable page 134 (How to Make Cheese Sandwiches).	Identify phoneme cluster ch.	1: Follow a recipe to make sandwiches; find ch words. 2*: Generate 'food' words beginning with ch. 3*: Search texts to find ch phoneme.	Eat sandwiches and discuss whether the recipe instructions could be improved.
HOUR 3	Shared reading of lists of food beginning with ch. Correct spellings.	Spell words through identifying the phoneme ch within words.	1*: Make 'ch' menus. 2*: Find 'ch' words in reading books. Make list. 3: Match word labels to utensils/ recipe ingredients.	Group 2 pupil reads aloud list of 'ch' words. Group 1 pupils share their menus.

RESOURCES

Board or flip chart, writing and drawing materials, OHP and acetate sheets (optional), card, photocopiable page 134 (How to Make Cheese Sandwiches), reading books (Groups 1 and 2).
    Tray containing a sliced wholemeal loaf, a piece of cheddar cheese, some cherry tomatoes, a jar of chutney and a bunch of chives; a cloth for covering the items; utensils for making sandwiches (see photocopiable page 134 as above).

PREPARATION

Hour 1

Before the session, place all the ingredients for making cheese sandwiches (see Resources) on a tray and cover with a cloth to play a memory game (Kim's Game). For each child in Group 3, write the following list of words: sliced wholemeal loaf, cheddar cheese, cherry tomatoes, chutney, chives. Include some missing letters in these words for children to fill in if appropriate.

Hour 2

Prepare an OHT or enlarged version of the cheese sandwich recipe on photocopiable page 134. Collect together the ingredients and utensils required for three pairs of children in Group 1 to make enough sandwiches for the whole class, then prepare one set of corresponding word labels for each ingredient and utensil. [NB: Ensure that you are aware of any children with food allergies or special diets, and provide alternative foods for them to eat in the conclusion to Hour 2.] Make three copies of the photocopiable recipe for use by Group 1. The other children in Group 1 will need reading books to work on (see activity) until they swap over to making sandwiches.

Hour 3
Choose one of the lists of *ch* foods compiled by a child from Group 2 in Hour 2. Prepare an OHT or enlarged version of this list for whole-class use. Make a simple blank menu for each pair of children in Group 1 by folding a sheet of A4 paper cut to fit inside a piece of folded A4 card. Have ready for Group 3 the word labels made in Hour 2. Gather the ingredients and utensils for the cheese sandwich recipe for use by Group 3.

Introduction
Begin by showing the children all the items on the tray. Can they name all of these things? What could be made using these items? Establish that these are the ingredients for making cheese sandwiches.

Now tell the children they are going to play a memory game. Explain that you will hide one of the items on the tray under the cloth and they must guess which one has been taken away. Give them some time to try to memorize the items, then cover the tray with a cloth. Discreetly remove one of the items, hiding it under the cloth, then uncover the tray and ask the children what is missing. Repeat this several times. Now ask the children what might help them to remember all the things on the tray, and introduce the idea of a list.

Whole-class skills work
Now ask the children to help you write a list on the board of all the items used in the memory game. Read the words together as you write them, pointing out particular features of sound/ symbol relationships that will help the children remember the look of the word, for example:
- the *l* sounds and tall shape of the *l* that sticks up in 'sliced wholemeal loaf'.
- the long shape of the word 'margarine', with the descender in the middle.
- the *ch* and double *dd* and *ee* phonemes in 'cheddar cheese'.
- although 'cherry' and 'chutney' look a little similar, point out the double *rr* in 'cherry'. Also point out that the word 'tomatoes' follows 'cherry' to give 'cherry tomatoes', whereas no word follows 'chutney'.

Finally, discuss with the children some other occasions when lists can be useful, for example, when packing for a holiday, when planning things that need doing, when going shopping and so on.

Differentiated group activities
1: In pairs, children make a shopping list of items they need to make a favourite meal or snack.
2*: Working with the teacher, children read the shopping list created at the beginning of the session and in the same way (ie drawing form phonic and graphic knowledge) create another shopping list from their experiences of shopping for food.
3: Give each child a selection of the words and phrases written on card. They should make a word and picture list by reading the cards, writing down the text and drawing an appropriate picture for each item.

Conclusion
Choose a child from Group 1 to read his/her shopping list. Take the list and make teaching points related to the phonic and graphic features of the words included, as in the skills session.

Introduction
Display an OHT or enlarged version of the cheese sandwich recipe (photocopiable page 134) and ask the children what they think it is. Establish that it is a recipe, then read it together, encouraging the children to interpret the picture and word instructions. Next, display the ingredients, utensils and corresponding word labels (see Preparation) and select children to read and place a label next to the appropriate item. They should also point to where the same word occurs in the recipe.

Whole-class skills work

Ask the children if they have noticed anything special about the sounds of the words for the recipe ingredients: cheddar cheese, chutney, cherry tomatoes, chives. Write the words on the board as you say them. The children should easily recognize that they all begin with *ch*. Ask them if they can think of other foods beginning with *ch*. List them on the board, encouraging the class to sound out and predict the letters as you write each word. Examples could include: chicken, chocolate, cheesecake, chops, cherries, chapati, cheese, cherry tomatoes, cherry cake, chocolate cake, and cherry cheesecake.

Differentiated group activities

1: A maximum of three pairs of children read and follow the photocopiable recipe to make cheese sandwiches, supervised by an adult helper. The other children should search their reading books to find words containing the soft *ch* sound, sorting them into words that begin with this sound and words that end with it. The children should swap activities half-way through the session if appropriate.

2*: The teacher supports this group after working with Group 3. Children work in threes to make a list of all the foods they can think of beginning with *ch*. One child in each three should act as scribe, but all should help with spelling the words.

3*: The teacher works with this group first in a guided reading session, in which children search their reading books for words beginning with *ch*. Together, they should compile a list scribed by the teacher.

Conclusion

The whole class can now eat the sandwiches made by Group 1! [NB: Provide alternative foods for those children who may require them.] Children from the group should say how easy the sandwiches were to make, and whether the instructions could be improved.

Introduction

Display an OHT or enlarged version of one of the lists compiled by Group 2 in Hour 2. Read this together and discuss how children arrived at the spellings, offering opportunities for correction which can be done by children using a different coloured pen.

Whole-class skills work

Explain that the sound *ch* can be found at the end of many words as well as at the beginning. Write on the board a list of examples (such, much, each, peach, reach, etc) and read the words together. Then ask if *ch* can occur elsewhere in some words, for example can the children hear the *ch* sound in 'reaching'? Repeat the word, lengthening the individual sounds to help the children hear them (rea-ch-ing). Ask: Is the *ch* at the beginning of the word? Is it at the end? Help them to decide that the sound is somewhere in the middle. Repeat this with another word such as 'searching'.

End by briefly pointing out that some 'ch' words do not have a 'soft' sound as in 'chicken' and 'chocolate', but sound hard as in 'chemist', 'Christmas' and 'Christine'.

Differentiated group activities

1*: The teacher works with this group first. Children work in pairs to create their own *ch* word menus. On the left-hand side of their blank menu (see Preparation) they write a main course, comprising foods beginning with *ch*. On the other side, they include a dessert and a drink also beginning with *ch*. They can refer to the list used in the Introduction to help them, perhaps mixing words, for example 'chocolate chip cookie', 'chocolate cheesecake', etc.

2*: The teacher supports this group after working with Group 1. Children work in pairs, searching their reading books for words beginning with and containing the soft *ch* sound. With your help, they compile a list of words beginning with *ch*, ending in *ch* and containing *ch* elsewhere.

3: Children work in pairs to match word labels (from Hour 2) to the ingredients and utensils for making sandwiches. If appropriate, the children could go on to make sandwiches following the recipe, with adult assistance.

Conclusion

Ask a child from Group 2 to present the list of *ch* words. Let children from Group 1 share their menus - how many different *ch* food words have they used between them?

HOW TO MAKE CHEESE SANDWICHES

For two people.

1. Spread margarine onto four slices of bread.

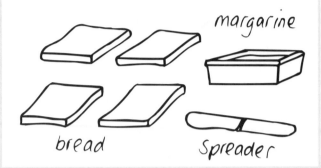

margarine

bread

Spreader

2. Grate cheese onto two slices of bread.

cheddar cheese

grater

3. Spread chutney over cheese.

chutney

Spoon

4. Slice tomatoes and put on top of chutney.

cherry tomatoes

knife

5. Chop chives and sprinkle over tomatoes.

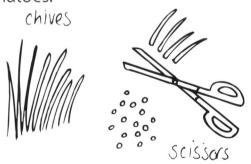

chives

Scissors

6. Place other two slices of bread on top.

7. Cut.

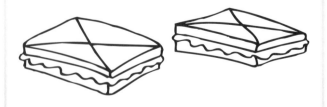

8. Serve.

INFORMATION BOOKS

OBJECTIVES

UNIT	SPELLING/ VOCABULARY	GRAMMAR/ PUNCTUATION	COMPREHENSION/ COMPOSITION
READING NON-FICTION Information books.	Blend phonemes in words with clusters. Extend vocabulary through reading. Collect words of interest, including those from topic work. Use initial letters for alphabetic organization.	Identify sentences in texts, ie those demarcated by capital letters and full stops.	Use terms 'fiction' and 'non-fiction', noting different features. Read non-fiction books and understand that reading can be selective according to readers' needs. Predict a book's contents from the covers. Understand purpose of contents/indexes.

ORGANIZATION (5 HOURS)

	INTRODUCTION	WHOLE-CLASS SKILLS WORK	DIFFERENTIATED GROUP ACTIVITIES	CONCLUSION
HOUR 1	Show differences between fiction and non-fiction books by comparing front and back covers.	Use new words associated with current topic. Sound them out for reading and spelling.	1*: Sort fiction from non-fiction books. 2: Read and spell new words linked with current topic. 3*: Guided reading: non-fiction book.	Display Group 1's work. Identify key words from cards used by Group 2.
HOUR 2	Demonstrate how to access non-fiction books by flicking through pages.	Identify and locate key words in text.	1: Locate key words in non-fiction book by flicking pages and scanning texts. 2*: Locate and match headings, captions, etc, in non-fiction books. 3*: Guided reading: learn to scan texts.	Group 1 explain where their key words occur in text. Group 3 explain the differences between non-fiction and fiction texts.
HOUR 3	Demonstrate how to use index.	Use indexes to show relevance of alphabetical order.	1: Locate words in index, find and read appropriate page. 2*: Re-arrange key topic words into alphabetical order. 3*: Guided reading: using an index.	Pupils from Group 1 describe how to use an index. Discuss how Group 2 decided on alphabetical order of key words.
HOUR 4	Show difference between index and contents page.	Consider second letters when ordering words in alphabetical order.	1*: Locate and match headings to contents page. Find and read correct section. 2: Re-order jumbled words into alphabetical order. 3*: Guided reading: contents page.	Selected pupils from Group 1 show how to use contents page. Selected pupils from Group 2 share their work.
HOUR 5	Pick out information contained in a sentence.	Identify sentences and use capital letters and full stops.	1: Read and identify information in given sentences. 2*: Punctuate texts. 3*: Guided reading.	Selected pupils from Groups 1 and 2 share their work. Class checks punctuated text for accuracy.

RESOURCES

Big Book of a traditional story; Big Book and smaller version of an information text relevant to the current topic, for example *How Cows Make Milk* by Katherine A Smith (Heinemann *Magic Bean* series, ISBN 0-947212-27-2), a selection of fiction and non-fiction books and some that are both, for example: *Doctor Xargle's Book of Earthlets* by Jeanne Willis and Tony Ross (Red Fox, ISBN 0-09-964010-4), *Dinosaurs and All That Rubbish* by Michael Foreman (Puffin, ISBN 0-14-05-5260-X), *The Very Hungry Caterpillar* by Eric Carle (Puffin, ISBN 0-14-05-0087-1), *The Bad Tempered Ladybird* by Eric Carle (Puffin, ISBN 0-14-05-0398-1), Big Book stand, board or flip chart, writing and drawing materials, card, glue, two PE hoops, photocopiable pages 141 (Alphabetical Order: 1) and 142 (Alphabetical Order: 2).

PREPARATION

Hour 1
Choose two Big Books: one containing a traditional story and the other a non-fiction text linked to a current topic. Gather a selection of factual books (see Resources). Write on cards a selection of words (in large print) associated with your chosen topic. Make a set of similar cards for each pair of children in Group 2, but include some additional topic words. You will also need some blank cards for writing further words on. For each pair in Group 1, provide a selection of books including fiction, non-fiction and some titles that are a mixture of both (see Resources).

Hour 2
Prepare a copy of the grid shown below for each pair in Group 1 to record their results.

Word	Label	In a list	In a heading	In a sentence	Another place

Write cards containing a range of key words related to the chosen topic for each pair in Group 1 to look up in the information book. For each pair in Group 2, make photocopies of specific headings, captions, diagrams, drawings and photographs from the Big Book information text for children to to locate and match in small versions of the book.

Hour 3
Add any additional new and relevant words to the card collection used in Hour 1. For each pair of children in Group 1, write a selection of six words on cards taken from the index of the non-fiction Big Book. For each child in Group 2, write a series of ten key words (linked to the chosen topic) on cards, each with a different initial letter, for them to rearrange into alphabetical order.

Hour 4
Make an enlarged photocopy of the index page in the non-fiction Big Book. Photocopy two headings from the Big Book's contents page and cut into separate strips for each pair of children in Group 1. For each child in Group 2, make a copy of either photocopiable page 141 (Alphabetical Order: 1) or 142 (Alphabetical Order: 2), depending on their ability (see activity). For Group 3, prepare a selection of headings from the Big Book contents page, cut into separate strips.

Hour 5
Word process a section of three or four sentences from the non-fiction Big Book, using the same print size as in the original. Replace all the capital letters with lower case and omit all the full stops. Stick onto card and laminate. For each child in Group 2, word

process a section of familiar text from the same Big Book, again replacing the capital letters and omitting the full stops. (Match the text length and complexity to the children's ability.) For each pair of children in Group 1, provide about six sentences from the Big Book, each on a separate strip of paper. Also for each pair, create a simple A4 grid marked as follows:

One piece of information	More than one piece of information

Allow plenty of space in each column for the children to stick on the sentences. For each child in Group 3, you will need to provide a copy of photocopiable page 141 (Alphabetical Order: 1).

Introduction

Note that in this Unit, reference is made to *How Cows Make Milk*, a typical non-fiction Big Book (see Resources), but you can use the activities with any appropriate non-fiction book you choose.

Start by displaying the fiction and non-fiction Big Books. Ask the children if they can tell from the covers what the books might be about. Encourage them to compare the two books by:
■ interpreting the illustrations on the front covers;
■ considering the shape of the print used in the titles;
■ comparing the wording of the titles;
■ comparing back covers, including blurbs.
Discuss the differences fully, encouraging the children to determine which book is a story book and which is an information book. Explain that there are lots of books written about interesting subjects such as horses, butterflies, sportsmen and women, etc, and show them your collection of factual books. Tell the children that these are called information books – they do not tell a story, but contain real, factual information, and use this opportunity to introduce the term 'non-fiction'.

Whole-class skills work

Explain to the children that later in the week, they are going to use important words linked to the chosen topic to help them find out more information about the subject. Then show them the cards containing the topic words. Encourage them to think about the phonemic structure of the words and to sound them out as they say them aloud. Ask them to suggest other words associated with the topic and sound them out for you to scribe onto blank cards in order to extend the word collection.

Differentiated group activities

1*: The teacher supports this group after working with Group 3. Children work in pairs, sorting a selection of books into fiction, non-fiction and a mixture of both. They record their findings in a Venn diagram. (You may need to show them how to set up the diagram outline and headings, and briefly explain or remind them how it works.)
2: Give each pair a set of cards with key words linked to the chosen topic. With the cards face down, children take it in turn to choose a card and read the word. They then practise spelling the words using the 'Look, say, cover, write, check' strategy.
3*: Demonstrate for the children how with information books, the reader can 'dip in' anywhere rather than having to start at the beginning. Read aloud from a suitable text and ask the children to suggest how listening to pieces of information differs from listening to stories.

Conclusion

Engage everyone in identifying key words from the cards used by Group 2. Using two PE hoops positioned as for a Venn diagram, ask children from Group 1 to display their findings and explain to the class how they made their decisions.

Introduction

Display the Big Book information text and ask the children if they can remember what sort of book this is (an information book). Find out what they already know about information books by asking questions such as:
- Have you got an information book at home?
- What is the book about?
- Have you seen information books in the school library?
- How do you read an information book?
- Do you need to start at the beginning?
- How do you find what you are looking for?

Using a small version of the Big Book, demonstrate how flicking through the pages enables you to spot eye-catching features such as a diagram, photograph or heading that interests you. Then choose a particular page in the Big Book (not the beginning) and read it aloud, alerting the children to the language structures, in particular the way that some sentences can stand alone.

Whole-class skills work

Ask a child to come out to the front and hold up a card (from Hour 1) containing a key word linked to the topic. Then, using a small version of your chosen information text, demonstrate again how to flick through the pages, this time in order to spot the key word on the card being held up by the child. Select children to flick through the book to try to spot the selected key word. Then ask them to find out where the word occurs – is it in a heading, as a label, in a list, in a sentence, etc? Repeat this activity using another key word.

Differentiated group activities

1: Give each pair a key word linked to the class topic and ask them to locate where it occurs in a small version of the Big Book. They should record their findings on a grid (see Preparation).

2*: The teacher supports this group after working with Group 3. Each pair should be given a selection of photocopied headings, labels, captions and diagrams from the Big Book (see Preparation) which they then locate and match in small versions of the book.

3*: The teacher works with this group first in a guided reading session as for Hour 1, ie reading aloud, with the children hearing how information text differs from story text. Reiterate identifying key words in a text.

Conclusion

Children from Group 1 explain where their key word occurred in the information text. A child from Group 3 explains the differences between using a non-fiction book and a story book.

Introduction

Ask the children if they know another way of finding information in an information book other than flicking through the pages. Turn to the index in the non-fiction Big Book and point to the words, reading them with the children. Introduce the term 'index', pointing to it in the Big Book. Ask the children if anyone knows what an index is, then pose questions such as:
- Are there any words in the index that you recognize?
- What do you notice about the order of the words?
- What do the numbers tell you?
- How might we use this 'index'?

Then choose a word associated with the topic and show the children how to locate it in the index and then find the relevant page. Repeat the process several times using different key words. Provide an opportunity for the children to explain what they know and understand about indexes.

Whole-class skills work

Tell the children they are going to make an index. First, show them a selection of key words written on separate cards. Ask several of them to come out to the front and hold up a word card. Then ask how they can arrange themselves so that their words are in alphabetical order as in an index. Let them move into the correct positions, then repeat the exercise using different words.

Differentiated group activities

1: Children work in pairs to develop their skills in using indexes. Give each pair the word cards from the index of the Big Book (see Preparation) and let them take turns to locate the word in the index of their small version of the book. They then refer to the right page and read the information together.

2*: The teacher supports this group after working with Group 3. Each child rearranges the word cards provided (see Preparation) into alphabetical order. They could record the final order in list form.

3*: The teacher works with this group first in a guided reading session, reinforcing looking up key words in the index.

Conclusion

Ask children from Group 2 to explain how they decided on the alphabetical order of the key words they were given. Link their explanations to Group 1's work by asking the children in that group if the alphabetical ordering of the index helped them to find their selected words more easily.

Introduction

Display the non-fiction Big Book again. Remind the children how to use an index, then show them the contents page at the beginning of the book. Point to the word 'contents', reading it with the children. Do they know what it means, or can they make a guess?

Next, place an enlarged photocopied version of the Big Book index next to the contents page for comparison. Do the children notice any difference in the way the two lists are ordered? What about the way in which the numbers are ordered? What other differences can they see? (For example, the index may contain single words on each line, whereas the contents list may contain several.)

Now demonstrate how the contents page works, asking children to help you. Provide opportunities for them to:

■ run their fingers along to the page number;
■ locate the page in the book;
■ read the heading;
■ match the heading to the contents.

Whole-class skills work

Some children may already be aware of the need to consider second letters when placing words in alphabetical order. Choose three or four words (linked with your topic) that have the same initial letter but a different second letter, for example: cattle, cows, cream, cheese. Write the words on the board in random order and ask the children how these can be sorted into alphabetical order when they all start with the same letter. Help them to establish the need to look at the second letter, then let them help you put them in the right order. Repeat the activity with another set of words.

Differentiated group activities

1*: The teacher supports this group after working with Group 3. Give each pair two headings from the contents page of the non-fiction Big Book for them to locate and match in the contents page of the smaller version of the book. They should find the appropriate page number, then turn to the page and read it together.

2: Depending on their ability, give each child a copy of either photocopiable page 141 (Alphabetical Order: 1) which requires only three words to be sorted by the second letter only, or page 142 (Alphabetical Order: 2), which requires sorting four words by the second letter.

3*: The teacher works with this group first in a guided reading session, reinforcing how to use the contents page by searching for given headings (see Preparation) on the contents page of the Big Book. Then give each pair a contents heading, and ask them to locate and read the information by themselves.

Conclusion

Ask two children from Group 1 to read aloud their contents headings from the cards and then show how to use the contents page to find that heading in the book. Reinforce alphabetical ordering using first and second letters by asking two children from Group 2 to share their work.

Introduction

Most sentences in non-fiction books for young readers will contain one piece of information, for example: *'The place where cows are milked is called a dairy'*. Some will contain more than one piece of information, for example: *'Cows graze in paddocks and fields eating grasses and clover'* (both sentences from *How Cows Make Milk*) where we learn both where cows graze and what they eat.

Now choose a section of the chosen non-fiction Big Book to read to the children and discuss the amount of information contained in each sentence.

Whole-class skills work

Display the non-fiction Big Book section from which all the capitals and full stops have been removed (see Preparation). Begin pointing and reading with the children, asking them what is wrong with the text. Encourage them to work out that the capital letters and full stops are missing. Select children to correct the text with a marker pen as the whole class read together.

Differentiated group activities

1: Give each pair of children a selection of sentences from the chosen non-fiction Big Book (see Preparation). Ask them to read each sentence together and decide whether it contains one piece of information or more. They can than stick their sentences into the appropriate section of the grid (see Preparation).

2*: The teacher supports this group after working with Group 3. Children should correct familiar sections of text from the non-fiction Big Book, adding in capital letters and full stops (see Preparation).

3*: The teacher works with this group first in a guided reading session, reinforcing the teaching points made in the Introduction and Whole-class skills sessions. The children should then work independently to complete photocopiable page 141 (Alphabetical Order: 1).

Conclusion

Choose a couple of children from Group 1 to talk about how they made decisions about whether their sentences contained one or more pieces of information. Then use a piece of punctuated text from a child in Group 2 and check it for accuracy as a whole class.

ALPHABETICAL ORDER: 1

■ Write the words below in alphabetical order.

jar	ball	feet	ring
juice	bow	face	rain
jelly	blue	fly	rug

1. _____   1. _____   1. _____   1. _____

2. _____   2. _____   2. _____   2. _____

3. _____   3. _____   3. _____   3. _____

nail	all	one	mouse
nut	at	out	mat
nest	are	oat	melt

1. _____   1. _____   1. _____   1. _____

2. _____   2. _____   2. _____   2. _____

3. _____   3. _____   3. _____   3. _____

pink	door	house	clown
posy	desk	hat	can
pat	drum	hen	come

1. _____   1. _____   1. _____   1. _____

2. _____   2. _____   2. _____   2. _____

3. _____   3. _____   3. _____   3. _____

ALPHABETICAL ORDER: 2

■ Write the words below in alphabetical order.

slam, spoon sack, shake	pram, pole pick, plum	clock, crack chair, cave	lace, love leaf, luck
1. _____	1. _____	1. _____	1. _____
2. _____	2. _____	2. _____	2. _____
3. _____	3. _____	3. _____	3. _____
4. _____	4. _____	4. _____	4. _____
tree, two tap, ten	whale, wing wool, wet	goal, grain glow, give	bring, bounce back, blame
1. _____	1. _____	1. _____	1. _____
2. _____	2. _____	2. _____	2. _____
3. _____	3. _____	3. _____	3. _____
4. _____	4. _____	4. _____	4. _____
dart, dress dim, duck	flower, feather fudge, frill	meat, malt might, mother	river, rung rake, roll
1. _____	1. _____	1. _____	1. _____
2. _____	2. _____	2. _____	2. _____
3. _____	3. _____	3. _____	3. _____
4. _____	4. _____	4. _____	4. _____

ORDER! ORDER!

OBJECTIVES

UNIT	SPELLING/ VOCABULARY	GRAMMAR/ PUNCTUATION	COMPREHENSION/ COMPOSITION
READING NON-FICTION Ordered texts: simple dictionaries.	Secure identification, spelling and reading of simple cvc words. Secure alphabetical order.	Expect reading to make sense when accessing information in dictionaries.	Use simple dictionaries and understand their alphabetical arrangement.

ORGANIZATION (2 HOURS)

	INTRODUCTION	WHOLE-CLASS SKILLS WORK	DIFFERENTIATED GROUP ACTIVITIES	CONCLUSION
HOUR 1	Demonstrate how to use dictionaries.	Reinforce alphabetical knowledge and its application using dictionaries. Reinforce reading simple cvc words.	1: Locate words in simple dictionaries. 2*: Put simple cvc words into alphabetical order. 3*: Access words in the dictionary.	Selected pupils from Group 3 explain how to use dictionaries.
HOUR 2	Revise how to use a dictionary.	Use onset and rimes dice to make new words.	1*: Make own dictionaries. 2: Make words using onset and rime; check meaning in picture dictionaries. 3*: Arrange new topic words into alphabetical order. Find their meaning using a dictionary.	Selected pupil from Group 1 reads the definition of a word in his/her dictionary. Arrange and display new topic words in alphabetical order as a reference.

RESOURCES

Multiple copies of simple dictionaries, writing materials, card, board or flip chart, photocopiable pages 145 (Word Lists) and 146 (Dice Net).

PREPARATION

Hour 1

Using large print, write the words 'bun', 'ten', 'man' and 'sun' on separate cards. For each pair of children in Group 1, prepare a list of about ten simple words, preferably linked to your current topic. For each child in Group 2, select and copy one of the lists of simple cvc words provided on photocopiable page 145 (Word Lists).

Hour 2

For each child in Group 1, make a simple 'mini dictionary'. Prepare a master copy by dividing each side of an A4 page into two rows of six columns with a letter in each column as shown above. Copy both sides onto single sheets of A4 paper and fold in half. Make four dice for each pair of children in Group 2 using photocopiable page 146 (Dice Net). On the first die write or stick the onsets c, b, s, r, m, f. On the second die, use the rimes at, an, un, ug, it, ap. On the third die, use the onsets: cl, st, pr, br, th, fl. On the fourth die, write the rimes: ick, ing, ain, ump, ank, ash. Finally, write new topic words in large print on cards for the children to arrange alphabetically as part of a display.

Introduction

Begin by showing the children a simple dictionary and ask them what sort of a book they think it is. Ask questions such as: How do you think you might use this book? Do you know what a book like this is called? How do you know it isn't a story book?

Reinforce the idea that dictionaries are used to find out what a word means or to check the spelling. Suggest a word associated with a current topic (check it is included in the chosen dictionary) and demonstrate how to find the word in the dictionary. Slowly talk through the process, emphasizing how the alphabetical arrangement of the words helps you to find the chosen word. Repeat the process using a different word.

Whole-class skills work

Write 'bun' and 'ten' on the board. Ask the children where in the dictionary they would find each word – the beginning, the middle or the end? Select children to explain the reasoning behind their answers, making clear the link between the order of the words in the dictionary and alphabetical order. Now choose four children to come to the front and hold up the word cards (see Preparation). Ask them to change positions so that the words are in alphabetical order. Ask the other children: Which word would come first in the dictionary? Which would come last? Where would you expect to find 'man'?

Differentiated group activities

1: Children work in pairs with a given list of simple words (linked to a current topic, if possible) looking them up in a simple dictionary and reading the definition together.
2*: After working with Group 3, give each child a list of simple cvc words (see Preparation) to place in alphabetical order. Let the children use dictionaries to help.
3*: Work with this group first. Give each child a copy of a simple dictionary, and take them step-by-step through the process of using the dictionary, looking up the meaning of two words linked to the current topic.

Conclusion

Select one or two children from Group 3 to explain how to use a dictionary.

Introduction

Begin by reminding the children how the alphabetical order of a dictionary makes it easier to find words. Demonstrate again how to look up a word to find its meaning. Then ask the children to suggest some new words linked to the current topic and write these on the board in random order. Now select some children to help you re-write the words in alphabetical order. Keep the list of words for the group activities.

Whole-class skills work

Tell the children you are going to show them an exciting way of making words by using two dice. First, remind them of how some words can be split into onset and rime by writing 'run' on the board. Identify -un as the rime and r as the onset (r/un). Then ask the children for words that rhyme with 'run' and identify the onset and rime in each.

Now select two children to roll the dice with the single letter onsets and the rimes (see Preparation) in order to make a word. Let several children take a turn, then explain that some combinations of onset and rime will make nonsense words. Ask the children what they could use to find out if the words make sense or not.

Differentiated group activities

All groups will need access to simple dictionaries for these activities.
1*: The teacher supports this group after working with Group 3. Give each child a blank 'mini dictionary' (see Preparation). The children should think of some more 'topic words' and write them in the appropriate section of their blank dictionaries. They then look up the definitions in the published dictionary and write them in their own dictionary.
2: In pairs, children roll the dice to make words (using the die with single-letter onsets before moving on to the one with double-letter onsets). They should decide whether or not the word makes sense, using a simple dictionary to check. They can record the words they make on a three-column grid with the headings 'word', 'sense' and 'nonsense'.
3*: Work with this group first. Children use simple dictionaries to find the meaning of new 'topic words' collected in the Introduction and any other suitable words.

Conclusion

Select a child from Group 1 to read the meaning of one of the topic words in his/her dictionary. Give the children some new topic words written on cards (see Preparation) and together, look up their meanings. Display them in alphabetical order along a suitable wall as reference for the topic work.

WORD LISTS

bun ☐	ant ☐	cap ☐	sat ☐	pie ☐
sun ☐	tap ☐	bin ☐	toe ☐	car ☐
ten ☐	lid ☐	tie ☐	pin ☐	tin ☐
hen ☐	rip ☐	pat ☐	lip ☐	den ☐
man ☐	hat ☐	eye ☐	bus ☐	lad ☐
run ☐	pot ☐	van ☐	jar ☐	bat ☐
log ☐	dog ☐	rat ☐	wet ☐	pop ☐
bar ☐	hay ☐	can ☐	top ☐	cat ☐
fat ☐	ham ☐	let ☐	fig ☐	dot ☐
nap ☐	bag ☐	net ☐	hot ☐	red ☐

DICE NET

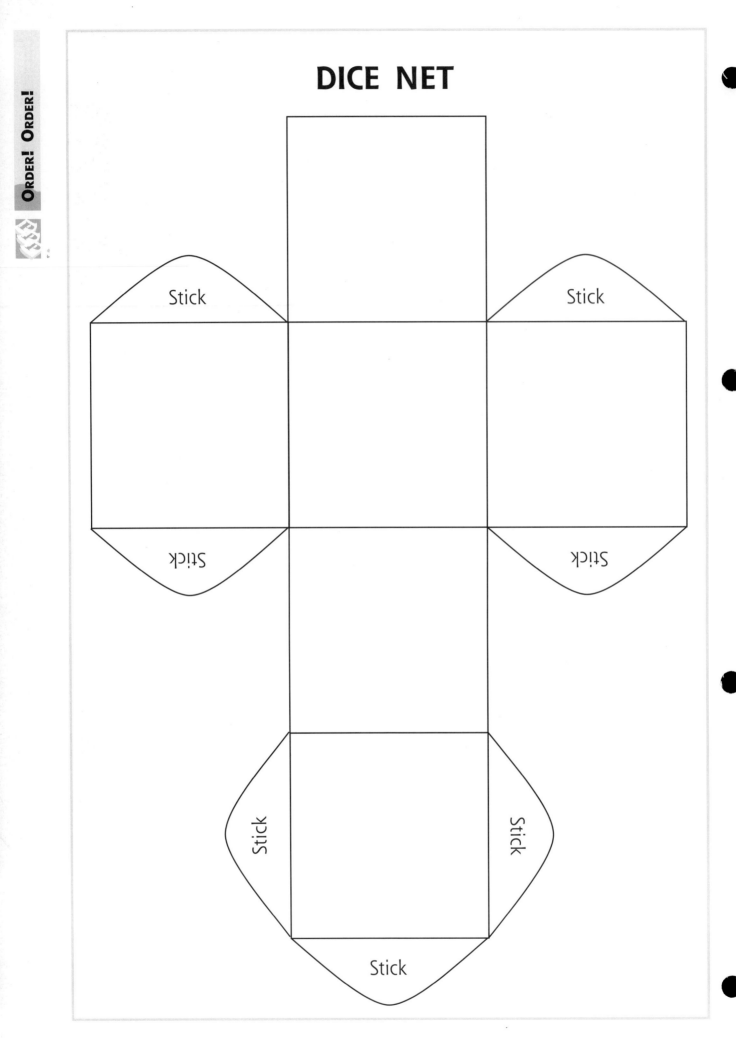

Stick

Stick

Stick

Stick

Stick

Stick

Stick

Stick

POLAR BEAR, POLAR BEAR

OBJECTIVES

UNIT	SPELLING/ VOCABULARY	GRAMMAR/ PUNCTUATION	COMPREHENSION/ COMPOSITION
READING FICTION AND POETRY *Polar Bear, Polar Bear, What Do You Hear?* and *Brown Bear, Brown Bear, What Do You See?* both by Bill Martin and Eric Carle.	Investigate verbs with -*ed* (past tense) and -*ing* (present tense) endings. Encounter new words from reading. Spell new and familiar words using graphic and phonic knowledge.	Use awareness of grammar to decipher new and high frequency words. Identify questions and use question marks appropriately. Read with pace and expression appropriate to grammar and punctuation.	Use titles, covers and 'blurb' to predict story content. Read poetry aloud. Compose poetic sentences using imagination. Enact and tell imagined stories, with expression.

ORGANIZATION (5 HOURS)

	INTRODUCTION	WHOLE-CLASS SKILLS WORK	DIFFERENTIATED GROUP ACTIVITIES	CONCLUSION
HOUR 1	Display cover of *Polar Bear, Polar Bear, What Do You Hear?* Big Book; pupils try to predict story. Shared reading of the book.	Investigate the spelling pattern of -*ing* words using the story text.	1*: Make list of animal sounds ending in -*ing*. Use them to write sentences. 2: Fill in -*ing* words on photocopiable sheet. 3*: Match animal and sound cards.	Two pupils from Group 1 read some of their sentences.
HOUR 2	Shared reading of *Brown Bear, Brown Bear, What Do You See?* Use syntactic frame as a model for composing own books.	Consider -*ed* and -*ing* endings in relation to past and present tense.	1*: Change root words to past and present tense on photocopiable sheet. 2: Choose suitable tense to complete sentences on photocopiable sheet. 3*: Compose own stories.	Two pupils from Group 2 explain some of their sentences. Two pupils from Group 3 share their stories.
HOUR 3	Shared reading of the poem 'Polar Bear' on photocopiable page 157. Discuss meaning of phrases in poem.	Cover words at the end of each line of poem for pupils to predict rhyming words.	1*: Interpret poem, using words and pictures. 2: Fill in missing rhyming words. 3: Put poem in correct sequence.	Two pupils from Group 1 explain their pictures and phrases. Selected pupils read sections of poem aloud.
HOUR 4	Shared reading of *Polar Bear Cubs* story on photocopiable page 158, with pupils acting it out using models in water tray.	Predict meaning of new and interesting words in *Polar Bear Cubs*.	1: Re-enact *Polar Bear Cubs* and re-order text. 2: Create story map of *Polar Bear Cubs*. 3*: Guided reading.	Two pupils from Group 1 re-tell *Polar Bear Cubs* using Arctic scene to help them.
HOUR 5	Pupils create own stories based on *Polar Bear Cubs*.	Cloze activity: pupils predict and spell high frequency words occurring in text.	1: Create new Polar Bear stories. 2: Create story maps of new Polar Bear stories. 3*: Guided reading: Polar Bear text.	Selected pupils from Group 2 tell their story. Selected pupils spell various high frequency words.

RESOURCES

Polar Bear, Polar Bear, What Do You Hear? by Bill Martin and Eric Carle (Puffin, ISBN 0-14-05-4519-0) – enough copies for group work, *Brown Bear, Brown Bear, What Do You See?* by Bill Martin and Eric Carle (Puffin, ISBN 0-14-05-0296-3), writing and drawing materials, board or flip chart, OHP and acetate sheets (optional), 'Post its', Big Book stand, glue, materials for making small books, a world map or globe, water tray set up as an Arctic scene (see Preparation).

Photocopiable pages 154 (What Do You Hear?), 155 (Now or Then?), 156 (Past and Present), 157 ('Polar Bear' Poem), 158 ('Polar Bear Cubs') and 159 (Story Map).

PREPARATION

Hour 1

Make a Big Book version of *Polar Bear, Polar Bear, What Do You Hear?* (see page 10 in main Introduction) and cover all the verbs/animal sounds ending with *-ing* with large 'Post-its'. Make one copy of photocopiable page 154 (What Do You Hear?) for each child in Group 2. Prepare a set of cards with the animal names and their corresponding sounds from the *Polar Bear* story for use with Group 3.

Hour 2

Prepare for whole-class use an enlarged version of the following syntactic frame based on the *Polar* Bear and *Brown Bear* stories:

_____, _____,
What do you do?
I _____ my _____.
That's what I do.

Make a smaller card version of this frame and a blank book (four pages plus front and back cover – see main Introduction, page 10 for further guidance) for each child in Group 3. For each pair of children in Group 2, make a copy of photocopiable page 155 (Now or Then?). For each pair in Group 1, make a copy of photocopiable page 156 (Past and Present).

Hour 3

Make an OHT or an enlarged version of the 'Polar Bear' poem on photocopiable page 157. Write some words/phrases from the poem on strips of card, for example: *Arctic skies, Arctic seas, snowstorms, frozen seas, floating land, homeland* (one for each pair in Group 1). Cover up the last word on each line of the poem and make a copy for each child in Group 2. If necessary, provide a jumbled list of the missing words for them to refer to. Provide a jumbled version of part of the poem text for each pair in Group 3, for example:

About snowstorms
About Arctic skies
Polar Bear in the Arctic snow
And frozen seas
Tell us all the things you know
And Arctic seas

Make sure that you leave enough space in between each line so that the children are able to cut up the text. Choose the text length according to the children's ability.

Hour 4

Before the session, set out the water tray as an Arctic landscape. Do this by placing in the tray wooden/plastic blocks covered in white fluffy hand towels to represent snow-covered land. Make large, mis-shapen ice-cubes to serve as icebergs by putting water in plastic bags and freezing. Use some water and model polar bears, cubs and seals to complete the scene.

Make an OHT or enlarged version of photocopiable page 158 (Polar Bear Cubs). Jumble up short sections of the 'Polar Bear Cubs' story text and make a copy for each pair in Group 1. Make a copy of the story strip on photocopiable page 159 (Story Map) for each child in Group 2, cutting and sticking them together as per the instructions on the photocopiable page. For each pair in Group 3, provide a copy of the 'Polar Bear Cubs' text omitting the following words: *flurries, inquisitive, ice-floes, reassuringly, whimper, drifted, seeks, lee, suckle*. Make a set of cards containing these words.

Hour 5
Set up the water tray as for Hour 4. Prepare an OHT or enlarged version of the 'Polar Bear Cubs' text with the high frequency words covered/omitted:

for, she, are, her, when, them, two, they, their,
will, has, must, who, out, down, next, first.

Make another smaller copy of this text for each pair of children in Group 3. Provide a prepared copy of photocopiable page 159 (Story Map) for each pair of children in Group 1 and each child in Group 2.

Introduction
Begin by displaying the *Polar Bear, Polar Bear, What Do You Hear?* Big Book and let the children read the title with you. Ask them what the mark at the end of the sentence means. Do they know what the answer to the question might be? Where could they look to find out more about the story? The children may suggest looking at the back of the book, but point out that in this book, some information is provided on the inside front cover instead. Read the information. Does it alter their opinion about what the polar bear might hear?

Whole-class skills work
Now begin reading the *Polar Bear* story. Each time you get to a covered up verb (see Preparation), ask the children to guess what the word might be. Slowly uncover it, highlighting the spelling and any phonic or graphic features that help the children to read the word. Now ask if they have noticed a spelling pattern that occurs in all these words (-*ing*). Can they think of some other sounds animals make that might end in -*ing*, for example barking, purring, grunting, squeaking, croaking? Ask them to help you with the spelling as you write their suggested words on the board.

Differentiated group activities
1*: The teacher works with this group first. Children work in pairs, making a list of animal sound words ending in -*ing*. They then include the words in sentences modelled on the *Polar Bear* text, for example: 'I hear children barking like a dog'; 'I hear children purring like a cat', etc. (Write the frame on the board for them to refer to.)
2: Children work independently to complete photocopiable page 154 (What Do You Hear?).
3*: The teacher supports this group after working with Group 1. Children work in pairs matching cards with the animal names to the animal sounds from the *Polar Bear* book (see Preparation). Read the story together so that they can check their work.

Conclusion
Choose two children from Group 1 to read some of their sentences aloud.

Introduction
Display the book *Brown Bear, Brown Bear, What Do You See?*. Read the first few pages aloud and ask the children if it reminds them of another book they know. Make the link with the *Polar Bear* story from Hour 1, then read them the rest of the *Brown Bear* story. Afterwards, show them the enlarged version of the syntactic frame (see Preparation). Say that together you are going to use these sentences from the story but instead of writing about 'Polar Bear' or 'Brown Bear', you will use a child's name and write about what he or she likes doing.

Choose a child and insert his or her name into the question from the story, for example: Sarah Peterson, Sarah Peterson, What do you do? Write this on the board, emphasizing the need to use a question mark. Then, together, substitute the selected child's details, for example:

I *ride* my *bicycle.*
That's what I do.
I *skate* on my *skates.*
That's what I do.

Repeat this with two or three children's names, encouraging the class to join in with sounding out and spelling the words each time.

Whole-class skills work
Display the sound words from the *Polar Bear* story on the board:

growling	roaring	snorting	braying
hissing	trumpeting	snarling	fluting
yelping	whistling	bellowing	

Remind the children how all the sound words they looked at previously ended in *-ing*. Refer to the list of 'sound' words on the board and ask what happens when you remove the *-ing*. (Rub out the letters.) Encourage children to see the 'root' words: *growl*, *roar*, *snort*, *flute*, *bray*, etc. (Explain that the e in *flute* was dropped to make *fluting*.)
Now ask the children if they know of any other endings they could add onto the words. Let them make suggestions, but focus on *-ed*, and apply this to the list of words, for example *roared*, *snorted*, etc. Then write on the board:

The lion _____ at the polar bear.
The lion is _____ at the polar bear.

Ask the children to choose *roared/roaring* appropriately. Repeat this again for:

The hippopotamus _____ at the lion.
The hippopotamus is _____ at the lion.

Ask the children what the difference is between the two sentences. Help them to establish that one sentence is about something that has already happened, while the other is about something that is happening now. You may wish to introduce the terms 'past tense' and 'present tense' at this point, depending on the children's abilities.

Differentiated group activities
1*: The teacher supports this group after working with Group 3. Children work in pairs to complete photocopiable page 156 (Past and Present).
2: Children work in pairs sharing a small version of the *Polar Bear* book to complete photocopiable page 155 (Now or Then?).
3*: The teacher works with this group first. Give each child a blank book for them to write their 'mini story' in, modelled on the *Polar Bear* and *Brown Bear* books. Show them the question and answer frames from the story (see Preparation) and ask them to write the question on the title page, filling in their name (repeating it twice). They should then use the answer frame to respond on the following pages in their books.

Conclusion
Reinforce the notion of past and present by asking children from Group 2 to explain the sentences they have worked on. Ask two children from Group 3 to read out their 'mini stories' based on the *Polar Bear* book.

Introduction

Remind the children of how the *Polar Bear* story (Hour 1) was set in a zoo. Ask them where polar bears really live. Use a globe to show them the Arctic and find out what they already know about this region. Now display the OHT or enlarged version of the poem 'Polar Bear' (photocopiable page 157) and read it to the children. Make your reading as expressive as possible, emphasizing the questions with your tone of voice, and linking this with the question marks in the text.
Discuss the poem, asking the children if it has helped them to imagine what it must be like to live in the Arctic. Can they imagine what the Arctic skies might look like, or how it would feel to be caught in a snowstorm? Encourage them to describe their

imagined pictures of a 'frozen sea', and to discuss what a 'floating land' might mean. Do they know what the word 'homeland' means? Can they imagine and picture the homeland of the Polar Bear?

Whole-class skills section

Read the poem together, with the children joining in the rhymes, then quickly cover the last word at the end of each line of the poem with large 'Post its'. Read the poem with the children, asking them to predict the covered words. Encourage them to hear the rhyming words and to use the rhyme to help them predict. Select one child to remove the 'Post its' as the words are predicted.

Differentiated group activities

1*: Give one of the phrases from the poem to each pair of children. Together, they should draw a picture of what the phrase evokes in their imaginations and write a couple of sentences about the special things in their picture. The teacher works with the group to stimulate discussion and ideas through questionning, and to model the transposition of speech to writing.

2: Children work independently filling in the missing words in the poem (see Preparation), using their memory and ability to predict the rhyme. They should then work in pairs to read the poem to one another.

3: Children work in pairs on a jumbled version of a poem extract (see Preparation) which they re-sequence by cutting into strips and sticking them onto paper. They then practise reading the extract to each other with appropriate expression and intonation, as you did in the Introduction.

Conclusion

Ask two children from Group 1 to share their poetic sentences and explain their pictures. Select three or four children to each read a section of the poem aloud with appropriate expression and intonation.

HOUR 4

Introduction

Show the children the Arctic scene in the water tray that you have prepared and say that you are going to read a story about a Mother Polar Bear and her cubs (photocopiable page 158). Now read the story aloud, choosing three children (to represent Mother Polar Bear and her two cubs) to use the polar bears in the water tray to act out what you are reading.

Whole-class skills work

Next, display an OHT or enlarged version of the 'Polar Bear Cubs' story (photocopiable page 158 and engage the children in following the text as you read. Ask them to suggest meanings for some interesting words in the text, encouraging them to use previous knowledge and context cues:

flurries	inquisitive	ice-floes	reassuringly	whimper
drifted	seeks	lee	suckle	

Differentiated group activities

1: Pairs of children take turns to use the water tray to act out the 'Polar Bear Cubs' story. The other pairs re-arrange jumbled sections of the story text into the correct sequence, and then read it together.

2: Provide each child with a copy of the 'Polar Bear Cubs' story and a story strip made from photocopiable page 159 (Story Map). Ask them to map out the story events in words and pictures.

3*: Guided reading of the story text that has some of the words missing for the children to fill in (see Preparation). Provide these words on cards in order that children can select appropriately.

Conclusion

Ask two children from Group 1 to tell and re-enact the story 'Polar Bear Cubs' using the Arctic scene in the water tray.

Introduction
Display the 'Polar Bear Cubs' story and read it through again with the children. Now ask them how they could use the text to make a different story. Ask them to think of an event which could make a whole new story, for example:

■ one of the cubs gets left behind;
■ one of the cubs drifts away on an ice-floe;
■ a terrible snowstorms occurs.

Record the children's ideas on the board and select some children to act out their suggestions using the Arctic scene in the water tray. Keep the list of suggestions for the group activities.

Whole-class skills work
Tell the children that they are going to look at some familiar words in the 'Polar Bear Cubs' story and learn how to spell them. Display the OHT or enlarged version of the text with the high frequency words covered (see Preparation) and read it together. As you do so, let the children predict and spell the missing words as you scribe them on the board.

Differentiated group activities
1: Each pair decides on an event to make a new Polar Bear 'mini story', using their own ideas or those discussed in the Introduction. One pair at a time re-enacts their event using the water tray set up as in Hour 4. The other pairs record their story idea on the photocopiable story strip using complete sentences and pictures.
2: Provide the children with the story map (photocopiable page 159) to map and sequence their own 'mini stories' in words/phrases and pictures, drawing from one of the suggestions (or their own ideas) recorded on the board in the Introduction.
3*: Guided reading with the teacher using the photocopiable 'Polar Bear Cubs' text with the high frequency words missing (see Preparation). Let the children predict and attempt to spell the missing words.

Conclusion
Ask a child from Group 2 to tell his or her story using their story map as a prompt. Select children to spell some high frequency words from 'Polar Bear Cubs' and display these words on the wall for future reference.

WHAT DO YOU HEAR?

■ Match the sounds in the box below to the right animal.
Use the storybook to help you.
■ Write the sounds in the spaces provided.

I hear children...

_____ like a polar bear.

_____ like a lion.

_____ like a hippopotamus.

_____ like a flamingo.

_____ like a zebra.

_____ like a boa constrictor.

_____ like an elephant.

_____ like a leopard.

_____ like a peacock.

_____ like a walrus.

that's what I hear.

yelping   hissing   trumpeting   roaring

bellowing   fluting   growling

snarling   snorting   braying

NOW OR THEN?

■ Look at the list of words below.
■ Use the right word in each sentence, adding *ing* or *ed*.
The first one has been done for you.

The lion _____ **roared** _____ at the polar bear.

The lion is _____ **roaring** _____ at the polar bear.

The hippopotamus _____ at the lion.

The hippopotamus is _____ at the lion.

The elephant _____ at the boa constrictor.

The elephant is _____ at the boa constrictor.

The leopard _____ at the elephant.

The leopard is _____ at the elephant.

The boa constrictor _____ at the zebra.

The boa constrictor is _____ at the zebra.

trumpet   **snarl**   **roar**   **hiss**   **snort**

PAST AND PRESENT

- Look carefully at the root words in the table below.
- Write each word in the past tense in the space provided.
- Now write each word in the present tense.
- The first one has been done for you.

Root word	Then (Past)	Now (Present)
growl	growled	growling
roar		
snort		
bray		
hiss		
trumpet		
snarl		
flute		
yelp		
whistle		
bellow		

'POLAR BEAR' POEM

Polar Bear

Polar Bear in the Arctic snow
Tell us all the things you know.

About Arctic skies
And Arctic seas

About snowstorms
And frozen seas.

What do you eat?
Where do you sleep?

Who are your friends?
Who do you meet?

Cold breaking ice.
A floating land.

Polar Bear
In your homeland.

Kathleen Taylor

POLAR BEAR CUBS

*O*utside the polar bears' den the heavy snows of winter have given way to spring's lighter snow flurries. Mother Polar Bear decides it's a good time to hunt for food and take her two cubs out into the Arctic snow for the first time.

The cubs are playful and inquisitive. They tumble along in the snow behind mother as she makes her way to the ice-floes to hunt for seal. At times the cubs ride on her back, especially when she leaps across the breaking ice. Mother Polar Bear purrs reassuringly as she leaves them on firm land while she hunts for seal.

The two little polar bears chase each other in the snow, slipping and sliding, rolling and tumbling, but after a while, they miss their mother and begin to whimper, hoping she will hear them.

Mother Polar Bear has drifted far away on the ice-floes and must swim through the freezing Arctic Sea to get back to her cubs. She is a strong swimmer and soon reaches the cubs who are now whimpering loudly. After shaking her fur, she seeks out a bank of snow in the lee of a hill and settles down with her cubs. The cubs suckle her milk and fall asleep next to her warm body.

STORY MAP

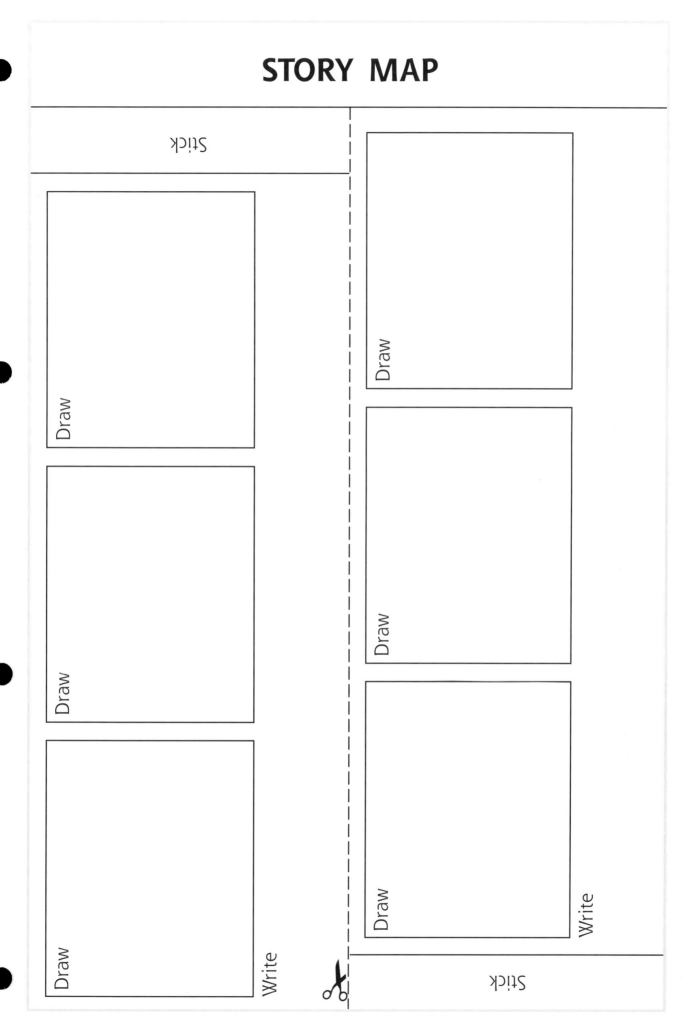

Stick

Draw

Draw

Draw

Write

Stick

Draw

Draw

Draw

Write

NON-FICTION: POLAR BEARS

OBJECTIVES

UNIT	SPELLING/ VOCABULARY	GRAMMAR/ PUNCTUATION	COMPREHENSION/ COMPOSITION
READING AND WRITING NON-FICTION Polar Bears.	Recognize words by common spelling patterns. Read and spell new words from reading. Identify special or significant words linked to the topic.	Identify questions. Read familiar texts aloud with pace and expression appropriate to the grammar. Add question marks to questions. Reinforce knowledge of the term 'sentence'.	Recognize non-fiction books. Read and write recounts and begin to recognize ordered sequence of events/words. Identify questions and use texts to find answers. Make group/class non-fiction books.

ORGANIZATION (5 HOURS)

	INTRODUCTION	WHOLE-CLASS SKILLS WORK	DIFFERENTIATED GROUP ACTIVITIES	CONCLUSION
HOUR 1	Identify questions in the poem 'Polar Bear' (photocopiable page 157 from previous unit).	Shared reading of 'Facts About Polar Bears' in order to answer questions.	1: Read fact sheet; answer questions. 2: Read fact sheet; answer questions. 3*: Guided reading and writing.	Selected pupils from Group 1 read out sentences in answer to questions. Display examples of each group's work.
HOUR 2	Shared reading of 'Facts About Polar Bears'. Find out if some facts can be grouped together. Group facts together under appropriate headings.	Re-order words in jumbled sentences.	1: Make information books. Match facts to headings. 2*: Begin making a class Big Book. 3*: Re-order jumbled sentences.	Display a page from a class Big Book and ask a pupil to explain why information has been grouped together.
HOUR 3	Discuss how the list of headings from Hour 2 can form a contents page. Explore contents pages from other information books.	Draw on pupil's graphic and phonic knowledge to list useful words to do with polar bears, and to order words alphabetically.	1: Reassemble list of headings to make a contents page. 2: Make an index. 3*: As for Group 1, but for the class Big Book with the teacher's support.	Select pupils to use contents page in class Big Book in order to find and read information in the book.
HOUR 4	Discuss what to include on class Big Book cover, referring to covers on other books.	Use alphabetically -ordered lists of useful words to make index.	1*: Make an index. 2: Make book covers. 3: Design covers for class Big Book.	Pupils from Group 1 demonstrate how to use an index.
HOUR 5	Discuss important features of front and back covers.	Model writing, using a recount writing frame.	1: Write about what has been learned. 2: Read little books; make improvements. 3*: Create index for class Big Book.	Pupils from Group 1 read their work. Display class Big Book and pupils' little books for future reading.

RESOURCES

A selection of 'early reader' information books about polar bears and/or other subjects currently being studied, writing and drawing materials, including pack of large coloured felt-tipped pens and chinagraph pencil, board or flip chart, card, glue, OHP and acetate sheets (optional), Big Book stand, laminator or sticky-backed plastic, materials for small books and class Big Book (see main Introduction, page 10, for guidance).

Photocopiable pages 157 ('Polar Bear' Poem) from previous unit 'Polar Bear, Polar Bear' and 166 (Facts About Polar Bears).

PREPARATION

Hour 1

Make an OHT or enlarged version of the 'Polar Bear' poem from the previous unit if you have not already done so. Prepare a large laminated version of 'Facts About Polar Bears' on photocopiable page 166 and prepare A4 copies for each pair of children in the class. For each child in Group 2, prepare a simple three-column grid with these three headings: What do you eat?; Where do you sleep?; Who do you meet? Prepare an enlarged version of the following sentence starters for use with Group 3:

The polar bear eats...
The polar bear sleeps...
We don't know if polar bears have friends but we do know that...
The polar bear might meet....

Hour 2

Laminate a blank sheet of card measuring about 64cm x 45cm.
Make a blank eight-page book for each pair of children in Group 1 (see main Introduction, page 12, for guidance). Provide one copy of the 'Facts About Polar Bears' sheet on photocopiable page 166 for each pair in Group 1.

For Group 2, enlarge the 'Facts About Polar Bears' sheet and list of headings suitable for including in a class Big Book. For each pair in Group 3, provide a list of the simpler sentences from the photocopiable fact sheet, jumbling up the word order and including capitals (for first words, etc) and full stops (next to the final word), for example:

eat Polar bears and seals fish.
layer thick the cold. out keeps A fat of
with stay two years. Cubs for mother their
pelts. Man polar their bears for hunts

Hour 3

Gather a selection of 'early reader' information books on polar bears, containing contents pages and indexes. Sew or staple a folded sheet of A4 paper to Group 1's books (Hour 2) to create two outer pages. Make a jumbled contents list based on the headings in their books (see Skills session, Hour 2) and photocopy for each pair in Group 1. Also make a single enlarged copy for Group 3. For each pair in Group 2, make a jumbled list of useful words for a Polar Bear facts sheet index as follows: polar bear, seal, summer, Arctic, swimmer, cubs, pelts, man, sleep, ice-floes, food, winter. (Leave enough space for cutting up the words.)

Hour 4

Choose one of the indexes made by children in Group 2 (Hour 3) and enlarge it for whole-class use. Provide the originals or make photocopies of these indexes for each pair of children in Group 1. Prepare some blank front and back covers cut to size for Group 1's books.

Hour 5

Make an enlarged laminated recount writing frame with the following text, leaving plenty of space between each section:

I already knew that...
I have found out that...
I have also found out that...
The most interesting thing I have found out is...

Make some smaller photocopied versions of the frame, enough for one per child in Group 1. Rub out the numbers on the enlarged index from Hour 4, ready for use with Group 3.

Introduction
Display the 'Polar Bear' poem from the previous unit and discuss what the children already know about polar bears. Read the poem together, then look again at the questions:

What do you eat?
Where do you sleep?
Who are your friends?
Who do you meet?

Ask the children how they know they are questions.

Whole-class skills work
Display a large laminated version of 'Facts About Polar Bears' (photocopiable page 166) next to the poem. Engage the children in reading the facts to find answers to the questions in the poem. Select individual children to 'spot' relevant pieces of information. Ask them if they can find an answer to the question 'Who are your friends?' on the fact sheet. Encourage the children to see that the illustrations in the margins provide some information on other animals that polar bears meet, but stress that this does not tell us who Polar Bear's friends are. Now ask if the sheet tell us about the enemies of polar bears. Encourage the children to look carefully for the information – ie man and the Arctic Sea are enemies to polar bears.

Differentiated group activities
Give pairs of children in all groups a copy of photocopiable page 166 (Facts About Polar Bears). Write the questions from the poem on the board for them to refer to.
1: Each child answers the questions from the poem, using the photocopiable fact sheet to help them. They should answer using complete sentences.
2: Each child answers the questions from the poem using the fact sheet. They select relevant pieces of information and write or stick them into the appropriate column of their grid (see Preparation).
3*: In this guided reading and writing session, children answer the questions from the poem by referring to the fact sheet. They should be shown how to construct simple sentences using sentence starters (see Preparation).

Conclusion
Select children from Group 1 to read out their answers to the questions in the poem. Display some of each group's work for children to refer to during the week.

Introduction
Display the large laminated version of 'Facts about Polar Bears'. Select children to read out some of the facts. Point out that the facts are not in any particular order and ask if the children think it would be useful to group some of the facts together. Invite suggestions for grouping the facts by asking which ones tell us what polar bears eat.
  Now use a coloured felt-tipped pen to write 'What polar bears eat' near the top (leaving a gap) of a blank laminated card placed next to the fact sheet. Then ask a child to find, read and then draw a circle around the relevant facts (on the fact sheet) using the same felt-tipped pen. Ask other children to read out the circled facts, and to say whether there are any other facts to include. Repeat this with the following headings, using a different coloured pen for each one:

■ Where polar bears live
■ Where polar bears sleep

- Dangers
- About the cubs
- Special facts about polar bears
- Other animals that live in the Arctic.

Whole-class skills work

Write a jumbled-up sentence from the 'Facts About Polar Bears' sheet (photocopiable page 166) on the board, for example:

stay mother for two about years. with Cubs their

Now ask the children to help you put the sentence in the correct order. Begin by asking what sort of letter normally appears at the start of a sentence. Let them look for the capital letter (in 'Cubs') and ask someone to read the word aloud. Next, ask what symbol or mark normally appears at the end of a sentence and let the children search for the word with the full stop at the end. Ask a child to read the word. Establish that the sentence begins with 'Cubs' and ends with 'years.' (write these words on the board, leaving a gap in the middle).

Then target individual children as appropriate to help you re-arrange the rest of the words in the sentence and write these on the board. If time allows, repeat the activity using a different sentence from the fact sheet.

Differentiated group activities

1: Give each pair a blank book to make an information book about polar bears. The first page is the title page, for example: Information about Polar Bears by... The children should then write the headings derived from the Introduction session of this Hour at the top of each page, referring to the laminated list. Next, they select information from the fact sheet to stick on the appropriate page and add illustrations.

2*: As for Group 1, but this time work with the children to create a class Big Book using enlarged text (see Preparation), guiding them through the reading of both the headings and facts.

3: Give each pair the jumbled sentences from the fact sheet (see Preparation) to re-order, working on one at a time.

Conclusion

Display a page of the class Big Book made by Group 2. Then select children to read out some of the information grouped under the different headings and explain why it has been grouped in this way.

Introduction

Display the different coloured headings on the laminated sheet from Hour 2 and select children to read the list. Ask if it reminds them of other lists they have seen in information books. If they mention indexes, ask if the list of headings is in alphabetical order. It isn't and this should help them to determine that the list is like a contents page rather than an index. Write 'Contents' above the list, sounding out the letters as you write them. Select children to find the contents pages in a selection of simple information books on any subject.

Now show the children the class Big Book made by Group 2 (Hour 2) and ask them where they would put a contents page. Then fold a large sheet of paper to make further outer pages, and show how a contents page could go adjacent to the inner title page, as in many information books. Place the laminated 'Contents' card appropriately in the book to emphasize this point.

Whole-class skills work

Explain that as well as a contents page, an information book needs an index. Look at some indexes in your collection of information books about polar bears (see Resources). Refer to the enlarged version of the 'Facts About Polar Bears' sheet and ask what useful words could be included in an index for this sheet. Invite some suggestions and write a list on the board, sounding out the words and pointing out any significant graphic features. Then select children to sort out the words into alphabetical order, drawing on their knowledge about ordering some words by second letters.

Differentiated group activities

1: Children continue to work in pairs on own information books begun in Hour 2. Give them a jumbled contents list based on the headings used. They should cut out and reassemble the list, sticking it down to make a contents page for their book. Finally, they number each page and add these numbers to complete their contents page.

2: Children work in pairs reassembling a list of jumbled words (see Preparation) in alphabetical order to create an index (numbers will be added in Hour 4). They can add in any words from the fact sheet that they think would be useful.

3*: With the teacher's help, children should create a contents page together for the class Big Book, numbering the pages appropriately.

Conclusion

Share the development of the class Big Book, using it to reinforce the teaching points about contents pages. Ask a child to select a heading from the contents page, then locate the appropriate page and read it aloud.

Introduction

HOUR 4

Display the class Big Book about polar bears (Hour 2) and tell the children that it needs a cover. Explain that the cover tells the reader about what is inside the book. Show them examples of 'early reader' information books and examine the front covers focusing on illustrations, colour and impact. Look particularly at the layout of the text – point out how the title is often at the top of the cover and is usually in larger print than the other cover text. Authors' names may also be included. Look at the illustrations – what clues do they give to the content? Tell the children that often, information books include photographs on the covers, unlike fiction books. Together, examine the back covers for any 'blurb' and pictures. How are these linked to the content of the books?

Now invite the children's suggestions about what features to include on the cover of the class Big Book. Write a list of these – for example, title, picture, authors' details, back cover blurb and picture – and display it clearly for children to refer to later. Now ask for suggestions about a title for the class Big Book and write them on the board. Discuss what should go in the 'blurb', and compose simple frames for sentences, such as:

> This book is about _____.
> You will find information on _____, _____ and _____ in this book.
> What do polar bears _____?
> Where do polar bears_____?
> Find out, read this _____.

Keep the information for reference during the group activities.

Whole-class skills work

Show the children an enlarged version of an index made by a child in Group 2, Hour 3 (see Preparation). Ask a child to choose and read a word from the index then, together, find all the places where it occurs in one of the books made by a child in Group 1 (Hour 2) and write the page numbers alongside the word in the index. Repeat this several times to demonstrate the nature of an index.

Differentiated group activities

1*: Using the indexes made by Group 2 in Hour 3, each pair works systematically to find the words as they occur in their own books. They add in the page numbers to complete the indexes which are then stuck onto the inside back page of their books.

2: Children work in pairs, one designing a front cover and the other designing a back cover for the books made by Group 1. (Join the covers together with sticky tape before sewing or stapling them to the books.) Encourage the children to refer to the suggested titles, 'blurbs' and sentence starters on display (see Skills session).

3: Individual children make a first draft of a design for the front cover of the class Big Book, using A4 paper. (Provide them with the title, for example 'Our Book About Polar Bears', and the name of the class as the 'authors'.)

Conclusion

Reinforce the concept of indexes by asking children from Group 1 to show how they located where particular words occurred in their books.

Introduction

Display the front cover designs made by Group 3 in Hour 4. Begin by asking the children their opinions on the colours used in the pictures. Which colours make them think of the cold? Now look at the position of the titles on the covers – can they be clearly seen? Discuss what information the covers convey through words and pictures. Explain that one of the covers will be used for the class Big Book, and then invite the children to give some advice to Group 3 on how they could improve their work.

Whole-class skills work

Display an enlarged laminated version of the recount writing frame (see Preparation). Discuss each section of the frame in turn in relation to what the children know about polar bears. Take an example of something that a child already knows about the subject, then model the writing process by writing a complete sentence for this on the frame (using a chinagraph pen). Select children to complete the other parts of the writing frame and ask individuals to contribute spellings of some commonly-used words and to sound out new words.

Differentiated group activities

1: Children work independently using a photocopy of the recount writing frame to record what they have learned about polar bears.
2: Children in pairs read the Group 1's books about polar bears. They should decide if further illustrations would enhance the text or if any further text needs adding. They should then work together to provide any additions on separate pieces of paper.
3*: Show the children the enlarged index from the Skills section in Hour 4. Ask a child to read the first word from the list then, placing the Big Book on a stand, track the text with the children to find the pages where this word occurs. Make a note of the page number next to the word on the index. Repeat until the index for the Big Book is complete.

Conclusion

Select children from Group 1 to read their accounts of what they have learned about polar bears. Add a front cover to the class Big Book when Group 3 have completed their work on the covers, and display this and the children's information books for future reading.

FACTS ABOUT POLAR BEARS

- Polar bears can walk easily over ice because they have hairy soles on their feet.

- Polar bears are expert swimmers and divers.

- Polar bears eat seals and fish.

- The Arctic Sea can be dangerous for polar bear cubs.

- In summer, polar bears also eat grass and berries.

- A thick layer of fat keeps out the cold.

- In summer polar bears live on the Arctic ice-floes, from which they dive to catch seals.

- Polar bears sleep in sheltered places, but in winter they dig into the snow to sleep.

- Cubs stay with their mother for about two years.

- Man hunts polar bears for their pelts.

- Other animals polar bears might meet in the Arctic are walruses, Arctic hares, Arctic foxes, Arctic owls, caribou, lemmings, wolves and wolverines.

MISTER MAGNOLIA

OBJECTIVES

UNIT	SPELLING/ VOCABULARY	GRAMMAR/ PUNCTUATION	COMPREHENSION/ COMPOSITION
READING AND WRITING FICTION AND POETRY *Mister Magnolia* by Quentin Blake.	Explore words with different spellings of the same phoneme.	Choose and collect significant/ favourite sentences. Discuss, re-read and use to adapt and extend.	Use the context of reading and grammatical and phonemic cues to predict texts. Use a poem/ story as a model for writing by adapting the text.

ORGANIZATION (3 HOURS)

	INTRODUCTION	WHOLE-CLASS SKILLS WORK	DIFFERENTIATED GROUP ACTIVITIES	CONCLUSION
HOUR 1	Shared reading of *Mister Magnolia*, with pupils predicting the rhyme.	Develop awareness of different spellings for same phoneme.	1: Track text for words with oo sound and note spellings. 2: Spell rhyming words from memory and check. 3*: Guided reading and sorting words.	Group 1 reiterate the various ways of spelling the oo sound. Display grids from Groups 1 and 3's work for future reference.
HOUR 2	Pupils read aloud from *Mister Magnolia*. They make direct reference to text and use it to construct sentences.	Model writing by extending storyline rhymes.	1*: Choose favourite lines to extend story and rhyme. 2: Complete some sentences. 3: Make a rhyming flap book.	Selected pupils from Group 1 share their extended story lines. Display Group 3's flap books.
HOUR 3	Gather and write suggestions for a new story. Pupils read back their suggestions.	Develop awareness of different spelling of long vowel phoneme oa.	1: Make a rhyming flap book. 2*: Guided reading, searching for the oa sound. 3: Make oat words and use in sentences.	Selected pupils from Group 1 read aloud their flap books. Display oa grids.

RESOURCES

Copies of *Mister Magnolia* by Quentin Blake (Picture Lions, ISBN 0-00-661879-0) – ideally one between two pupils – writing materials, board or flip chart, 'Post its', reading books (for Groups 1 and 3), card, A4 paper for making simple flap books (see Preparation).

PREPARATION

Hour 1

Take a copy of *Mister Magnolia* and cover with 'Post its' all the rhyming words at the end of the lines, for example *boot, flute, newt*, etc. Make a photocopy of this text for each pair of children in Group 2. Next, draw a simple five-column grid to fill an A4 sheet of paper. Use the following column headings: *oo, ui, ew, u(t)e, other*. Make enough photocopies of the grid for each pair in Group 1 and each child in Group 3.

Hour 2

Make an enlarged version of the following adapted rhymes (based on *Mister Magnolia*) with missing words:

> He has some very fat owls who are learning to hoot
> And all of them wearing only one _____
> And a dinosaur called a MAGNIFICENT _____.
>
> He sometimes likes quiet at the pond with the newt
> Or noise at the pool when he slides down the _____
> Or dancing to music played on the _____.

Make a card containing the sentence starter 'A good/ funny thing happens to Mister Magnolia when...' for each child in Group 2.

For each child in Group 3, make a simple flap book by folding a sheet of A4 paper in half. Make a fold 2cm from the seam, then cut the pages in half up to the fold to make separate top and bottom pages (Figure 1). (The top and bottom pages can then be mixed by turning one and not the other.) Write *Mister Magnolia has only one boot* on the top part of the cover page of each book.

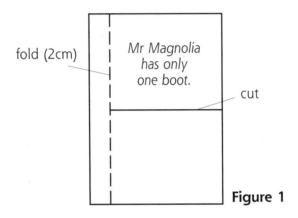

Figure 1

Hour 3

Make a flap book for each child in Group 1 as described above for Hour 2, but change the sentence on the top part of the cover to: *Mister Magnolia has only one coat*. Draw a simple four-column grid to fill an A4 page. Use the following column headings: *oa (coat)*, *o(l)e (pole)*, *ow (show)*, *others*. Make a copy of this for each child in Group 2. For each pair in Group 3, make a word wheel as shown in Figure 2.

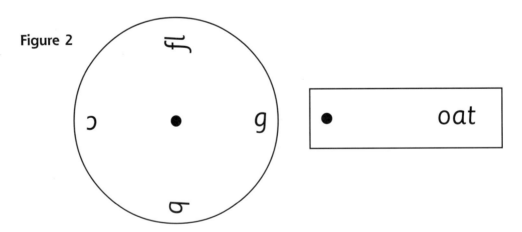

Figure 2

Introduction

Introduce *Mister Magnolia* to the children and read it together. Then read it again, using the copy with end-of-line rhymes masked (see Preparation). Ask the children to guess the rhyming words. Now talk about the story, asking the children what Mister Magnolia might be thinking when he looks down at his one boot (page 1). Did he seem to mind having only the one? Turn to pages 6 and 7 and ask what is happening. How does Mister Magnolia react to having his feet tickled? Look at page 13. How does Mister Magnolia manage to ride the scooter with only one boot? What has he had to do?

Finish by discussing what makes Mister Magnolia want another boot. What do the children think of his new boot?

Whole-class skills work

Read *Mister Magnolia* again, this time asking the children to offer spellings for the rhyming words. Write these on the board, then check the spellings together by referring back to the book. Now focus on all the *oo* sound words and explain that there are several different spellings for it, in this case *oo*, *ui*, *ew*, and *u(t)e*. Draw a simple four-column grid and write each of these spellings as a heading. Then help the children to sort the words with the *oo* sound into the appropriate columns on the grid, scribing for them. Suggest other words such as 'hoop', so that the children hear the *oo* sound with alternative consonant endings. Other examples could include: moon, spoon, flew, chew, chute, root.

Differentiated group activities

1: Children work in pairs searching in their reading books for words with the *oo* sound. They record their findings onto the grid (see Preparation). Other spellings for 'oo' that they encounter should be written in the last column of the grid. Stress that the words they find don't have to have a 't' sound as in the *u(t)e* column, but they must have the *oo* sound.
2*: The teacher supports this group after working with Group 3. Children work in pairs with a copy of the *Mister Magnolia* text from which the rhyming words have been omitted (see Preparation). They should try to spell the missing words correctly from memory, then consult the book together to check spellings. The group then do a guided reading of the text for the final ten minutes.
3*: Guided reading: give each child a copy of *Mister Magnolia* and a grid (as for Group 1) in order to collect and sort the words by their spellings.

Conclusion

Children from Group 1 share their findings on the different spelling patterns of the *oo* sound. Display a selection of the children's grids for future reference.

Introduction

Read *Mister Magnolia* again, selecting different children to read aloud parts of the text. Talk about the fact that although Mister Magnolia has only one boot, lots of good things happen to him which are often amusing. Ask what these things are and where they occur in the text, encouraging the children to locate and read the relevant text to support the points they are making.
   Then, to enable the children to write their comments, write the following sentence starter on the board for them to extend: 'A good thing that happens to Mister Magnolia is when...'. The children then add a phrase such as: 'his sisters play the flute' or 'he gives rides to his friends'. Then change 'good' to 'funny' in the starter so the children can extend it by referring to the amusing incidents, for example: 'A funny thing that happens to Mister Magnolia is when...he salutes the mice/ parakeets pick holes in his suit'.

Whole-class skills work

Ask several children to tell you their favourite rhyme in the book. Write these on the board, then read them together. Now show the children the enlarged version of the adapted rhymes (see Preparation) and ask them to predict the missing words. Encourage them to refer to the grids of rhyming words from Hour 1 on display.

Differentiated group activities

1*: Children work in pairs sharing a copy of *Mister Magnolia*. They choose their favourite rhyming sentences/phrases from the book and use them to extend the storyline, as in the Skills session, choosing words that fit the rhyme if possible.
2: Children work independently, sharing copies of *Mister Magnolia*. They use a sentence starter (see Preparation) to write about the incidents that happen to this character.
3: Give each child a flap book (see Preparation). Children refer to *Mister Magnolia* and choose rhyming lines to match the sentence *Mister Magnolia has only one boot* written on the cover. They write these in their books and read them in pairs.

Conclusion
Select children from Group 1 to share their extended storyline and rhymes as appropriate. Display Group 3's books for reading by other children.

Introduction
Ask the children what might occur in the story if Mister Magnolia had only one coat. Give some examples to elicit a response from them, for example:

Mister Magnolia has only one coat...

He keeps sheep and cows but only one _____ (goat)
He likes going to sea and sailing his _____ (boat)
He sings so loudly he gets a sore _____ (throat)
He goes to the pool where he likes to _____ (float).

Collect the rhyming words on the board ready to add to during the Skills session.

Whole-class skills work
Ask the children if they can think of other words that rhyme with *coat*, for example: oat, moat, quote, note, vote, wrote. Then focus on the *oa* sound, encouraging them to hear it by saying it together. What about the word *Magnolia*? Can the children hear the o sound in that? Explain that just as there are different spellings for the oo sound they explored previously, there are also different spellings for the *oa* sound. Say that a group of them are going to find some different spellings for this sound and report back to the rest of the class later.

Finally, remind the children that the consonant ending can be different from the *t* ending in *coat* and ask them to suggest *oa* sounding words without a *t* ending. Mention words such as 'poke', 'hose', 'posy', and 'show' to reiterate the teaching point.

Differentiated group activities
1: Give each child a flap book (see Preparation). Ask them to compose simple sentences that complement the opening line (*Mister Magnolia has only one coat*) in the same way as in the Introduction, using rhyming words at the end of each new line.
2*: Guided reading: children work in pairs searching their reading books to find words containing the *oa* sound. They record the words on a simple grid (see Preparation).
3: Children work in pairs using a word wheel (see Preparation) to make different words which they read together and then include in written sentences.

Conclusion
Selected children from Group 1 read aloud their rhyming books. Display the *oa* grids for future reference.

MR McGEE GOES TO SEA

OBJECTIVES

UNIT	SPELLING/ VOCABULARY	GRAMMAR/ PUNCTUATION	COMPREHENSION/ COMPOSITION
READING AND WRITING FICTION AND POETRY *Mr. McGee Goes to Sea* by Pamela Allen.	Explore words with different spellings of the long vowel phonemes ee and *ie*.	Extend rhyming sentences. Construct sentences for given words.	Use the context of reading as a cue in conjunction with grammatical and phonemic cues to predict texts. Explore element of fantasy in story.

ORGANIZATION (2 HOURS)

	INTRODUCTION	WHOLE-CLASS SKILLS WORK	DIFFERENTIATED GROUP ACTIVITIES	CONCLUSION
HOUR 1	Shared reading of *Mr McGee Goes to Sea*, with pupils predicting the rhyme.	Develop awareness of different spellings of long vowel phoneme ee.	1: Read and sort ee and ea words. 2: Find and sort words with ee sound in *Mr McGee* text. 3*: Guided reading: collect and sort words with ee sound.	Selected pupils from Group 1 read their sentences. Display Group 3's work.
HOUR 2	Discuss the word 'absurd' and explore fantasy in *Mr McGee Goes to Sea*. Compare with other similar stories.	Develop awareness of different spellings of the long vowel phoneme *ie*. Extend rhymes.	1: Extend/adapt opening lines using new character Mr McGie. 2*: Find and sort words with *ie* sound in *Mr McGee* text. 3: Read and sort *igh* words and construct sentences.	Selected pupils from Group 1 read their rhyming openings. Display large grid from Group 2 for reference.

RESOURCES

Copies of *Mr McGee Goes to Sea* by Pamela Allen (Picture Puffins, ISBN 0-14-054403-8) – ideally, reading books (for Group 3), photocopiable pages 174 (Word Grid: 1) and 175 (Word Grid: 2), writing materials, including coloured felt-tipped pens, A3 paper, card, board or flip chart, red and blue counters.

PREPARATION

Hour 1

Prepare a copy of *Mr McGee Goes to Sea* by covering up the rhyming words at the end of the lines. Enlarge the first two lines from the story: *Mr McGee was sipping tea/beneath his spreading apple tree*. Make a copy of photocopiable page 174 (Word Grid: 1) for each child in Group 1. Draw a simple three-column grid to fill an A4 page. Use the following column headings: ee *(tree), ea (tea), others*. Copy this for each pair in Group 2, then make a single enlarged copy for use with Group 3.

Hour 2

Make an enlarged copy of the 'blurb' on the inside front cover of *Mr McGee Goes to Sea*: *Here is a story, absurd as can be of Mr McGee who's swallowed at sea*. Write the following adapted sentence opening on a strip of card for each child in Group 1: *Mr McGie was...* (note the different spelling). For Group 2, draw a large five-column grid on an A3 sheet of paper Use these column headings: *y (sky), i_e (quite), ie (pie), igh (high), others*. Make a copy of photocopiable page 175 (Word Grid: 2) for each child in Group 3.

Introduction
Introduce the book *Mr McGee Goes to Sea* to the children. Tell them that the story is about Mr McGee trying to have a cup of tea when it begins to rain, and ask them to watch the teapot as you read the story. Explain that there is a rhyming word at the end of each line, and as you read the story, you would like the children to try to guess the word by using the predictable rhymes and any clues from the illustrations. Then read the story together.

Finish by asking the children if the story reminds them of another – for example, 'Noah's Ark'. (Some children may also know 'Jonah and the Whale'). Ask them to explain what Mr McGee was most worried about. What would they have been most worried about if they were Mr McGee?

Whole-class skills work
Display the enlarged version of the first two lines from the story:

Mr McGee was sipping tea
beneath his spreading apple tree

Select children to underline the words with the ee sound, (*McGee, tea, beneath, tree*). Ask the children to take a closer look at the spellings of the ee sound and select individuals to circle the ee spellings in blue and the ea spellings in red. Then ask them to think of other words that have an ee sound, for example 'please', 'keep', 'cheap', 'sleep', and so on. Encourage them to attempt the spelling of the words they suggest and correct it for them if necessary. Be prepared to discuss ee sounding words that have other spellings, such as 'me', 'ski', 'shriek'.

Differentiated group activities
1: Children work individually using photocopiable page 174 (Word Grid: 1) which focuses on words with the ee sound.
2: Each pair shares a copy of *Mr McGee Goes to Sea* and hunts for words with the ee sound. They record their findings on a grid (see Preparation) and then write sentences using some of the words.
3*: Each child should have a copy of *Mr McGee Goes to Sea* for guided reading. They should search the text for words with the ee sound and record these on an enlarged grid (see Preparation).

Conclusion
Select children from Group 1 to read aloud some of their sentences. Discuss how they knew the meaning of the words on the grid and whether their sentences reflect the meanings accurately. Which ones did they find difficult? Display the large grid of words with the ee sound compiled by Group 3 for future reference.

Introduction
Read *Mr McGee Goes to Sea* again, pausing before each rhyming word so that the children can predict it. Afterwards, ask a child to say what the story is about in just a few words. Then show the children the enlarged version of the book's 'blurb' on the inside of the cover page:

Here is a story, absurd as can be
of Mr McGee who's swallowed at sea.

Ask the children what *absurd* means. Offer support by asking other questions such as:

■ Do you really think that the drips and drops of rain became a sea?
■ Did Mr McGee really sail away?
■ Can it be true that a huge fish swallowed Mr McGee and then spat him out?

Whole-class skills work

Suggest to the children that by changing Mr McGee's name to Mr McGie (the long vowel phoneme *ie* as in 'lie'), they can devise their own 'absurd' story. Begin by writing on the board an opening line for Mr McGie, for example *Mr McGie was...*, and ask the children to extend the line, ending with a rhyming word. Some examples might include *Mr McGie was...*

learning to fly
scoring a try
hanging to dry
learning to fry
going to buy
sailing to Skye
heaving a sigh

Continue with the last line: *beneath his spreading apple...* – the children will probably offer 'pie'! Use the opportunity to draw their attention to the different spellings of the *ie* sound, for example *igh, uy, y, ye*.

Differentiated group activities

1: Children work in pairs to extend and adapt the opening lines of the story using the new character Mr McGie (see Preparation). Encourage them to develop the nonsense element and experiment with rhyming words to create the beginning of their own 'absurd' rhyming story.
2*: Guided reading: children each have a copy of *Mr McGee Goes to Sea* which they read together, searching for *ie* sounding words. They record their findings on a large grid (see Preparation). They can continue the activity by searching for more words in their reading books if necessary.
3: Children work in pairs using photocopiable page 175 (Word Grid: 2) which focuses on *ie* sounding words.

Conclusion

Select children from Group 1 to read their rhyming openings to a new story about Mr McGie. Display the large grid of *ie* sounding words compiled by Group 2 for future reference.

WORD GRID: 1

- ■ Read aloud the words below.
- ■ Cover ee words with blue counters.
- ■ Cover ea words with red counters.

tea	meet	he	sea	feet
seen	me	meat	mean	sleet
been	we	seat	lean	sheet
peel	ski	seal	bee	queen
heat	see	wheat	glee	pea
green	flea	street	plea	sweet

- ■ How many different spellings can you find for the sound ee?
- ■ Use some of the words to make sentences. Write them on the back of this sheet.

WORD GRID: 2

■ Read aloud the words below.
■ Cover *igh* words with blue counters.
■ Cover *i_e* words with red counters.

high	smile	lie	dry	why
sigh		my	pipe	kite
sky		tie	light	shine
slime	pie	line	tight	shy
time	crime	cry	rhyme	while

■ How many different spellings can you find for the sound *ie*?
■ Use some of the words to make sentences.

CATS

OBJECTIVES

UNIT	SPELLING/ VOCABULARY	GRAMMAR/ PUNCTUATION	COMPREHENSION/ COMPOSITION
READING AND WRITING POETRY 'Cats' by Eleanor Farjeon and 'Cat' by Vernon Scannell.	Identify rhyming words including those which have same sounds but different spellings. Understand the terms 'vowel' and 'consonant'. Learn some of the common spellings for the long vowel phoneme *ai*.	Use awareness of grammar to decipher new or unfamiliar words.	Read a variety of poems on similar themes.

ORGANIZATION (3 HOURS)

	INTRODUCTION	WHOLE-CLASS SKILLS WORK	DIFFERENTIATED GROUP ACTIVITIES	CONCLUSION
HOUR 1	Shared reading of 'Cats' by Eleanor Farjeon on photocopiable page 179.	Raise phonological awareness, particularly by focusing on rhymes.	1: Explore rhyming words. Invent rhymes. 2*: Read and sequence poem text. 3*: Shared and guided reading of poem, focusing on expression. Prepare to read to an audience.	Selected pupils from each group read and present their work, and discuss responses. Display Group 1's rhyming words. Group 3 read 'Cats' poem aloud.
HOUR 2	Shared writing of a poem based on 'Cats', substituting words and elaborating on text.	Look at the terms 'vowel' and 'consonant' in the rhyming words used in the class poem.	1*: Write poems based upon 'Cats'. 2*: Shared and guided reading of poem, focusing on expression. Prepare to read to an audience. 3: Read and sequence poem text.	Look at Group 1's poems. Group 2 read 'Cats' poem aloud. Look at how Group 3 sequenced the poem text.
HOUR 3	Shared reading of 'Cat' by Vernon Scannell on photocopiable page 180. Compare with 'Cats' by Eleanor Farjeon.	Look at words which contain the grapheme *ai*.	1*: Shared and guided reading of 'Cat', focusing on expression. 2: Identify rhyming words in 'Cat'. 3*: Invent names for cats and write them phonetically.	Look at Group 3's cat names and write them on the board. Talk about the possible spellings for these, and discuss vowels and consonants.

RESOURCES

Writing materials, board or flip chart, OHP and acetate sheets (optional), photocopiable pages 179 ('Cats') and 180 ('Cat').

PREPARATION

For Hour 1, make an OHT or enlarged copy of the poem 'Cats' on photocopiable page 179. Make an A4 copy of the poem for each child in Groups 1 and 3. For each child in Group 2, prepare a version of the poem with the lines arranged in the wrong order for re-sequencing.

For Hour 2, you could produce a word bank to help children in Group 1 to write their own poems (see main Introduction, page 11). Copy the 'Cats' poem for each child in Group 2. Prepare a jumbled version of the poem for Group 3, as above, but differentiate as necessary by giving children sections to re-sequence rather than the whole poem. The length of the sections can be varied to match the children's ability.

Introduction

Read the poem 'Cats' (photocopiable page 179) to the children and ask them to listen to it carefully. Together, discuss the things that cats do. Do they think the poem is an accurate description of cats' sleeping habits? Now display the OHT or enlarged version of the poem and re-read it with the children following the text.

Whole-class skills session

Now say that you are going to read the poem again, but this time you want the children to help you. As you read, pause before the second rhyming word in each couplet and let the children say the word. Then ask them to look closely at the poem and pick out the words which rhyme together. Ask them if they can see an example of two different words rhyming with another (*chair* at the beginning and *care* at the end rhyme with *anywhere*). Can they think of any other rhyming words which the poet could have used in place of these? Make a list of their suggestions on the board.

Differentiated group activities

1: Give each child a copy of 'Cats'. The children should pick out the rhyming words and write them across the top of the page, then list other rhyming words they can think of underneath. For example:

anywhere	ledge	shoe	box
chair	edge	do	frocks
care	dredge	who	socks

2*: The teacher works with this group first. Give each child a copy of the poem with the lines in the wrong order (see Preparation). Ask them to use the rhyming words to help them re-order the text. Those who finish early could try writing additional couplets for the poem. Encourage them to look at the structure of the text and at the overall meaning as they write the couplets. Talk about the repetition of the first lines at the end of the poem. (Some pairs could use the computer cut and paste facility for this activity.)
3*: After working with Group 2, the teacher supports this group in both a shared and guided reading of the poem, focusing on expression and preparing to read it to an audience. They could learn the poem in pairs and practise reading together for a joint presentation. One child could read the first part of each couplet; the other the second.

Conclusion

Ask each group to tell the rest of the class about what they have been doing. Choose some children from Group 3 to read the 'Cats' poem aloud. Children from Group 2 should read any additional couplets they have composed and Group 1 could show their rhyming lists and invite the rest of the class to add to them.

Introduction

Display and re-read 'Cats' with the children, asking them to look at it carefully. Explain that, with their help, you are going to write a cats poem like Eleanor Farjeon's but using your own words. Your poem might begin *Cats sleep anywhere...*, and then tell of other places where cats might sleep, or it may be about other feline activities. Ask the children to tell you about some of the things which cats do and note their ideas on the board. These can then be turned into short lines for the poem, for example:

> Cats eat
> Fishy things,
> Play with balls,
> Wool and strings,
> Drink milk,
> Eat up mice,
> Which they think,
> Taste very nice.

Whole-class skills work

Use the newly composed class poem to focus on rhyming words again and look closely at the spelling of these. Write the words on the board and ask the children to listen carefully to the sounds as you say them. Now ask them to say the words too, and introduce the terms 'vowel' and 'consonant'. Explain these by talking about the way in which the vowels are sounded against the consonants. Show the children using simple three-letter examples such as 'cat', 'dog', 'bed' and 'pet' and ask them to tell you which letters represent the vowel sounds and which represent the consonants. Look at an alphabet with the children and help them to identify the letters which are vowels and those which are consonants. Although *a*, *e*, *i*, o and *u* are usually thought of as being the vowels, you may, at some stage, need to explain that *y* can also be used as a vowel in words like 'hymn', 'by', 'try' and 'baby'.

Differentiated group activities

1*: The teacher works with this group first. The children write their own poems based on 'Cats', supported by you as necessary. Begin by discussing the behaviour of pet cats to stimulate ideas. Provide a word bank to help them if appropriate (see Preparation).
 2*: After working with Group 1, the teacher supports this group in both a shared and guided reading of the 'Cats' poem, focusing on expression and preparing to read it to an audience (see Hour 1, Group 3).
3: Give each child a copy of the poem with the lines in the wrong order (see Preparation). Ask them to use the rhyming words to help them re-order the text (see Hour 1, Group 2).

Conclusion

Look at the poems written by Group 1 and write some of the lines on the board. Give children from Group 2 an opportunity to read the poem to the class. Children from Group 3 should show the class how they sequenced the poem text.

Introduction

Display an OHT or enlarged version of the poem 'Cat' by Vernon Scannell (photocopiable page 180). Read it to the children, then compare it with 'Cats' by Eleanor Farjeon. Display both poems side by side, and ask the children to look at the different ways in which they are set out. 'Cat' has four verses; 'Cats' has only one.

Discuss what the poets are telling us about cats in each poem. In 'Cat', the poet says that names do not mean much to cats. Ask the children if their pet cats respond when their names are called - does this contrast with the way that dogs react? Invite the class to tell you what they have discovered about cats from reading the two poems.

Whole-class skills work

The Vernon Scannell poem provides an opportunity to look at the long vowel phoneme *ai* as in *afraid* and *mislaid*, and to show children that this phoneme can be created in a different way in *name*, *blame* and *flame*. In the Eleanor Farjeon poem, the *ai* grapheme represents a different phoneme in *chair*, and this should be explored with the children as they look at the poems side by side.

Differentiated group activities

1*: The teacher works with this group first in a shared reading of the 'Cat' poem. Children then re-read it as a group and individually. You may need to discuss some words such as *vanish*, *require*, *stare* and *Black Buzz*.
2: Children identify the rhyming words in the 'Cat' poem and write them down in rhyming pairs. Encourage them to try to think of any further rhyming words and to write these down, too.
3*: Ask the children to make up names for cats and to write them phonetically. Explain that there may be many different ways of spelling the same name and encourage them to use their knowledge of phonics to attempt different spellings. There may be children in the class who have the same names with different spellings. For example, 'Sean' and 'Shaun', 'Claire' and 'Clare', 'Catherine', 'Katherine', 'Katharine' and 'Kathryn'. Use some of these examples to reassure the children that their attempts at the spellings may be perfectly correct even if they differ from the most common spellings of the names.

Conclusion

Look with the class at Group 3's cat names and write them on the board. Talk about the different spellings for these names with the children and use the opportunity to discuss vowels and consonants.

CATS

Cats sleep
Anywhere,
Any table,
Any chair,
Top of piano,
Window-ledge,
In the middle,
On the edge,
Open drawer,
Empty shoe,
Anybody's
Lap will do,
Fitted in a
Cardboard box,
In the cupboard
With your frocks –
Anywhere!
They don't care!
Cats sleep
Anywhere.

Eleanor Farjeon

CAT

My cat has got no name,
We simply call him Cat;
He doesn't seem to blame
Anyone for that.

For he is not like us
Who often, I'm afraid,
Kick up quite a fuss
If *our* names are mislaid.

As if, without a name,
We'd be no longer there
But like a tiny flame
Vanish in bright air.

My pet, he doesn't care
About such things as that:
Black buzz and golden stare
Require no name but Cat.

Vernon Scannell

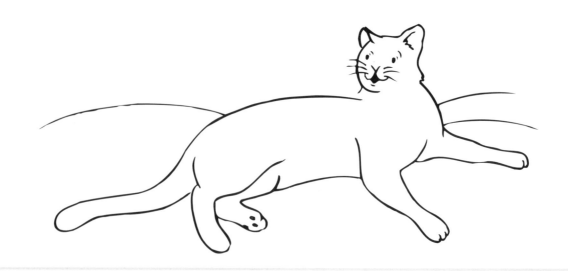

I WONDER

OBJECTIVES

UNIT	SPELLING/ VOCABULARY	GRAMMAR/ PUNCTUATION	COMPREHENSION/ COMPOSITION
READING AND WRITING POETRY 'I Wonder' by Kathleen Taylor.	Build individual collections of words for alliterative value from given double consonant blends. Build collections of words that rhyme. Investigate spellings of vowel phonemes *ai*, *ow* and *i_e*.	Read aloud with pace and expression appropriate to grammar.	Use poem as a model for composing own poetry.

ORGANIZATION (3 HOURS)

	INTRODUCTION	WHOLE-CLASS SKILLS WORK	DIFFERENTIATED GROUP ACTIVITIES	CONCLUSION
HOUR 1	Shared reading and discussion of the poem 'I Wonder' on photocopiable page 184 .	Identify rhyming words in the poem.	1*: Re-read and recite with expression, ready to present to an audience. 2*: Extend lines from poem using their own ideas. 3: Collect rhyming words.	Selected pupils from Group 1 perform the poem. Display Group 2's work on extended lines from the poem for others to read.
HOUR 2	Shared re-reading of 'I Wonder'. Use graphic and phonic knowledge to spell words.	Investigate initial double consonant blends: *sh, bl, sw, fl*.	1*: Collect and write new words linked with *rain*, *sun*, *wind*. 2: Read and re-order poem text. 3: Collect and write words with initial blends *sh, bl, sw, fl*.	Selected pupils from Group 2 read their re-ordered poems. Reinforce spelling strategies. Display work from Group 1.
HOUR 3	Extend opening lines of the poem using pupils' ideas.	Investigate the rhyming long vowel sounds *ai, i_e, ow*.	1: Extend lines from the poem. 2: Compose short poems. 3*: Search for various spellings of the long vowel sounds *a*, *i*, and *o*.	Selected pupils from Groups 1 and 2 read their poems. Display Group 3's work for future reference.

RESOURCES

Writing materials, including A3 paper, OHP and acetate sheets (optional), board or flip chart, Big Book stand, sheets of A3 paper, reading books (for Group 3), photocopiable pages 184 (I Wonder) and 185 (Vowel Phonemes).

PREPARATION

Hour 1

Prepare an OHT or enlargement of the poem 'I Wonder' on photocopiable page 184. Make a copy of this poem for each pair of children in Group 1. For Group 2, write the opening line of the poem (*I wonder what would happen...*) in large print on card to use as a writing frame. Draw a simple four-column grid to fill a sheet of A4 paper and use the following column headings: *rain, shine, blow, fly*. Make a copy for each pair in Group 3.

Hour 2

Write either *rain*, *sun* or *wind* in large letters on an A3 sheet for each sub-group of two or three children in Group 1. Prepare a jumbled version of the 'I Wonder' poem where a middle line in each verse has been taken from one of the other verses, for example:

> I wonder what would happen
> if the sun forgot to shine?
> If they never ever swam again
> I wonder what would happen?

Make a copy of this jumbled version of the poem for each child in Group 2. Draw a simple four-column grid to fill an A4 sheet. Use the following column headings: *sh (shine), bl (blow), fl (fly), (sw) swim*. Make a copy of the grid for each pair in Group 3.

Hour 3
Produce a writing frame with the first three lines of the first three verses of 'I Wonder'. Adapt each fourth line and add a blank space as follows:

> I wonder what would happen
> if the clouds forgot to rain?
> If it never ever rained again
> I would never ever_____.

Copy this version for each child in Group 1. For Group 2, provide enlarged syntactic frames on cards to stimulate ideas for a fourth line in each verse of their own poems based on 'I Wonder'. For example: I would never ever...; There would never ever.... Make a copy of photocopiable page 185 (Vowel Phonemes) for each pair in Group 3.

HOUR 1

Introduction
Display an OHT or enlarged version of the poem 'I Wonder' (photocopiable page 184) and read it aloud using appropriate expression. Now ask some children to join in with a second reading, using the text. Afterwards, discuss what other things we take for granted in nature that would be a source of wonder if they didn't happen any more. Point to the opening line *I wonder what would happen...* and invite some suggestions, recording them on the board. For example: *I wonder what would happen if...*the flowers never opened/ if the stars never shone/ if the grass never grew, etc. Encourage the children to think of more ordinary, everyday occurrences, for instance: *I wonder what would happen if...*the shops never opened/cars didn't start, and so on.

Whole-class skills work
Ask the children to identify the parts of the poem that rhyme. Help them to establish that these include *rain/ again* and *never/ ever*. Then ask them to suggest other words that rhyme with *rain* and write them on the board, for example: train, brain, main, lane, cane. Repeat this exercise using another word from the poem such as *shine*.

Differentiated group activities
1*: The teacher supports this group after working with Group 2. In pairs, the children learn and practise reciting verses of the poem, preparing to perform to the class as a group. Each pair could learn two verses, depending on the number of children in the group. Encourage them to recite the verses with appropriate expression.
2*: The teacher works with this group first. The children work independently or in pairs, depending on their ability. They use the opening line of the poem *I wonder what would happen...* and extend the sentence with their own ideas.
3: Children work in pairs to find words that rhyme with four words taken from the poem and record them on a grid (see Preparation).

Conclusion
Group 1 performs the 'I Wonder' poem to the rest of the class. Display Group 2's work for other children to read.

HOUR 2

Introduction
Read the poem 'I Wonder' again to the children, then point to specific words and select individuals to read them according to their ability. Next, write *rain* in the centre of the board and ask the children to tell you all the words that come into their heads when they think about rain. Stress that you want their ideas in just one word; for instance, if

rain reminds them of umbrellas, they should just say 'umbrella'. Write their suggestions on the board, referring to phonic and graphic spelling strategies as appropriate.

Whole-class skills work

Now ask the children to pick out the words beginning with *w* in the poem and point to them. Ask them why they think the words are repeated. Are the *w* sounds hard or soft? What effect does this have on the sound of the poem? (It gives it a 'whispering' feel.) Can they see other initial sounds that are repeated (*shine/ shone, swim/ swam*)? In the case of *fly, flew* and *fish*, point out the double consonant letter blends *fl* and *sh*. Explain that the *sh* in *fish* is the same as the double consonant letter blend *sh* in *shine* and *shone*. Look at the blend *sw* in *swim* and *swam*.

Differentiated group activities

1*: Children work in twos or threes, sharing a sheet of A3 paper with either *rain, sun* or *wind* written in the centre. They then brainstorm and write down all the words they associate with the given word, as in the Introduction to this Hour.
2: Each child re-orders a jumbled version of the poem (see Preparation).
3: In pairs children use a grid of four words taken from the poem (see Preparation) and write other words beginning with the same double consonant blends, *sh, bl, fl, sw*.

Conclusion

Select children from Group 2 to read their re-ordered versions of the poem. Reinforce the skills work by selecting children from Group 3 to read some of the words from their list, asking them to identify the double consonant phonemes and to spell the words by referring to the phonemic structure. Display Group 1's work.

HOUR 3

Introduction

Display the poem 'I Wonder' and read the opening verse. Remind the children of their previous ideas (Hour 1) about what other things would be a source of wonder if they stopped working/happening. Refer to Group 2's display of extended opening lines.

Now ask the children what they would do if it never rained again, and display one of the sheets with *rain* words from Group 1 (Hour 2) as a stimulus for ideas. Demonstrate an example using the following sentence: 'I would never ever need my umbrella again' and write this on the board. Then encourage the children's responses, for example: 'I would never ever need my wellingtons again'; 'I would never ever play in puddles again'.

Whole-class skills work

Focus on picking out rhyming vowel sounds from the poem. Remind the children that the letter or letters that make the sound are called 'phonemes'. Then ask which two words have the same rhyming vowel phoneme (i.e. *shine* and *fly*). Point out how in *shine* and *fly*, the vowel phonemes are spelled differently although they sound exactly the same. Look at other vowel phonemes such as *ai* in *rain* – what about the *ai* sound in cake, lane, came? Write these words on the board to demonstrate the different spellings for this phoneme. Finally, refer to one of the lists made by children in Group 3 (Hour 1) and check spellings together, correcting where necessary with the children's assistance.

Differentiated group activities

1: Children work independently to complete the fourth (adapted) line of the first three verses of the 'I Wonder' poem (see Preparation).
2: The children use their ideas from the group activity in Hour 1 to write their own short poems. They combine their suggestions for extended opening lines with ideas for closing lines based on simple syntactic frames (see Preparation).
3*: Each pair of children search their reading books for one of the long vowel sounds which you have sounded out for them before they begin – for example, one pair will search for *a* sounds, another for *i* sounds and another for *o* sounds. They use the relevant spelling grid on photocopiable page 185 to sort the phonemes by spelling.

Conclusion

Ask several children from Groups 1 and 2 to read aloud their poems. Display their work and allow some time afterwards for illustrating their poems. As an extension to work undertaken by Group 3, display large versions of their grids at a suitable height for children to contribute appropriate words as they encounter them in their reading.

I WONDER

I wonder what would happen
if the clouds forgot to rain?
If it never ever rained again
I wonder what would happen?

I wonder what would happen
if the sun forgot to shine?
If it never ever shone again
I wonder what would happen?

I wonder what would happen
if the wind forgot to blow?
If it never ever blew again
I wonder what would happen?

I wonder what would happen
if the birds forgot to fly?
If they never ever flew again
I wonder what would happen?

I wonder what would happen
if the fish forgot to swim?
If they never ever swam again
I wonder what would happen?

I wonder what would happen
if I forgot to wonder?
If I never ever wondered again
I wonder what would happen?

Kathleen Taylor

VOWEL PHONEMES

a_e (lane)	ai (rain)	ay (day)	others

ie (lie)	i_e (like)	igh (high)	y (fly)	others

oa (boat)	o_e (pole)	ow (blow)	others

THE LITTLE BOX

OBJECTIVES

UNIT	SPELLING/ VOCABULARY	GRAMMAR/ PUNCTUATION	COMPREHENSION/ COMPOSITION
READING FICTION 'The Little Box' by Kathleen Taylor.	Investigate, read and spell words by onset and rime, drawing on knowledge about initial consonant letter blends and word endings.	Reinforce knowledge through reading of the term 'sentence'.	Re-tell stories to give the main points in sequence and to pick out significant incidents.

ORGANIZATION (2 HOURS)

	INTRODUCTION	WHOLE-CLASS SKILLS WORK	DIFFERENTIATED GROUP ACTIVITIES	CONCLUSION
HOUR 1	Shared reading of 'The Little Box' story on photocopiable page 189.	Identify story structure and main events.	1: Sequence events in the story to a story pattern. 2: Put sections of story text in correct order. 3*: Track story text to find sentences.	Selected pupils re-tell the story.
HOUR 2	Tell the story of 'The Little Box' from memory with some deliberate mistakes to test pupils' memory skills.	Spell words using onsets and rimes.	1*: Re-tell the story using prompt cards. 2*: Sort out true statements from false. Re-write false statements to make them true. 3: Make and spell words using onsets and rimes.	Selected pupils from Group 2 explain their work and reinforce how to structure sentences.

RESOURCES

Writing materials, board or flip chart, OHP and acetate sheets (optional), card, including large sheet (64cm x 45cm), laminator (optional) or sticky-backed plastic, glue, A3 paper, small cloth bag, tape recorder (optional), Blu-Tack.

Photocopiable pages 189 (The Little Box), 190 (Story Map), 191 (The Little Box Story Pattern), 192 (True or False?) and 146 (Dice Net) from 'Order! Order!' unit (Term 2, page 192).

PREPARATION

Hour 1

Prepare an OHT or enlarged version of 'The Little Box' story on photocopiable page 189, and make an A4 copy for each pair of children in the class. Cut up the photocopiable story into long or short sections (depending on the children's ability) for each pair in Group 2 to reassemble in the correct order. Make an enlarged version of the story map on photocopiable page 190, cut it into five separate strips and then paste it onto a large sheet of card. Laminate or cover in sticky-backed plastic. Make an A3 photocopy of the story map for each child in Group 1, and a copy of photocopiable page 191 ('The Little Box' Story Pattern). Select a variety of sentences from the text of 'The Little Box' and provide a list of these for each child in Group 3. Differentiate the number and complexity of the sentences according to each child's ability.

Hour 2

Fill a cloth bag with small cards, each containing a simple word ending in *ing* or *ink* (make four of each word type). Make some simple blank prompt cards for each pair of children in Group 1 to write on. Make a copy of photocopiable page 192 (True or False?) for each child in Group 2. For each pair in Group 3, prepare two dice using the net on photocopiable page 146 (Dice Net – from 'Order! Order!' unit, Term 2). On one of the dice, write the rime *ing* on three of the faces and the rime *ink* on the other three faces. On the other dice, write the following double/triple consonant blends (onsets) on the faces: *shr, dr, br, th, st, str*. Finally, draw a simple three-column grid to fill an A4 page. Use the following column headings: word, makes sense, nonsense. Provide a copy for each pair in Group 3.

Introduction and whole-class skills work

NB: This session will take the full 30 minutes and includes the skills work for this hour.

Read the story of 'The Little Box' to the children. Give a photocopy of the text to each pair and display the enlarged version of the story map (see Preparation). Now discuss the sequence of events in relation to the questions in the story map. As the children answer the questions, encourage them to refer to the text so that they have to locate and read the relevant information. Write their suggestions in the appropriate section of the laminated story map, so that the story pattern emerges. Go through the story map questions establishing the points below. Suggested questions to ask the children are included in brackets.

■ The main character is introduced. (Who is the main character? What does it tell you about her at the beginning of the story?)
■ An item of interest is also intoduced: the little box. (What important thing are we told about at the beginning? Why do we think it's important or special?)
■ Some background information is given that helps to set the scene. (How does Julia feel about the little box? Why is it so special?)
■ The task is set: Julia wants to collect special things for her box. (What do you think about Julia's idea? What sort of things would you want to collect if you had a little box?)
■ A problem is identified. (What happens to affect Julia's idea? What problem does she encounter?)
■ The story develops. (What happens next? How does this make Julia feel? What happens to make Julia feel better?)
■ A further problem is identified. (Why doesn't the story end when Mrs Embles talks to Julia in the playground?)
■ The story reaches its conclusion. (How does the ending leave you feeling? What do you think Julia's next story might be?)

Differentiated group activities

1: Children work independently, cutting out the sentences from photocopiable page 191 ('Little Box' Story Pattern) and arranging them in order in the appropriate place on an A3 version of the story map (see Preparation).
2: Children work in pairs arranging sections of the story text in the correct order. They staple the sections together one behind the other to make a little book. (Covers could be made later and the books used for guided reading.)
3*: Each child has a copy of the story text and a selection of sentences from the text (see Preparation). They track the story text to locate each of the given sentences, which they then colour over in the main text with a felt-tipped pen.

Conclusion

Select one or two children to re-tell the main events in the 'The Little Box' story.

Introduction

Remind the children of the story of 'The Little Box' by telling the story from memory. Make some deliberate mistakes in your telling in order to elicit a reaction from the children, for example using the name 'Susan' instead of 'Julia', saying that the character didn't like the little box and so on. Then ask if they could tell the story from memory, and give some children the opportunity to try this. Afterwards, explain that some 'prompt cards' might be useful to help them remember the story. Make sure the children understand how prompt cards are used, then invite some suggestions for what would be useful to include on them, such as names of characters, brief details of important items such as the little box with a fox and cockerel painted on and a tiny stone, and important events summed up in a few words.

Whole-class skills work

Start by discussing how the children sometimes bring things to school, just as Julia does in the story. Say the words 'bring' and 'thing' and discuss their meaning. Ask what the children notice about the sound of these two words, and establish that they rhyme. Write the words on one side of the board, then orally segment them into onset and rime and say them together with the children, i.e. 'br/ing', 'th/ing'.

Now ask the children if they can hear the difference between 'thing' and 'think'. Segment both words ('th/i/n/k', 'th/i/n/g') to draw the children's attention to the different letter and sound at the end of the word. Write 'think' on the other side of the board, and underneath write 'brink'. As you write, refer to the word 'bring' – ask the children if they can hear the difference between 'bring' and 'brink' and to think about what 'brink' might mean so that the difference is made clearer.

Finally, select children to choose words from a cloth bag (see Preparation), read them and stick them (using Blu-Tack) under the *ing* or *ink* list on the board as appropriate.

Differentiated group activities

1*: The teacher works with this group first. Pairs of children work together to learn the story of 'The Little Box' and re-tell it from memory. They should write characters' names and other important information from the story on prompt cards. The group could use a tape recorder to record their stories.

2*: The teacher supports this group after working with Group 1. Children work independently to complete photocopiable page 192 (True or False?). They should put a tick next to the true statements and a cross next to the false statements. They should then re-write the false statements so that they are true, or simply change the words on the photocopiable sheet.

3: Children work in pairs using two dice, one containing six onsets and the other containing the rimes *ing* and *ink* written on three faces each (see Preparation for full details of this activity). Each child rolls both dice to make a word. The pairs record their words on a grid, sorting them into 'makes sense' and 'nonsense' words by ticking the relevant column.

Conclusion

Select children from Group 2 to explain how they corrected the false sentences on their photocopiable sheets. Ask children from other groups to correct some of the false statements, re-writing them on the board to reinforce how to structure sentences.

THE LITTLE BOX

One day, Julia arrived at school with a little box. It was a little box that fitted snugly in her hand. The little box was decorated with tiny pictures of brightly coloured cockerels and crafty looking foxes. Her Uncle William, who had given her the box on her fifth birthday, had told her a story of how the cockerel had outwitted the fox. She loved that story and she loved the box.

For Julia, the box held lots of stories: stories about Uncle William, stories Uncle William had told her and stories about all the people who had enquired about the box and what it held. On this particular day, though, the little box held nothing – except for the stories, that is – but Julia had a very special reason for bringing it to school. She wanted to put inside the box; not any old things, but special, tiny things. Things that she might find, things she might be given, things she might make.

By playtime, quite a few of the children knew about Julia's box.

"You can have this to put in your box, Julia," said Karen.

"What is it, Karen?" asked Julia.

Karen smirked as she handed Julia a dirty little stone. "Ha ha ha ha ha!" she sang as she ran off.

Julia's teacher, Mrs Embles, saw what had happened. She went over to Julia and told her not to take any notice of Karen's teasing. Mrs Embles could see how upset and disappointed Julia was about what had happened.

"Never mind, Julia, what was it Karen gave you that upset you so?"

Julia answered, trying very hard not to show how upset she was. "I'm collecting special things to put in my box, special tiny things and Karen gave me a dirty stone and laughed at me."

"Oh dear, I see," said Mrs Embles. "Let me look at the stone, Julia". Julia gave the stone to Mrs Embles who held it between her thumb and forefinger. She looked at it for several moments, then carefully placed it in Julia's palm.

"Julia," she said. "You're holding millions of years in your hand, did you know that?"

"Millions of years? What do you mean, Mrs Embles?" asked Julia, surprised.

At that moment, Vanessa and Lee ran up to Mrs Embles to tell her about a fight starting round the corner. So Julia had to wait until it was almost home time before she could ask Mrs Embles again what she meant by 'holding millions of years'. Mrs Embles explained that the little stone was millions of years old, because it was part of the Earth which was very, very old. So, when you held the stone in your hand, you also held millions of years.

Julia was amazed at what Mrs Embles had just told her. It was a wonderful story and she happily put the stone in her little box. Now the box held even more stories, and she wondered how many others she might collect. After all, the stone was only tiny; it didn't take up much space at all.

Kathleen Taylor

STORY MAP

■ What happens at the beginning of the story?

■ What is the main problem?

■ What happens next?

■ Is there a further problem?

■ How does the story end?

'THE LITTLE BOX' STORY PATTERN

Julia arrived at school with a little box.

The little box was a present from Uncle William.

Julia wanted to collect things to put in the little box.

Karen gave Julia a dirty little stone.

Julia was upset.

Mrs Embles held the stone between her thumb and forefinger.

Mrs Embles said, "You're holding millions of years in your hand."

Julia wanted to know more about the stone.

Julia knew that when she held the stone she held millions of years.

Julia put the stone in her box.

TRUE OR FALSE?

■ Read the sentences below.
■ Put a tick next to those sentences that are true.
■ Put a cross next to those sentences that are false.
■ Re-write or correct the false sentences so that they are true.

1. One day Julia arrived at school with a big box. ☐

2. Uncle William had given Julia the box on her sixth birthday. ☐

3. The little box was decorated with tiny pictures of brightly coloured foxes and crafty looking cockerels. ☐

4. Julia wanted to collect only special things to put in the box. ☐

5. Karen gave Julia a tiny bright button. ☐

6. Mrs Embles held the button in her hand. ☐

7. Vanessa and Lee told Mrs Embles about a playground fight. ☐

8. Julia had to wait quite a while before she could ask Mrs Embles again about the stone. ☐

FUNNYBONES

OBJECTIVES

UNIT	SPELLING/ VOCABULARY	GRAMMAR/ PUNCTUATION	COMPREHENSION/ COMPOSITION
READING FICTION *Funnybones* by Janet and Allan Ahlberg.	Use the term 'phoneme' and identify phonemes in speech and words.	Reinforce knowledge of a sentence by re-writing upper case letters in lower case, placing capital letters correctly. Read familiar parts of text with expression.	Use covers to compare similarities and differences within the *Funnybones* series. Identify preferences in the different stories of *Funnybones*.

ORGANIZATION (2 HOURS)

	INTRODUCTION	WHOLE-CLASS SKILLS WORK	DIFFERENTIATED GROUP ACTIVITIES	CONCLUSION
HOUR 1	Introduce the *Funnybones* book. Discuss cover and predict contents. Shared reading of the book and comparison with other books in the same series.	Use the word 'phoneme' in relation to the sounds in words.	1*: Read various *Funnybones* books; make comparisons. 2: Compare *Funnybones* books by studying covers. 3: Identify phonemes in a list of words.	Selected pupils from Group 1 explain how they compared books. Reinforce long vowel sounds and other digraphs in words.
HOUR 2	Demonstrate reading with expression, using *Funnybones* text.	Convert upper case writing in speech bubbles to lower case and position capital letters at the beginning of sentences.	1: Prepare to read text with expression before an audience. 2: Convert upper case letters to lower case and place capital letters appropriately. 3*: Guided reading, focusing on phonemes.	Select pupils from Group 1 to read *Funnybones* with expression. Reinforce using capital letters at the beginning of sentences and punctuation at the end of a sentence.

RESOURCES

Copies of *Funnybones* by Janet and Allan Ahlberg (Mammoth, ISBN 0-7497-0304-0), including your own Big Book of this text (see main Introduction, page 10, for guidance), a selection of other *Funnybones* books, such as *The Black Cat* (ISBN 0-7497-1040-3), *Dinosaur Dreams* (ISBN 0-7497-0910-3), *Mystery Tour* (ISBN 0-7497-0911-1), *The Pet Shop* (ISBN 0-7497-1034-9), writing materials, board or flip chart, 'Post-its', tape recorder, photocopiable pages 196 (Book Covers) and 197 (Looking at Phonemes).

PREPARATION

Hour 1
Make a Big Book version of *Funnybones* (see instructions on page 10 of the main Introduction). Make one copy of photocopiable page 196 (Book Covers) per pair in Group 2 and one copy of page 197 (Looking at Phonemes) per pair in Group 3.

Hour 2
Use 'Post-its' to mark out a separate section of the *Funnybones* text for each pair of children in Group 1 to practise reading aloud.

Introduction
Show the children the front cover of *Funnybones* (use a Big Book version if you have made one) and encourage them to predict what kind of book it is going to be, using the following questions:

- Is it going to be a true story? Why/why not?
- Is it going to be scary? Why/why not? How can you tell?
- Is it going to be funny? Why/why not?

Now read the story to the children and enjoy it! Afterwards, ask them if they have read any other books like this one. Show them a selection of other *Funnybones* books (see Resources). Compare the covers asking: How are they the same? How are they different? Write their ideas on the board and keep these for the group activities.

Whole-class skills work

Select words from the *Funnybones* text to segment by sound. Ask the children to identify the sounds in, for example, the word *dark*. Begin with the initial sound *d*, then the final sound *k*, followed by the middle sound *ar*. Do this orally first, then write the sounds on the board as you say them, making the whole word. Continue to take words from the text and segment them by sound, for example *d/ar/k, h/ou/se, s/t/r/ee/t, t/ow/n*. Use the word 'phoneme' to describe the sounds in each word.

Differentiated group activites

1*: Children read together a selection of *Funnybones* books to make comparisons and identify preferences. They should prepare to present their opinions at the end of the session.

2: Children work in pairs with a copy of *Funnybones*, together with another book from the series (see Resources). They compare the front covers, identifying similarities and differences and predicting what they think the other book is about. They should then record their ideas on photocopiable page 196 (Book Covers). The children can refer to the suggestions on the board made in the Introduction to this Hour.

3: Children work in pairs to segment the words on photocopiable page 197 (Looking at Phonemes) by drawing a hash line between the phonemes. They should start with the simple CVC words (part A) at the beginning of the activity and move on to the long vowel phonemes (part B) if appropriate.

Conclusion

Select children from Group 1 to explain how they compared the *Funnybones* books and to identify which books they particularly like. Reinforce the skills work by asking children from Groups 1 and 2 to identify some of the phonemes in Group 3's list of words.

Introduction

Tell the children that you will be asking some of them to help you read *Funnybones* aloud. Demonstrate how to build up the tension in the opening of the story by exaggerating and drawing out the length of words such as *dark*, or reading this word in a low whisper to make it sound scary. Then select a child to read the opening part of the story with appropriate expression. Continue to involve the children in reading parts of the story, encouraging them to use appropriate expression and guiding them as necessary.

Whole-class skills work

Draw the children's attention to the speech bubbles in the *Funnybones* text and show them how you used these to enhance the reading of the story, reading aloud some of the characters' thoughts or speeches. Ask the children what they notice about the writing in the speech bubbles; they should be able to see that it is all in capital letters. Write a speech bubble in capitals on the board, for example:

WHAT SHALL WE DO TONIGHT?

Then select a child to re-write it in lower case letters. Ask where a capital letter should be included as a way of encouraging children to explain that sentences begin with capital letters. Continue to involve the children in re-writing other speech bubbles quoted from the book and remind them of where to use full stops. Finish by discussing the use of other punctuation such as question marks and exclamation marks.

Differentiated group activities

1: Children work in pairs with a section of the *Funnybones* text which they practise reading aloud with expression. They should prepare to read the text before the class at the end of the session. Let the children record their readings on a tape recorder so they can play them back and think about how to improve them.

2: Ask the children to work in pairs to look through the *Funnybones* book for more examples of speech bubbles. They should re-write the speech bubble text in lower case and place a capital letter correctly at the beginning of each sentence.

3*: Guided reading of the *Funnybones* text, with the children using phonemic knowledge to decipher new words.

Conclusion

Select children from Group 1 to read extracts from the story with expression. Reinforce the need to put capital letters at the beginning of a sentence, and ask children about other punctuation used at the end of the sentence, including full stops, question marks and exclamation marks.

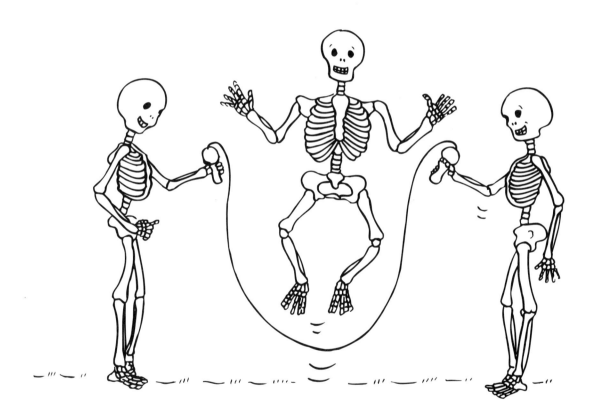

BOOK COVERS

■ Look at the covers of your chosen books. Then answer the questions.

In what ways are the books the same?

_____

_____

In what ways are they different?

_____

_____

■ What do you think each book is about? Answer using the grid below.

Book title:	Book title:

LOOKING AT PHONEMES

- Look at the words below.
- Separate the phonemes using lines like this: f/a/t, d/ow/n.
- Do this for each word.

PART A

fat	dog	cot	peg
pin	rug	win	rat
run	tin	let	top
van	fit	sat	put
den	cup	pot	fan

PART B

down	found	me	peel
town	tree	rain	coat
hook	flute	pool	mice
toe	ice	day	seat
dark	star	clown	ground

ALEX AND ROY

OBJECTIVES

UNIT	SPELLING/ VOCABULARY	GRAMMAR/ PUNCTUATION	COMPREHENSION/ COMPOSITION
READING AND WRITING FICTION *Alex and Roy* by Mary Dickinson.	Be able to read on sight words from List 1. Investigate compound words. Investigate spellings of verbs with -*ed* and -*ing* endings.	Read familiar texts aloud with pace and expression appropriate to the grammar. Understand common uses of capitalization.	Write about significant incidents from known stories.

ORGANIZATION (5 HOURS)

	INTRODUCTION	WHOLE-CLASS SKILLS WORK	DIFFERENTIATED GROUP ACTIVITIES	CONCLUSION
HOUR 1	Shared reading of *Alex and Roy* (pages 1–12). Discuss title, cover pages, pictures and 'blurbs'.	Discuss high frequency words and new words, including character's names. Discuss invented onomatopoeic words *brrring* and *brrrum*.	1: Write about key events and characters in story. 2*: Guided reading with expression. Strategies for unknown words. 3: Identify high frequency and new words in story text.	Discuss key events and characters in story; pupils from Group 1 read their sentences. Learn spellings of new words (refer to Group 3). Pupils from Group 2 read extracts of the story aloud.
HOUR 2	Shared re-reading of pages 1–12 of *Alex and Roy*, focusing on names and other words with capital letters.	Discuss the use of capital letters.	1*: Guided reading, identifying capital letters. Write down speeches. 2: Write about key events and characters in story. 3*: Guided reading with expression. Strategies for unknown words.	Shared reading with Group 3, focusing on using grammar to predict unfamiliar words.
HOUR 3	Shared reading of pages 13–22 of *Alex and Roy*. Discuss significant incidents.	Discuss capital letters further. Predict ending of story.	1: Write notes predicting the ending of the story. 2*: Guided reading, identifying capital letters and sentences. 3: Complete sentences about the story.	Discuss Group 1's predictions for the story's ending. Look at sentences completed by Group 3.
HOUR 4	Re-read *Alex and Roy* up to page 22. Discuss how it might end, then read the end of the story. Discuss compound words.	Look at verbs with -*ed* and -*ing* endings.	1: Write an ending for the story using notes made in Hour 1. 2: Complete sentences about the story. 3*: Guided reading of story, focusing on verbs with -*ed* and -*ing* endings.	Selected pupils from Group 1 read their story endings aloud. Write sentences together, focusing on verbs with -*ed* and -*ing* endings.
HOUR 5	Look at a book cover and identify features. Reinforce use of capital letters.	Complete sentences which require verbs with -*ed* and -*ing* endings. Revise the week's work.	1*: Guided reading of story focusing on verbs with -*ed* and -*ing* endings. 2: Write sentences using verbs with -*ed* and -*ing* endings. 3: Place capital letters correctly in a passage of text.	Look at Group 3's work on capital letters, using an enlarged version of the text. Discuss Group 2's sentences, identifying whether they are in the past or present tense.

RESOURCES

Enough copies of *Alex and Roy* by Mary Dickinson (Scholastic, ISBN 0-590-13172-9), for group work, writing materials, board or flip chart, an OHP and acetate sheets (optional), photocopiable pages 203 (Finish the Sentences) and 204 (Capital Letters).

PREPARATION

Hour 1
Prepare a homemade Big Book version of *Alex and* Roy (see main Introduction, page 10). Compile a list of high frequency words (from List 1 of *National Literacy Strategy* framework) and new words which appear in *Alex and Roy* for each child in Group 3. These could include:

good	want	off	mother	door	sister
here	where	saw	help	out	could
pushed	one	now	Alex	Roy	

Hour 2
No special preparation is required.

Hour 3
Make enough copies of photocopiable page 203 (Finish the Sentences) for one for each child in Group 3.

Hour 4
Make enough copies of photocopiable page 203 (Finish the Sentences) for one for each child in Group 2.

Hour 5
Make enough copies of photocopiable page 204 (Capital Letters) for one for each child in Group 3. In addition, make an OHT or enlarged version of this sheet for whole-class work. You will also need to find a suitable book cover for display which includes details of the title, author, illustrator and publisher's blurb.

Introduction
Introduce the children to the book *Alex and Roy*. Show them the cover and ask them to tell you the title, the name of the author and the illustrator. Read the 'blurb' on the back cover and ask the children if it makes them want to know what happens in the story. Discuss what kinds of things on book covers encourage them to want to look inside.

Now look at pages 1 to 12 together, and ask the children to tell you about the story. Use the picture clues to encourage them to predict what the story might be about, then read the story aloud together. Discuss the reasons why they think Alex did not want to play with Roy and ask them to look for some of the words and phrases which show that Alex is unhappy. These include:

...he stomped off to his bedroom. (page 4)
Alex was sitting behind the door, looking very, very, very cross. (page 8)

Together, discuss the pictures and the clues which they give about Alex's mood.

Whole-class skills work
Look at the spellings of some of the key words in the story, including the names of the characters, and help the children to learn these. Remind them of how the 'Look, say, cover, write, check' strategy can help them to do this. There are two words *brrring* and *brrrum* which are included to give an onomatopoeic effect. Talk with the children about the way in which the words are written and point out that words do not usually have triple letters in them but that the author has used them here for effect.

Differentiated group activities
1: Each child writes sentences about the significant events and characters (appearance, behaviour, etc) in the story so far. You *may* need to discuss this with them initially and

provide some key words as a starting point for their sentences.

2*: Re-read the first 12 pages of the story together, encouraging the children to be expressive. Discuss strategies for working out unfamiliar words, ie using the grammar of the text to read around unknown words and then using phonic as well as semantic clues.

3: The children read the story up to page 12, identifying high frequency and new words. Provide them with a list of words to look for (see Preparation) and ask them to write the words and the pages on which each was found.

Conclusion

Discuss the key events and the characters in the story so far, and ask children from Group 1 to read some of their sentences aloud. Discuss the spellings of the characters' names and ask Group 3 to show the class how to spell 'Alex' and 'Roy'. Children from Group 2 should read some of the story aloud to the rest of the class, using appropriate expression.

Introduction

Begin by recapping and then re-reading the first 12 pages of *Alex and Roy* with the children. Ask one child to read the part of Alex and others to be Roy, Renee and Alex's mother. Discuss how the children can use the speech marks to help them know when to say each character's words.

As the children read the story with you, ask them to watch for speech marks and to stop when they reach these so that those playing the characters can say their lines.

Whole-class skills work

Talk about the names of the characters in the story and write them on the board. First, try writing them without capital letters to see if the children spot the mistake and correct you. Then try writing other words from the story with and without capital letters and ask the children to tell you which should have capitals and which should not. Use the text to emphasize that some words which are not names have capital letters when they are at the beginning of a sentence or speech.

Differentiated group activities

1*: The children read through the story text identifying capital letters. They then look back at the sentences which they wrote about characters and key events in the previous session and write some of the speeches which the characters made.

2: Each child writes sentences about the significant events and characters (appearance, behaviour, etc) in the story so far. You may need to discuss this with them initially and provide some key words as a starting point for their sentences.

3*: The teacher works with this group first. Re-read the first 12 pages of the story together, encouraging the children to be expressive. Discuss strategies for working out unfamiliar words, ie using the grammar of the text to read around the unknown word and then using phonic as well as semantic clues.

Conclusion

Look again at capital letters, and then ask two or three children from Group 3 to read aloud expressively to the class, with everyone following the text. Talk about using the whole sentence or text and the pictures to help to decipher unfamiliar words. Write some sentences on the board with words missed out and ask the children to use semantic clues to fill in the gaps. You could provide clues such as the first grapheme to help them and to focus attention on the importance of phonic clues.

Introduction

Begin by discussing the story so far and then read pages 13 to 22 to the children. Follow this by a class discussion about the new significant incidents in the story.

Whole-class skills work

Discuss capital letters again and ask the children to try to explain why some of the words in the story have capitals. For example, on page 13:

Suddenly has a capital because it begins a sentence.
Alex has a capital because it is someone's name.
Can has a capital because it begins speech and a sentence.

Next, ask the children how they think the story will end. You could follow this by reading the first line on page 24 which indicates that the story is coming to an end (it provides a clue to this).

Just as they had finished, the doorbell rang.

Differentiated group activities

1: The children write notes predicting how they think the story will end. (They will continue the activity in Hour 4.)
2*: In this guided reading session, ask the children to look for words with capital letters when they look through the story again and ask them to explain why the capitals have been used.
3: Children work independently to complete photocopiable page 203 (Finish the Sentences), using the story text to help them.

Conclusion

Ask Group 1 to talk about their ideas for the story ending and invite other children to make suggestions. Show the class some of the sentences worked on by Group 3 and ask if they can use their knowledge of the story to provide alternative and equally valid suggestions for completing the sentences.

Introduction

Re-read *Alex and Roy* up to page 22 and discuss again some possible endings, then read the rest of the story. Ask the children what they think about the ending and compare it with those suggested by Group 1 in the previous session. How accurate were the predictions? Did anyone guess the ending correctly?

Now take the opportunity to discuss the compound words in the book, introducing the idea that words can be formed by combining two words. Draw the children's attention to the following examples and, for each one, show how two words have been combined to make one: *doorbell, bedroom, hairdresser, nothing, anywhere, another, hairstyle, lunchtime.*

Whole-class skills work

Focus on some of the verbs in the story text. Talk about verbs with the children and demonstrate the use of the past and present tenses in a practical way by, for example, knocking on the table and saying:

I am going to knock *(then knock).*
I am knock... *(ask the children to complete the word and then stop knocking).*
I have just... *(ask the children to supply the word 'knocked').*

Repeat with various other regular verbs until the children understand. Then ask them to look at page 24 and find the words *finished, asked* and *cooked.* Ask them to tell you if the verbs are in the past or present tense and invite them to compose sentences which use these verbs in the present tense.

Differentiated group activities

1: The children write an ending for the story using the notes which they made in Hour 3. Encourage them to use capital letters appropriately and to write in complete sentences. Remind them to spell verbs with an *-ed* or *-ing* correctly.
2: Children work independently to complete photocopiable page 203 (Finish the Sentences), using the story text to help them.
3*: Guided reading of *Alex and Roy,* discussing the spelling and grammatical features which have been learned during the week, ie verbs with *-ed* and *-ing* endings and the uses of capital letters.

Conclusion

Ask Group 1 to read their story endings aloud and encourage the other children to discuss them. Write some of Group 1's sentences on the board and ask the class to identify some of the verbs which have *-ing* or *-ed* endings.

Introduction

The final lesson in this unit should provide an opportunity to revise learning and to assess the children's levels of understanding. Begin by showing them a display of an enlarged book cover (not *Alex and Roy*) and asking them questions such as:

- Who wrote the book?
- What is the special name for a person who writes books?
- Who provided the pictures?
- What is the book's title?
- What does the 'blurb' tell us?

Write the names of the author and illustrator on the board either with the children's help, or omitting the capitals and asking the children to correct what you have written. Talk again about the use of capital letters for names and ask the children to tell you when else capitals are used. Look again at the cover for *Alex and Roy* and ask them to identify the above features on it.

Whole-class skills work

Talk again about verb endings and write some sentences on the board which have verbs in the present tense with -*ing* endings. Ask the children to say the sentences aloud and then to repeat them, but this time changing them so that they are in the past tense. Finish by writing some sentences on the board which have the verbs missing. Ask the children to use the grammar of the sentences to work out what the covered word might be and to identify whether it should end with -*ing* or -*ed*.

Differentiated group activities

1*: Guided reading of *Alex and Roy*, discussing the spelling and grammatical features which have been learned during the week, i.e. verbs with -*ed* and -*ing* endings and the uses of capital letters.
2: Ask the children to write sentences which describe some things which have happened and some things which are happening now, drawing on their own personal experience. Emphasize that they should use verbs which end in -*ed* and -*ing* to do this.
3: Children work independently to complete photocopiable page 204 (Capital Letters), adding capital letters in the correct places in a piece of text.

Conclusion

Show the class an enlarged version of the text on photocopiable page 204 which Group 3 have worked on and ask members of the group to point to the places where capital letters are needed. Ask the rest of the class to point out any omissions. Ask children in Group 2 to read their sentences aloud and invite the others to say whether the sentences are in the present or the past tense.

FINISH THE SENTENCES

PART A
■ Look through the storybook of *Alex and Roy* and finish the sentences.

1. _____ came to play at Alex's house.

2. Alex did _____ want to play with _____.

3. When Roy came to his house Alex went to _____

_____.

4. Alex's _____ asked Roy to help her to put the _____

_____.

5. Roy played in two boxes and pretended he was _____

_____.

PART B
■ Write your own endings for these sentences.

1. Alex came into the kitchen and asked _____

_____

_____

2. Alex and Roy drove the car to lots of places. They went to _____

_____

_____

CAPITAL LETTERS

All the capital letters are missing in the text below!
■ Correct it by putting capital letters in the right places.

alex and roy were good friends but one day, alex did not seem to like roy very much. when roy came to play at alex's house, alex went to his bedroom and wouldn't play. roy helped alex's mother to put the shopping away. after that he played in some boxes. the boxes were roy's car.

soon alex came downstairs and he and roy played together. they were friends again. they drove the car to lots of interesting places. in africa they saw some lions.

when it was time for roy to go home, alex asked if he could stay for lunch. his mother had not cooked enough food so roy had to go home. each of the boys had a box to play with. roy put his on his head and alex pretended his was a car.

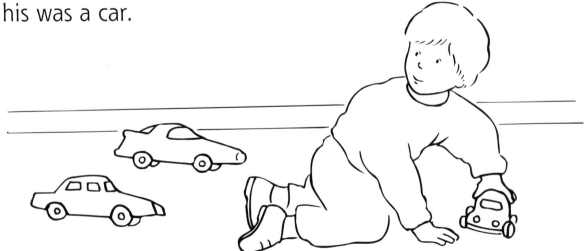

LOCATING INFORMATION

OBJECTIVES

UNIT	SPELLING/ VOCABULARY	GRAMMAR/ PUNCTUATION	COMPREHENSION/ COMPOSITION
READING AND WRITING NON-FICTION Charts.	Learn new words linked to a topic. Use simple dictionaries to check spelling.	Add question marks to questions.	Locate information using a chart. Use the language and features of non-fiction texts. Write questions related to a chart.

ORGANIZATION (3 HOURS)

	INTRODUCTION	WHOLE-CLASS SKILLS WORK	DIFFERENTIATED GROUP ACTIVITIES	CONCLUSION
HOUR 1	Examine together the chart 'Our Pets' on photocopiable page 208. Discuss the information presented and the layout.	Look at spellings of unfamiliar words. Segment them into phonemes to help with spelling and reading.	1: Read the chart and write questions to accompany it. 2: Locate information on the chart and answer questions. 3*: Look at the chart and answer questions orally.	Attempt to answer Group 1's questions using the enlarged chart. Discuss the use of question marks.
HOUR 2	Look again at the 'Our Pets' chart, discussing how a lot of information is presented in a concise and visual way.	Write questions. Revise use of question marks. Discuss spellings of words in questions.	1: Make charts of their own pets modelled on the photocopiable sheet. 2*: Read the chart and write questions to accompany it. 3. Locate information on the chart and answer questions in writing.	Match words on cards to those on the chart and look at spellings. Attempt to answer Group 2's questions.
HOUR 3	Create a pet chart together; look at those made by Group 1 in the previous session.	Learn to spell new words and use simple dictionaries to check spellings.	1*: Extend pet charts and discuss other ways of presenting the information. 2: Write sentences about information presented on the chart. 3: Complete sentences related to the chart.	Look at incomplete sentences about the chart. Discuss spellings of unfamiliar words.

RESOURCES

Writing materials, OHP and acetate sheets (optional), card, board or flip chart, a pointer (optional), computer database (optional), photocopiable page 208 (Our Pets).

PREPARATION

Hour 1

Prepare an OHT or enlarged version of the 'Our Pets' chart on photocopiable page 208. Make smaller copies of the chart (not the text below) for each child in the class. Devise a list of simple questions related to the chart and make a copy for each child or pair in Group 2.

Hour 2

Make a blank chart based on the format used on photocopiable page 208 (Our Pets). Include enough columns for each child in Group 1 to be included in the chart. Add the six headings in the first column, as on the 'Our Pets' chart and make a copy for each child in Group 1. Make a set of 'flash cards' containing high frequency words and new words used in the chart, or words which will be used during the whole unit.

Hour 3
Draw a blank chart on the board, in the same format as the 'Our Pets' chart. Make a copy of the whole of photocopiable page 208 (Our Pets) for each child in Group 3, and prepare an OHT or enlarged version of the sentences on this page.

Introduction
Begin by showing the children the OHT or enlarged version of the chart 'Our Pets' on photocopiable page 208. Ask them to look at it and to tell you what they think it shows. Talk about the way in which it is set out and ask the children to tell you some things which may be found out from it. Ask questions such as:

- What kind of pet does Usha have?
- Who has a pet rabbit?
- What does the canary eat?
- Where does Seema's pet live?

Whole-class skills work
The children will probably find some of the words on the chart difficult to read, so use the opportunity to talk about the spellings and to demonstrate how the words can be segmented and sounded. The word *aquarium* may present problems, but it is phonically regular enough for the children to learn it and to take satisfaction from being able to read and write a 'long' word. Show them how they can learn the words by focusing on the 'difficult' parts and learning those. Emphasize that using the 'look, say, cover, write, check' strategy will help them to remember the spellings.

Differentiated group activities
1: Ask the children to read the chart on photocopiable page 208 and to write some simple questions related to the information it provides. Give them some examples of questions to get them started, for example: What does Usha's cat like to drink? Who owns a pet dog? and so on. Encourage them to write in complete sentences. Explain that the rest of the class will try to answer some of these questions at the end of the session.
2: Provide the children with some simple questions (see Preparation) which they must answer by looking at the chart. Ask them to try to write their answers in complete sentences.
3*: Look at the 'Our Pets' chart together and ask the children questions which they can answer orally. You may wish to use a pointer to help them to locate and remember where the information can be found.

Conclusion
Let children from Group 1 ask the rest of the class some of their questions based on the 'Our Pets' chart. Write some of these on the board and discuss the use of question marks to show that sentences are questions.

Introduction
Display the 'Our Pets' chart again and discuss the way a chart can provide us with a lot of information using very little space. Talk about other ways in which the information could be presented, drawing on the children's experience of constructing bar charts and grouping information, for example 'pets which eat meat' and 'pets which eat vegetables'. If possible, show the children how the information could be entered into a computer database.

Whole-class skills work
Now ask the children to help you to write some simple questions related to the chart. First, identify a fact gleaned from the chart – for example, four pets drink water – then together, work out the question that will reveal that fact. Encourage the children to join in with spelling the words, and take the opportunity to reinforce the use of question marks. The questions should be phrased simply, as they will form the basis for Group 3's independent work.

Differentiated group activities

1: The children use the grid outline (see Preparation) to make their own charts showing which pets are owned by members of their group. (Some children could also use a computer database for this activity.) Children who do not have pets could either be entered in the chart as such, or could provide information about a pet owned by someone from their extended family.

2*: Look at the chart with the children and help them to write questions related to it. Pay particular attention to the use of question marks and to discussing spellings and strategies for learning them.

3: Show the children the list of questions which you wrote with the class in the Skills session and ask them to answer these, using complete sentences if possible.

Conclusion

Share some of the questions which you created with Group 2. Use some cards containing high frequency and new words (see Preparation) and hold them up for the children to take turns in reading aloud and then scanning the chart and questions to locate them.

Introduction

Together, look at the charts which Group 1 made in Hour 2. Talk about the way in which the children set out their information and explain that everyone is going to help them to extend their charts to include information about other children in the class.

Present a blank chart on the board (based on the format used by Group 1) and ask some children from Groups 2 and 3 to give details of their pets. Enter these on the chart, asking children to tell you where each piece of information should be placed. As you complete the chart, talk about the information which is being added and about the way in which it can be expressed very simply on a chart. For example, you might point out that a piece of information such as 'Helen has a pet dog which eats bones' could be expressed in just three words ('Helen', 'dog', 'bones') using the chart.

Whole-class skills work

As new words arise in the process of making the pets chart, discuss their spellings and encourage the use of dictionaries to check these. Where children give names for their pets, discuss possible spellings and look at alternatives. (It is quite possible that children may not know how to spell their pets' names, so you could ask them in advance to find out from their parents. If you have a 'THRASS' chart (see main Introduction, page 9), you might ask the children to use it to select as many alternative spellings as possible for a pet's name, and then offer these to the owner to take home and identify the correct one.)

Differentiated group activities

1*: Work with the children to help them each produce an extended chart about pets owned by children in the class. Again, some children could create a database to complete this activity.

2: Provide the children with a copy of the chart on photocopiable page 208. Ask them to select pieces of information and to write sentences to present this information in a different way, for example: 'Four pets drink water, and one pet drinks milk'.

3: Each child works to complete photocopiable page 208 (Our Pets), filling in the incomplete sentences using the information in the chart.

Conclusion

Look at an enlarged version of the incomplete sentences on photocopiable page 208 (Our Pets) and ask Group 3 to show the class how they filled the spaces. Ask other children to suggest some further incomplete sentences and write these on the board, inviting children to complete them. Use the opportunity to discuss the spellings of any new or unfamiliar words.

OUR PETS

■ Look at this chart about some children's pets.

Children's names	Adam	Usha	Ruth	Seema	Tony
Children's pets	dog	cat	rabbit	goldfish	canary
Pets' foods	bones dog food	fish cat food	lettuce grass	fish food	bird seed
Pets' drinks	water	milk	water	water	water
Pets' homes	kennel	basket	hutch	aquarium	cage
Pets' names	Rover	Tiddles	Eric	Goldy	Sammy

■ Use the chart to help you complete these sentences.

1. Adam's dog eats _____.

2. The animal which drinks milk is a _____.

3. Ruth's pet is called _____ and it lives in a _____.

4. Tony has a canary called _____ and it lives in a _____.

5. _____ has a pet goldfish and it eats _____.

6. _____ is the name of Adam's _____.

7. Tiddles eats _____ and _____ _____ and is

owned by _____.

8. The place where Seema's _____ lives is called

an _____.